City Watch

For

Sam Kuraishi

with very best wishes,

Don Anderson.

6. 14. 2001

Discovering
the
Uncommon
Chicago

City Watch

JON ANDERSON

University of Iowa Press ψ Iowa City

University of Iowa Press, Iowa City 52242
Printed in the United States of America
Design by Richard Hendel
http://www.uiowa.edu/~uipress

Columns dated from November 24, 1985, through September 29,
1999, are reprinted by permission of the *Chicago Tribune.*
Photographs on pages 4, 11, 18, 47, 54, 66, 122, 161, 170, 175, 179,
183, 187, 220, 245, and 249 courtesy the *Chicago Tribune.*

The publication of this book was generously supported
by the University of Iowa Foundation.

Printed on acid-free paper

Library of Congress Cataloging-in-Publication Data
Anderson, Jon.
City watch: discovering the uncommon Chicago / Jon Anderson.
p.   cm.
ISBN 0-87745-752-2 (pbk.)
1. Chicago (Ill.) — Social life and customs — 20th century.
2. City and town life — Illinois — Chicago — History — 20th century.
3. Chicago (Ill.) — Biography.   I. Title.
F548.52.A66   2001
977.3′11043 — dc21
00-053645

01 02 03 04 05 P 5 4 3 2 1

This book is dedicated
to my son, Jon Jr.,
who died early on the morning of
November 17, 1999.
In many, many ways, he inspired me.

CONTENTS

INTRODUCTION

When I came back to Chicago from Iowa City, after two years living in a wood-panelled coach house on South Dodge Street, my friend Jack Altman e-mailed me from Paris. "What was the single most important thing you learned there?" he wanted to know. Jack is like that. He has been through most of the writing stations I have, from *Time* magazine to the hurly-burly of daily journalism in Chicago. Like all writers everywhere, including me, he is still trying to master the mysterious practice of arranging twenty-six letters of an alphabet in ways that lead the mind towards new and interesting images. "I learned how to listen," I wrote back. And I left it at that, not going into how two years I spent in Iowa City in the early nineties changed my life. In one way, quitting the *Chicago Tribune*, cashing in my profit sharing and driving 235 miles west was going back to a sort of driver's ed class, a way to restore my vision, learn new ways, clean out old ones. Or, as Carl Klaus, the head of the non-fiction Master of Arts in Writing program at the University of Iowa, urged me when I sat down in his office to discuss this adventure: "Open up your mind, your senses." And that's what I did, at fifty-three, changing myself quite a bit.

Later, when I went back to Chicago, to be rehired by the *Chicago Tribune*, I was in many ways a different person. What I have tried to do, in my post-Iowa period, is to look for the deeper themes of life, as it is lived in Chicago, in what many people call "America's most typical big city." I wanted to take snapshots of people doing what they do. I wanted to get beneath the public clatter, the conflicts, the violence, the public issues and political debates. What interested me more were private obsessions, triumphs, fears and adjustments that shape people. On the South Side, for example, a man in Beverly paints the light poles in his neighborhood. He started with one. It bugged him because it was rusty. Then he did his block. Now he has done five thousand. Or a poet takes a job as a maid on the Gold Coast and records the strange demands of her employers, in verse. Or an artist, just out of the School of the Art Institute, knits forty-three mittens and makes a display of them, her way of remembering the elderly victims of a killer heat wave.

So, thus, this book.

I probably wouldn't be writing about these people if I hadn't taken two years to go to the University of Iowa. That's why having a collection of them published by the University of Iowa Press is, in many ways, a capstone for a career that (I don't know how) I seemed powerless to avoid. I grew up in Montreal, where the first explorers of Iowa started out from. I grew up with an uncle who worked for newspapers and, for some reason, I never thought seriously about doing anything else. Yes, I studied to be an engineer, though I switched my major after an English professor pointed out that I was in peril of spending the rest of my life in the northern Quebec, building dams for power companies. And I did finish law school, for reasons that I have never fully understood. But looking back, I realize that the course of my life was set at the age of nine when the man who was about to become my uncle arrived for a date with the woman who had always been my aunt. Together, they took me downtown, on a school night, to tour the offices of the Montreal *Gazette*. It was probably eight o'clock when we got there, a time when most offices would have closed down for the day, but there were typewriters clacking, people yakking into phones, bells going off and, down a long corridor, a whole row of clacking, whirly-gig machines, all grasshopper arms and smelling of oily dust. "What's your name, kid?" one of the grizzled linotype operators asked me. "Jon Anderson," I said, and he typed, pulled a lever and grunted, "Watch out. It's hot." He handed over a "slug," a by-line in raised letters, backwards, two ounces of warm lead, the most addictive substance that I, for one, have ever known.

On June 15, 1963, at 5 P.M., I arrived in Chicago, where I have lived, more or less, ever since. I was employed at the time by *Time* magazine. The chief of correspondents, Richard Clurman, suggested that, to broaden my horizons, I leave my post as Montreal bureau chief and move to the U.S. for a year, before going on to Paris. Of all the cities in the country, Chicago, he said, "had the most going on," which would give me a chance to perfect my craft by writing for every section of the magazine. This was not always easy. Writing, I confess it, is tough for me. There is always the search for form. What is this story about? How should it be told? On top of that, as I tell students when I teach, writers always have to struggle to move from the general to the specific. I once interviewed a man who had two hundred cats. He was separated from his wife. Another man collected twine and had a ball eleven feet high in his front yard. It used to be thirteen feet high, but it shrank in the rain. Those are the kind of people I like to start with when I write. Yes, I am aware of the great abstractions of the day — isolation, loneliness, the quest for meaning, the fear of being overwhelmed by a civilization that gets ever more clangorous. How do we learn to live in harmony with nature, not only what is outside of us but also what is inside? But what I really like to find are people whose daily lives and quiet obsessions point out interesting ways of identifying, handling, or being defeated by, the challenges that face all of us.

This search for the "meaningful detail," as one of my teachers once described it, is where it's at for me in all forms of writing, be it journalism, or essays, or fiction. It's what I like to see in print, in my own work or in that of others. Some call it "the glory of the specific fact." But to me it is the joy in finding, and writing down, a detail that sets a scene, pointing to some larger truth.

I believe that one can learn much about the workings of a civilization by studying its "micro" aspects. "Civilization," as historian Will Durant described it, "is a stream with banks. The stream is filled with blood from people killing, stealing, shouting and doing the things that historians record. On the banks, unnoticed, people build homes, make love, raise children, sing songs, write poetry and even whittle statues. The story of civilization is what happened on the banks."

This book collects some of my observations of what happens on "the banks" in Chicago. I first arrived there almost forty years ago at night, flying in over Lake Michigan, seeing through the airplane windows only blackness, a sense of nothing until I caught a first glimpse, on the horizon, of a stage set, a distant metropolis, a wall of glass and steel towers, gleaming with light and rising, as I flew closer, out of the vast, flat, black water. I came for a brief stay. Except for my Iowa years, I never left.

I would like to acknowledge the extraordinary debt I owe to editors, mentors, writers and wise friends who have told me really useful things, some of them about writing, over the years. That list would include Carl Klaus, who guided me through the University of Iowa with help from William Cotter Murray, David Hamilton, and Hans and Barbara Breder. My writing teacher for the past twenty years, Molly Daniels, has relentlessly pushed me to look for "the moments after which everything is different." At the *Chicago Tribune*, Colleen Dishon started me off, with great wisdom. For many years, Mary Elson edited my offerings with enormous skill and precision. I am also grateful to Bob Davis for suggesting that I be assigned the "City Watch" beat. My father, William, of Cape Cod, and my brother, Derek, of Montreal, have been constant sources of love and literary direction. I would like to thank Barbie Mann and Pamela Sherrod. Muses don't come any better than them. And, of course, my children Ashley, Abra and Anthony who, each in a special way, have helped me hear life's sweet song.

God is in the details.

Ludwig Mies van der Rohe

SPECIAL PLACES

TOUR THAT THOUGHT
IT'S SEEN IT ALL TAKES IN
REAL EYE-BOGGLER

"You're in for a wonderful treat," said tour leader Ellen O'Connor, as a chartered bus outside the Ogilvie Transportation Center filled up for the first "Know Your Chicago" outing of the year.

For fifty years, operating under the umbrella of the University of Chicago, such tours have taken civic-minded citizens on backstage visits to everything from the Deep Tunnel project to Cook County Jail where, once, they shared beef stew with prisoners.

The idea was thought up in the late 1940s by Mary Ward Wolkonsky, a doyenne of Chicago society, who had read in her Vassar College alumni magazine about "a class that had taken a trip along the Hudson stopping in major towns to study their government.

"I thought that a similar venture would be important in Chicago," she said in an interview before the bus took off. "Our aim was to appeal to educated women, offering information that would enhance whatever they were doing. Or encourage them to get going at something."

Along with speakers ranging from social activist Saul Alinsky to photographer Victor Skrebneski, many of the two hundred tours so far have delved into the underside of the city and suburbs.

"We've been through three steel mills, almost every city organization, City Hall, schools, social agencies, companies, plants, most of the courts, sewage disposal operations and water filtration plants," Wolkonsky recalled. "We've had on lots of hard hats."

This year, however, planners scheduled a rather more upbeat opener, to celebrate not only surviving fifty years but doing well, with a mailing list that now exceeds twenty-five hundred.

It was also something of an exploration of what happens, in the Chicago area, if one plays one's cards exactly right and makes a gigantic pile of money. Like, what then?

Tribune photo by Ovie Carter.

"I've been doing this tour for twenty-five years and I thought I'd seen everything," murmured Sheila Kalish, as the bus reached its destination, the private home of a couple whose fortune came from the nut and sesame-bar business. It is rarely open to outsiders and is known as "The Victorian Palace," hidden away on a sixty-one-acre private park amid the rolling fields of Barrington Hills.

They had not, as Al Jolson said when introducing talking pictures, seen anything yet.

Inside the front door, the 150 guests assembled around a grand staircase designed after the main one on the *Titanic*.

(SPECIAL PLACES)

Then, they were led into the music room, a twenty-seven thousand-square-foot addition finished in 1992, which includes the largest theater pipe organ ever built, set in front of a replica of the theater curtain of the old Paradise Theater, once a West Side landmark.

"Migod, it's like Balaban & Katz go to Versailles," whispered one visitor, recalling decorating touches favored by the late Chicago movie theater moguls and by France's Louis XIV.

Indeed, throughout the vast palace of a home, which covers a full acre of ground, were columns and frills saved, or copied, from such temples of the cinema as the Regal, the Granada, the Chicago, the Southtown, the United Artists and the Music Box.

Inside, in the main house and in a vast metal box known as the Carousel Building on the other side of the lagoon beyond the dozens of geese at rest on manicured lawns, were hundreds of automatic musical instruments, many of them driven by perforated paper rolls.

"Yes, there are lots of things to see," noted the hostess, Marian Sanfilippo, whose husband, Jasper, built the nut business, amiably greeting a crowd that broke up into four groups to examine everything from the old coin-operated tavern pianos to genuine Tiffany table lamps.

"Extraordinary," said one guest, as a 450-pipe organ, with flashing lights, clacking maracas, a tom-tom and three automated accordions, played "Blue Tango" while a restored carousel whirled next to a glittering two-story art-glass facade titled "Palace of Eden."

So, what's it like, living in a place like this? "Well, after dinner, they often snuggle up by themselves and listen to the organ," said Robert Ridgeway, the palace's in-house instrument curator, noting that the Sanfilippos have no live-in help.

Indeed, others said, the couple are still as straightforward and friendly as they were thirty years ago when they lived in a small house in Niles. That was when Jaspar Sanfilippo began working for a nut firm started by his father, an immigrant from Sicily.

After his father died, Sanfilippo, who was turned on to the possibilities of mechanization as a youth after viewing nickelodeon pianos in a North Side restaurant, built the company into the world's second-largest processor and distributor of nuts and sesame-seed bars. Sales of John B. Sanfilippo & Son, Inc., products rose from $320,000 in 1963 to over $300 million last year.

The change in fortune also gave Sanfilippo the chance, after the company went public in 1991, to indulge in his favorite hobby, collecting automatic music instruments. His collection now is valued at $75 million.

"This was certainly more fun than the morgue," Wolkonsky suggested later, summing up the buzz about the place. Though the home is not open to the public, its gates do swing wide for about thirty charity fundraisers each year. To get their group in, "Know Your Chicago" board members pulled strings, of which they have plenty.

Others, on the bus back into town, were wondering how to wangle another invitation — when a planned private railroad around the grounds is completed.

September 18, 1998

SAVING GRACE
OF A LONELY LIFE

When it comes to saving things, it is normal and prudent, psychiatrists assure us, to put aside small objects for later use, an occupation that often involves string, rubber bands, newspapers, wrapping paper, nails and a stack of *National Geographic* magazines for rainy day reading about Borneo.

On the other hand, some people just love clutter.

John Steinbeck did.

In *Travels with Charley*, he wrote lovingly about his garage "full of broken bits and pieces," which he kept that way so that if a toilet or motor or lawnmower broke down he could find a part to fix it. A person with a similar cast of mind was the late Elizabeth Cheney of Oak Park. She filled so much of her home with her possessions — from Oriental antiques to used cigarette packages carefully folded into brown paper bags — that two major auctions will be needed this spring just to dispose of the good stuff.

Her three-story mansion at 220 North Euclid Avenue was packed with furniture, paintings, silver, porcelain, boxes, mounds of rugs, 150 quilts, letters, postcards, yellowed newspapers and 100,000 books. The best things — among them, $250,000 worth of antique silver — are going to gavel, in two auction sales.

But there have been surprises as packers moved through rooms of the elegant old house in recent weeks. They found, for example, stacks of Oak Park newspapers, *Chicago* magazines, pre-World War II newspapers, enough *New Yorkers* to build a pillar of fiction a dozen feet high and, neatly packed, hundreds of empty cartons of instant breakfast, Cheney's major sustenance in the years before her death on September 20, 1985.

"She saved everything. I don't know if she ever threw anything away," says Leslie Hindman, whose staff of auctioneers, at 225 West Ohio Street, has been preparing the goods for sale. Was this another case of an obsession identified in the archives of Chicago's Institute for Psychoanalysis as "collector's mania," a compulsive need some people have to set up strange warehouses? Actually, no.

Unlike New York's wealthy Collyer brothers, whom police found lodged in a filthy Fifth Avenue mansion with fourteen pianos, two organs, toys, bicycles, empty bottles, cans, three tons of newspapers and a partly dismantled Model-T Ford, Cheney was cheerful, neat, often generous and meticulously organized. To keep track of her possessions, she invented her own inventory system, using cards with brief descriptions, code numbers, purchase prices and insurance estimates. She had, in the Victorian sense, a place for everything, with everything in its place. She just kept more than most people do, as was seen on recent tour of her home, a three-story building with a grand staircase, elegant ballroom and, in the major bathrooms, fireplaces.

Her kitchen bookcases, for example, contained five hundred cookbooks, with enough recipes to feed a gourmet army. On a living room mantel were a dozen miniature rooms by Narcissa Thorne whose work also fills much of a room at the Art Institute of Chicago. Hats from legendary Chicago milliner Bes-Ben filled a large closet upstairs. Her attic once contained three hundred rugs, obtained by her uncle when he helped out an Oriental rug company during the Depression.

Born in Chicago in 1902, Elizabeth Cheney was the only child of William Cheney Jr., whose father, a train engineer, drove the last locomotive out of Chicago before the Great Chicago Fire engulfed the railroad yards, and Florence Hooker Cheney, whose father founded a Chicago glass and paint company. When she was three, her mother died. Her father, undone by the loss, put her in a private school and seldom saw her.

"She had a very sad childhood," says Steffi Podmanik, her housekeeper. "That's why she was the way she was." Early years, friends agree, were not easy. She boarded with two teachers who set her to "doing the dirty work," cleaning stoves and the kitchen. Later, for twenty years, she worked in the book department at Carson Pirie Scott & Company, saving pennies for the movies by walking from El stations instead of buying bus transfers.

Her nearest relatives, with whom she often stayed, were her uncle and aunt, Andrew and Mary Dole, in Oak Park. A philanthropist and major donor to George Williams College, Chicago Theological Seminary and the Oak Park library system, Andrew Dole died in 1940. Mary Dole died, at age eighty, in 1949, leaving the family mansion to niece Elizabeth, then forty-seven. Following in her aunt's directions, Elizabeth added to the collections of art, books and antiques, became a regular in Loop

(SPECIAL PLACES)

silver departments and well-known in antique circles in New York and London.

"Dealers from all over remember her really well," Hindman says. "We get calls all the time saying, for example, 'I once sold her a covered soup tureen. Are you selling that?'" The answer, in most cases, is yes. The upcoming auctions will include a George III soup tureen worth, perhaps, twenty thousand dollars, as well as four hundred lots of jewelry, Chinese snuff boxes and several cases of good port from the basement. The Cheney home, given to the Park District of Oak Park under a life-lease agreement in 1975, probably will be restored and opened to tours and small receptions.

Besides her things, friends also remember an interested, compassionate woman, an avid reader and benefactor of many interests, including the White House, to which she made donations of fine china. "She loved to do things for people," says Mary McMenamin, a longtime friend. "She loved to take them out to eat, buy them clothes, give them books." Nor was she without a sense of humor.

Two years ago, for example, during the Christmas shopping season, she took two pals downtown to Neiman-Marcus for lunch, found she couldn't hear over a tinkling pianist, waved over a waiter and told him: "Tell that fellow I'll give him ten dollars to have a long drink or get lost for a while." Moments later, the waiter returned, bowed politely and said: "Madam, the piano player accepts." The rest of lunch, McMenamin recalls, was "lots of fun."

April 20, 1986

POET FINDS PAST JOB
MAID TO ORDER

Much later, long after she was fired, when poet Lisa Alvarado was asked what she remembered most about her six months as a maid on Chicago's Gold Coast, she always began with the closets.

For starters, she'd never seen ones that big. The two off the master bedroom, one for "him," one for "her," were larger than many apartments she had known. "Can you organize a walk-in closet?" she was asked, at her hiring interview. She could. She got the job.

Later, as a poet, Alvarado was to think about the meaning of closets. About "skeletons in the closet." About "coming out of the closet." About "Fibber McGee's closet," a reference to an old radio gag about a cluttered storage area whose opening always led to major clatter.

As a maid, her duties were, to put it mildly, anti-McGee.

The goal was perfect order — for the Richard Tyler cocktail gowns, the Gucci and Armani outfits, the rows of Manolo Blahnik shoes, the La Perla lace-edged undies. Everything was top drawer, sorted according to color, category and the advice of a specialist from New York.

"She had a person fly in to pull outfits, lay them out and shoot photos. She would keep files, like 'Here is the beige Gucci outfit, these are the right accessories,'" Alvarado said, recalling a world above going to stores. Clothing came on the arms of fashion consultants, such as "the Donna Karan person arriving with a load of cashmere to look at."

What was needed, Alvarado was told, was a person who understood the nuances of dusting lacquered furniture, of cleaning modern art, of scrubbing marble tubs, of taking care to wash and dry a dog's paws after outings to protect the all-white carpets.

So, how did a self-professed "lifelong scribbler" from Albany Park, with a growing reputation as a poet and a performance artist, the winner of grants from the Illinois Arts Council and the city's Department of Cultural Affairs, get into a spot like this?

"A poem begins with a lump in the throat," Robert Frost once suggested.

For Alvarado, it was more like hunger pangs.

Two years ago, after blowing her savings on a writing trip to Mexico, Alvarado answered a want ad in the *Tribune* placed by a head-hunting firm. The client was a Gold Coast family whose identity Alvarado agreed, at the time of her hiring, never to reveal.

Her previous employments had included factory jobs, union organizing, health-care advocacy, several stints as a psychiatric orderly at Mt. Sinai Hospital Medical Center — and cleaning.

It was only after she left the Gold Coast that she considered her experiences as poetry, specifically *The Housekeeper's Diary*, now out from La Onda Negra Press, a four-year-old local publishing enterprise "devoted to expanding markets for women writers of color."

The book, with images by Robin Barcus, a graduate of the School of the Art Institute, is available at Women and Children First, a bookstore in Andersonville.

Many of Alvarado's poems, with titles ranging from "Hand Laundry" and "Taking Instructions" to "Sons of the Very Rich" and "Home," have to do with her feelings of strangeness in a place where she dealt with the most private aspects of a family's life, from sexual habits to ways of sharing food, but felt herself invisible:

> You will not think of me.
> I am a whisper
> a shadow.
> Silently,
> I slip in and out of rooms
> bearing gifts
> you only see as a meal.

Not easily summarized, the poems deal with "panties thin as a lie." And what to make of "someone who buys birthday presents with trust fund money, by phone, and pays someone else to wrap and deliver them." The isolation of the wealthy. And how "with Tilex, (the maid becomes) police and conjurer. I protect the pristine. I make evidence disappear."

"Diary" also gives Alvarado a ranking place in a spreading form of literature. Call it dust-and-tell. It's a genre started by palace help in London, lately including Wendy Berry, who served for eight years as housekeeper to Prince Charles. She got three hundred thousand dollars for revealing that Princess Diana had, on certain distraught occasions, shouted obscenities at Prince Charles, smashed teacups "and retreated to the loo to vomit after lunch."

Thus far, there have been no big bucks for poet Alvarado, who leaves this week to polish her skills, working toward a master of fine arts degree at Vermont College.

Indeed, she laments that, before she lost her Gold Coast job after a mixup involving a misplaced key to the country house, she was making thirty thousand dollars a year — "the best-paying job I ever had."

September 9, 1999

WEDGWOOD SOCIETY DREAMS
STILL ON THE TABLE

A sense of Old English restraint is one of the hallmarks of the Wedgwood Society of Chicago. They got around to holding their first meeting of the new year last week over cocktails and dinner at the Tavern Club, a private retreat at 333 North Michigan Avenue.

Slowly, over the years, the members have been raising money to build an arts center and museum to pay tribute to people they call "Illustrious Moderns."

The project appears to be in no danger of completion.

But the group has, without doubt, the classiest letterhead in town.

At the top is Queen Elizabeth II, followed by sixty-four others, including Princess Grace of Monaco, Sir Winston Churchill, Douglas Fairbanks Jr., Clare Booth Luce, A. N. Pritzker and Jane Byrne. At the bottom: Lord Piers Wedgwood, a descendant of Josiah Wedgwood, an English potter (1730–1795) whose dream, he once said, was to be "Vasemaker to the Universe."

Josiah Wedgwood was also "the father of modern marketing," arguably the first person to understand fully the value of celebrity clients in positioning a mass-market brand name, as Sotheby's ceramic specialist Letitia Roberts has observed in writings on the subject.

In 1773, for example, one notable client, Catherine the Great of Russia, ordered a 952-piece dinner service to entertain guests at Chesmenski Palace, located near a frog swamp. Going all out, Wedgwood put a different frog, along with British castles and landscapes, on each hand-painted plate, bowl and cup, for 1,244 views in all.

The "Frog Service," as it quickly became known, was the talk of Europe.

Later, as Roberts notes, Wedgwood learned how to produce lower-priced crockery for the masses, allowing their guests to flip plates, check the label and feel special.

Last week, as five dozen members of the Wedgwood Society of Chicago, most of them wealthy locals, settled into an upstairs function room at the Tavern Club, a sense of wistful Anglophilia filled the air. It was not for the Britain of Tony Blair.

Rather, as several guests noted, it was a feeling brought about by faded memories of leather book bindings, tar soaps, old tweeds and bumpy plates, the kind of aged artifacts that once led sociologist Thorstein Veblen to speculate on "the leisure class's veneration of the archaic" as a way of separating from the lower orders who fly to the new.

The host at the meeting of the Wedgwood/Chicago was Lawrence Marshall Pucci, who, with his sister, Caryl Pucci Rettaliata, established the society in 1967.

Their father, Lawrence Rance Pucci, started the family's tailoring business on North Michigan Avenue in 1923 and, as the younger Pucci explains, "was obsessed with Wedgwood china." Along with collecting, the senior Pucci made his children aware of "Illustrious Moderns," a term coined more than two hundred years ago by Josiah Wedgwood as he did plaques and busts of those he called "outstanding statesmen, scientists and contributors of the age."

In 1972, the Chicago society started up a list of its own, to honor the "gentlemen and ladies who've enhanced the art and culture of this age," as the younger Pucci put it.

For example, when Princess Margaret came through town in 1980, she was added at a Wedgwood ceremony, even though she tangled, that same week, with another "Illustrious Modern," then-mayor Jane Byrne, over the topic of Irish contributions to world culture.

Others on the list now include Dame Margot Fonteyn, Victor Borge, Sir Michael Redgrave, Arthur Rubloff, Ruth Page, John Paul Getty and Bonnie Swearingen.

Picked as this year's "Illustrious Modern" was Dominique de Menil, a French-born, Houston-based heiress to a fortune built by her father, Conrad Schlumberger, who developed a geophysical tool that determined the location of underground oil deposits.

Mrs. de Menil was best known for building what architect Philip Johnson called "the greatest private museum in the world," the Menil Collection Museum near Houston, housing more than fifteen thousand works of art valued at upwards of $150 million. Mrs. de Menil died last New Year's Eve.

Pucci presented a plaque honoring her to two of her friends,

Count Rinaldo Petrini de Montfort, an Italian-born architect now based near Houston, and Carolyn Farb, a Houston social-ite and author of *How to Raise Millions: A Guide to Fundraising*.

Both promised to help with Chicago efforts to get the local "Illustrious Moderns" museum beyond the talking stage.

"Carolyn's just a whiz at raising money," whispered one guest as the evening came to a close. "One time, she pulled in a million dollars in one night, with a ball and silent auction."

"How did you do it?" a visitor asked Farb.

"I locked the doors," she said.

April 4, 1998

GENTS (AND LADIES)
IN WHITE RECLAIM TURF
AFTER DRY SPELL

The grass is back.

As sports bulletins go, the big news — from Hyde Park's courtly Lakeside Lawn Bowling Club — is not exactly earth-shaking, certainly not up there with "Tiger Wins" or "Bears Lose" or "Bulls Take Fifth."

On the other hand, that's one point of a game that has quite nicely survived tumultuous off-court events ranging from the collapse of the Roman Empire, where it was invented, to the recent transfer of Hong Kong.

Lawn bowling, to put it mildly, is sedate. Earth-calming, if anything.

"It's a gentlemanly game," club instructor Cal Wright was saying the other day, standing on a club green just south of the Museum of Science and Industry. Unlike contestants in other sports, he noted, lawn bowlers would never wave fists, shove one another, shout at referees — or bite.

"We wear white clothes, by tradition," he said. "Before every game, you shake hands with your partner and the competition and wish them 'Good bowling.' And afterwards, you shake hands with all of them again."

Wright did face a situation once in California where, after he won a match, his opponent "stomped off." That was wrong, he said, and as bad as anything he's ever seen in lawn bowling, at least among the players.

Nature, however, can be something else, because the essence of what one writer once called "the trickiest sport ever devised by the mind of man" is a level playing field. On that score, Lakeside, the only lawn bowling club in the Chicago area, has been through a bad patch recently.

Two summers ago, its two bowling greens, each a 120-foot square of impeccably tailored lawn, caught a double whammy. First, they were parched by a severe heat wave. Then, they were riddled by grass-eating fungus.

Only now, after resodding and care, are the greens back in decent shape, attracting new players to a strange little sport so

compelling that Sir Francis Drake, on July 19, 1588, insisted on completing his game before rounding up other sailing enthusiasts to beat back the Spanish armada.

On a recent sunny afternoon on the South Side, in an atmosphere of civility and politeness, a mix of old hands and novices came together, as they do on shaded greens around the world, to roll an odd-shaped ball.

"A degree in physics would help," quipped one bystander.

"It couldn't hurt," agreed another.

Unlike boccie, which uses a small round ball, or bowling, which uses a large ball and wooden alleys, lawn bowling uses a "bowl," shaped like a softball that someone has sat on — and smooshed.

Not quite round, it is heavier on the un-smooshed side — and curves that way as it loses speed, allowing for considerable tactics.

The game starts with a player throwing a small ball, a "jack," down one of seven "rinks," as lawn-bowling alleys are known. Bowlers roll four bowls, each about three pounds, placing them as close as possible to the jack.

"You can master the essentials in about an hour," Wright said. But, as in so much of life, getting one's curve just right can take a lifetime.

"I was jogging by here two years ago, saw this place — and it was deserted. When I saw it was operating again, I came right over," said one of a threesome new to the sport, Douglas Pinsky, a graduate student in political science at the nearby University of Chicago.

"It's frustrating at times," suggested one of his competitors, Jeannie Tan, a physician at Weiss Memorial Hospital. "You think you're aiming properly, then the ball turns and goes the other way."

Lawn bowling, noted a brochure passed out by Lakeside president Bill Nakagawa, "is a test of temper, a trial of honor, a revealer of character. It is a contest calling for courage, skill, strategy and self-control."

It is, others said, a game played "behind every pub in England" and in almost every corner of the world where the British Union Jack once flew. Indeed, a phone call this week to the sports department of the *South China Morning Post* brought news that, despite its British heritage, lawn bowling "is terrifically popular among the Chinese," with many clubs flourishing.

Lakeside, on the same site for seventy-three years, has score-cards back to 1928 when the club formally opened with a match against thirty-five touring bowlers from New Zealand. The visitors "let Lakeside look good the first day, shading them 134–100," a member wrote in the club report. On the second day, New Zealand, playing tougher, whomped their Chicago hosts, 202–107.

"Lawn bowling used to be big in this country," Wright said, noting that seven states have cities named for the sport and that George Washington once had a bowling green at Mt. Vernon. (In 1776, during a general nose-thumbing at England, it was converted into a square vegetable garden.)

These days, Lakeside staffers report, there are some 250 lawn bowling clubs across the U.S. That may be a pittance beside, say, Britain's 4,000 clubs but, without making a big fuss about it, Lakeside is reaching out, says its president, "to anyone who wants to take up the game."

On Tuesday and Thursday afternoons, those willing to learn, and wearing flat-soled shoes, can get free instruction from 1 to 3 P.M. A side bonus is a splendid view of the lake — in case an armada arrives.

July 9, 1997

LIMOUSINES:
NOT JUST FOR THE RICH

Back in the days when a million dollars still meant something, Chicago publishing executive Bailey K. Howard used to ride around town in a limousine so long that it had two telephones. "Just a minute," his chauffeur would tell callers, "I'll ring back there and see if he's in."

But, as they say, times change.

These days, not just the rich and famous have lifestyles that include the use of a limousine. Now, all sorts of people are easing back into a womb of plush, shutting doors on the day-to-day scuffle of life, gliding through traffic with a bar, color TV, footrests, reading lamps and darkened windows and making, through their choice of transport, a steel-and-chrome statement to those who gawk at street corners: "I am somebody."

Consider some figures. Best estimates are that the nation's limousine population has reached sixty-five thousand; forty-five thousand vehicles are operated by public livery services and twenty thousand more are under private command. That's a population growth of 100 percent in a decade. It's also quite a comeback since the darkest day in the history of American limousines: January 21, 1977.

That was the "afternoon of infamy," as some in the trade still call it, when newly-inaugurated President Jimmy Carter, his wife, Rosalynn, and daughter, Amy, nine — to make a point — abandoned their long limousine, joined crowds of marchers and actually walked in the winter's cold down Pennsylvania Avenue to the White House.

"When that happened," shudders James Centner, "every chauffeur in the country died a thousand deaths."

Centner is president and chief operating officer of Chicago's Moloney Manufacturing Corporation, a company that takes Cadillacs, Lincolns, Buicks, Oldsmobiles and Mercedeses, saws them down the middle, inserts body sections ranging from fourteen to fifty inches, customizes the interior and repaints the result — one more stretched luxury limousine.

These are different times, as Centner, a man with much to lose from such populist gestures, is quick to point out.

Last year, working out of a former pinball machine factory at 2640 West Belmont Avenue and two other plants, in Schaumburg and in Florida, Moloney finished 1,140 such vehicles, one-fifth of the nation's total. This year's company projection is 1,400 and, if the nation's economy holds up, Centner predicts that the company's output will double by 1990. The standard price for a reworked Cadillac Brougham or Lincoln Town Car is $40,000, though Moloney also offers a Mercedes, stretched by forty inches, for $135,000.

A limousine still is not the kind of transport that the penny-minded should consider for runs to the supermarket. Luxury vehicles consume fuel at a rate akin to the liner *Queen Mary*, which, before it was beached in California, got thirteen feet to the gallon. But these days renting a "canoe," as stretch limos are jocularly known, is not that expensive, about $50 to an airport or about $175 per night on the town, plus a tip for the driver.

Why are people into limousines?

For renters, crawling into one is a quest for grandeur, a nice addition to prom night, wedding day, bar mitzvah or barhopping. For owners, there are the special satisfactions that come from having a car that serves as a portable wing of a home, a haven of safety, an important mechanism for class-status display and a place to leave coats.

For revelers, limousines now make even more sense. Times were when people out on a toot accepted the possibility of being stopped by police while driving as just one more risk of a night on the town. "Now," Centner notes, "bright young couples chip in to hire a limousine for evenings. It beats some of the alternatives, such as three days in the slammer, your license suspended, a fine of four hundred dollars and loss of your reputation."

During the day, another business of limousines has become, well, business. Ultra Limousine Corporation of La Palma, Calif., for example, fits many of its vehicles with computer stands, cellular phones and conference tables so that two to four people can "take a meeting" while tooling along an expressway. "For executives," notes Ultra's marketing director Craig Hoelzel, "a limousine is efficient transportation, not a luxury. It is a mobile office. They can make decisions instead of doing the driving."

The talk of the industry these days is something else from Ultra, the "Super Ultra," a fifty-foot vehicle with gull-wing doors, a rumble seat—and a swimming pool. "The pool is about ten feet long, three feet deep and really more of a hot tub," Hoelzel admits. "But we have had eight people in it."

More practical, Hoelzel says, is a back seat microwave oven, a feature (along with a refrigerator and a sink) in a limousine used by actor Clint Eastwood, who likes hot hors d'oeuvres during his hundred-mile-or-so commute from home to work in the Los Angeles area. One African head of state recently bought an armored Mercedes limousine with a satellite communications system and a throne.

When fifteen hundred conventioneers gathered in Atlantic City last month to gawk at new limousines at the Second Annual Limousine and Chauffeur Show, what they liked were vibrator seats, laser-disc record players, safes, computerized bars, ice crushers, gold-plate wheel spokes, gull-wing doors, power moon-roofs and hard-plastic security windows.

When such limousines whoosh past — and whoosh past they will, sometime in the near future — try not to stare.

January 13, 1986

CHICAGO
PASSIONS AND
STYLES

"WILD ONES" SAY
IT SIMPLY ISN'T SO

In the basement of the Abbey Pub, below the din of the big biker party upstairs, a man known as Jo-mama stood by the row of chili pots and talked of Harleys, wrenches and the first night he'd ever felt close to his father.

It was years ago. He was fourteen. His father had torn apart his own Harley and laid out the parts on the floor of the family garage. Then, said Jo-mama, "my dad goes, 'Until you can put it together, you ain't ready to ride.'"

By dawn, Jo-mama had it ready. His father said he'd "better try it out first — to make sure it's safe." The old man "fired up the machine, kicked it into gear, flew out of the garage, sped across the street and spun out on the neighbor's front lawn, right under their bedroom window."

It was an important lesson, admitted Jo-mama, who got his nickname later for being a mechanic always willing to help out a biker in trouble.

"I forgot to hook up the brake rod."

For a bikers rally, the all-night scene last weekend on three floors of the Abbey, at 3420 West Grace Street, just off the Edens Expressway, was oddly peaceful, though it often resembled the space-jockey bar in "Star Wars."

Monitoring the crowd was about three thousand pounds of human flesh, on a dozen beefy bodies, wearing intercom headphones and orange shirts reading SECURITY.

Despite an engaging sense of menace, the purpose of the evening was peaceful enough to raise several thousand dollars through a dance, unisex tattoo competition and chili-making for a biker support group, ABATE, which stands for A Brotherhood Aimed Toward Education.

"It's not like Marlon Brando and 'The Wild One.' We don't like that image," said Michael Kerr, local chapter head of the national organization. These days, he noted, pointing to faces in the crowd, "we have every trade — plumbers, welders, electricians, firemen, cops." Others mentioned Dan Aykroyd, actor — and biker.

Representing 180,000 bikers licensed in Illinois, ABATE seeks to push interests threatened by ordinances banning bikers from some city streets, laws demanding helmet use and emerging technology that someday may limit highways to electronically-aimed cars and trucks.

To bikers, such weapons as support groups, fundraising and a political agenda are modern necessities. Without them, Kerr warned the crowd, "in twenty years, we might find ourselves off the road."

To many bikers, federal regulations requiring states to pass helmet-use laws or lose a portion of highway funding, smack of, as one put it, "the thin edge of a wedge" of government interference in biker affairs.

"We don't say helmets are good or bad," said Skip Robinson, another ABATE officer. "We say, 'Don't force us to wear them.' What we want is freedom of choice. Let each rider decide."

"We send a thousand bikers to Springfield every year for a rally in May," said Jay Schellerer, the group's legislative director who also is working to reverse biker bans on several streets in West Rogers Park and in an area around Navy Pier. "The police should deal with noisemakers like with anybody who makes a racket," he said, "not just ban all bikers."

These days, a hog can set a biker back ten to twenty-five thousand dollars, with up to twenty-five thousand more for customizing, principally chrome and mirrors, and suitable clothing and adornment. One woman, Kerry, was the hit of one corner when she pulled back her blouse to reveal a back tattoo of Emmett Kelly.

"All the stuff in your daily life, like mortgage payments, that's behind you," mused president Kerr. "You're out. All the elements around you. One with reality. If it rains, you get wet," he said.

Each year, ABATE members ride from the downtown lakefront to a Highland Park roadhouse for coffee. They gather Christmas toys for needy children.

Their "Spring Fling Picnic," in the LaBagh Woods Forest Preserve on the Northwest Side, provides competitions for riders.

Other bikers are into the arts, noted Santo, organizer of a Biker Poetry Slam to be held at the Outlaws Chicago Clubhouse, at 2601 West 25th Street, on Friday at 8 P.M. "We read poems about riding around, womanizing, drugs, the whole gamut," said Santo, who appeared last fall on "The David Letterman Show," illustrating one of the "Top Ten Biker Pickup Lines."

His line was, "I left my Volvo at home."

Often, bikers are misunderstood, said Dave "Dog Killer" White. "I ran over the only black and white dingo in the United States in Minnesota in 1984," he said, explaining his nickname. "We tried to comfort the owner. I told him, 'Look, you've still got the only black and white dingo in the United States. It's just that now he's dead.'"

February 2, 1997

CLOTHES FOUND IN
RUBBISH DON'T HAVE TO
LOOK TRASHY

In Dumpster-diving, as in much of life, timing is everything, as they were saying the other night at the big Dumpster-Diving Fashion Show at the St. Francis Catholic Worker House in Uptown.

Think May 1. And October 1.

"Moving days are terrific. There are tons of stuff," whispered a man named Larry, one of two dozen models hurriedly changing outfits backstage before parading through the stately old home at 4652 North Kenmore Avenue.

So, too, is end of term near any college with dormitories. Or end of summer where there are vacationers. Or end of season behind any good store.

"If you do it right, you can live really cheaply," said Ruthie, as she slipped into a floor-length white dress and, with a swing of her hips, hit the runway across the living room — to gasps and applause.

"I was Ruthie's roommate for a year," said a friend, "and I never saw her actually buy anything. But she always had ten outfits to show me."

It was an evening of considerable inventiveness.

Twirling, one woman showed off an outfit built around a found jacket that she said had been listed at seventy-five dollars in a recent Land's End catalog.

A man named Eric wore a safari hat with a leopard bandana (once someone's pillowcase) tied around the brim.

Another woman appeared in bowling shoes and tights that she had fished out of a garbage bin. After shining the shoes and washing the tights, she wore them with a pink suit, which, she acknowledged, cost her six dollars at a thrift shop.

"Thrift shopping is considered spring training," one veteran Dumpster-diver explained, helping a visitor understand an increasingly popular art form.

Some might find it yucky, but others see it as the kind of thing Henry Thoreau would be doing if he were alive and living downtown.

It was Thoreau — the Michael Jordan of cheap living — who put in two years and two months at a small pond in Massachusetts, living off a budget of $61.99 a year — an outlay some Dumpster-divers consider excessive.

"None is so poor that he need sit on a pumpkin," Thoreau wrote in *Economy* in 1845. "There is a plenty of such chairs as I like best in the village garrets to be had for taking them away."

Exactly, say Dumpster-divers.

"You look for a high correlation of disposable income, transience and stupidity," observed one model, noting that best finds are not necessarily on the Gold Coast. (There, old wealth families traditionally ship their unwanted treasures to resale shops, for a tax deduction.)

"She's talking Lincoln Park," said another. "That's the best."

There were tales of found furniture, computers, books, shelving and a child's car seat with one strap missing.

"I read that raising a child through college today can cost upwards of two hundred thousand dollars," said the car seat finder. "That's nonsense. I called the manufacturer and got them to send me a new strap. I'm already one car seat ahead."

The fashion show of sixty found outfits was put together by several dozen residents and volunteer helpers at the home, a shelter for homeless adults that preaches, among other virtues, self-reliance.

And street smarts. Or, in this case, alley smarts.

"It's important to keep your eyes open," said one man, noting that he had picked up a "wonderful bureau which I'm sanding and making into something else because it's missing a few drawers."

During a discussion period, some noted that Dumpster-diving has moved beyond economic necessity to become a sort of modern virtue, a thoughtful reuse of the world's resources — and its things.

"Ten years, ago I saw this TV report which equated Dumpster-diving with the dregs of society, and I thought, 'How tragic,'" one diver confessed. "Now, I'm like, 'Hey, get away. That's my favorite spot.'"

According to books on the subject, notably John Hoffman's *The Art & Science of Dumpster Diving*, seasoned divers avoid areas around hospitals, dentists' offices and pathology labs. Garbage bins there have a higher incidence of "sharpies," such as broken glass and used needles.

"Launder everything," Hoffman writes, "and forget anything with black spots. That's usually mildew, and it's hard to get out."

The Tightwad Gazette, another strong seller that is billed as a guide to "thrift as a viable alternative lifestyle," devotes six pages to Dumpster-diving.

"If you wear gloves and wash finds immediately after returning home, you face less of a health risk than riding a crowded subway in flu season," claims its editor, Amy Dacyczyn, also known as "the Frugal Zealot."

Asked to recount their Dumpster-diving experiences, one woman at the fashion show said she drew the line at "going through icky stuff, where it's messed in with chicken bones." She added, "I'm kind of wimpy."

But others reported amazing finds from digging deep.

"I found a whole case of condoms in a Dumpster behind a dormitory at Northwestern (University)," one man said. "It was the end of term."

"Our wedding gift was a set of knives that Jack found," reported Ruthie, speaking of her recent nuptials and a present from the best man.

April 25, 1997

FIVE GUYS IN THEIR FORTIES
SING ABOUT, WELL, GUYS
IN THEIR FORTIES

Moody, blue, they sing songs of paunch, of second marriages, of fading hopes, of job disenchantment — of downsizing.

These five guys — somewhat overweight, all in their forties, all from the suburbs — have been singing up a storm lately, tackling the concerns of a generation that is now slogging through middle age in an era of corporate upheaval and turmoil. They call it Boomer rock.

"We're the only group I'm aware of doing original stuff dedicated to our age group, the Baby Boomers," said Steve Wyrostek, guitarist, vocalist and songwriter for The Houndz.

Just out is the band's first CD, *2nd Adulthood*, available in many stores on their own label, Boomer Music. It addresses issues ranging from office angst to mid-life dreams of running away and becoming an artist, like maybe in Tahiti. They know whereof they sing.

"I had, like, four arrows to the brain in the past few years," said Wyrostek, taking time off from rehearsals for an interview. "Got divorced. Downsized. Eyesight got a bit fuzzy. And, tell me, why don't I care about the Bears any more? Since Ditka left?"

An operations manager for CNA Financial Corporation in Downers Grove, Wyrostek, forty-four, who lives in Des Plaines, will be laid off in the near future, after which, he says, "I'm going to take my severance and recognize that it's time to shift. No more corporate stuff for me."

Similarly, Tom Holler, forty-three, of Des Plaines, on guitar, now outsources as a database administrator for Ameritech, where he once worked.

Bob Reed, forty-two, of Elmhurst, on sax, became a management consultant after he was given a farewell package by Helene Curtis.

Jeff Plettau, forty-six, of Schiller Park, on bass and banjo, is currently a house husband, looking after a new baby at home while his wife teaches.

The fifth member, Ken White, forty-three, of Forest Park, on drums, is a payroll programmer at Household Finance Corporation in Elmhurst.

What links them all, said Reed, is "this band — something I've always wanted to do. We play the music we want to play." They've been at it for four years.

This summer, The Houndz have drawn applause in venues ranging from Naperville, where they did a church picnic, to Antioch, where they played a microbrew fest last weekend at Parrots Cove Resort. Along with party planners and corporate events organizers, who now book the band for thirty or more gatherings a year, critics are starting to take note, among them Diane Jessurun of Small Hall, an on-line review of "the newest artists, the latest tunes."

"These guys are in mid-life," Jessurun recently wrote, at www.smallhall.com, "and have set themselves on a journey of their dreams. I'll keep listening."

To Boomers, the concept of good music means paying due deference to the rhythms of the sixties, upgraded with relevant lyrics for the nineties.

"People our age are getting tired of the oldies, but the new stuff we just can't listen to," said Wyrostek, who has authored such tunes as "I'm Tired," "Day Job" and "I Am a Warrior," which defiantly reports that "a spirit beats beneath this suit."

While bands composed of, well, slightly older persons are nothing new, what sets The Houndz apart is "that we do a lot more originals," claims saxist Reed, noting that their work "often brings smiles of recognition.

"Midlife crisis has to do with dreams we had when we were young. Then, at forty or so, you say, 'Hey, maybe this isn't going to happen,'" noted Wyrostek. "We want to tell people in their forties and fifties that there is a lot of hope for their remaining years."

One problem is how to get the message out.

In former times, the musicians suggested, The Houndz would have started as a bar band. But, caught up in the demands of jobs, families or budget constraints, fewer members of the Boomer generation are hitting the clubs anymore.

"It's, 'Oh, I'd have to get a baby-sitter.' Or, 'Gotta take my kids to soccer practice,'" said Reed, listing excuses given by friends unable to make club dates. To reach their aging fans, The Houndz now specialize in weekend fests and parties during daylight hours.

And The Houndz get considerable airplay on an hour-long

radio program, *The Midlife Crisis Show*, at 7 P.M. each Wednesday, on WJKL/94.3, an FM station known as "The Fox!" in downtown Elgin. "It's a hot market," reported Mike Bellah, a phone-in guest, referring to Baby Boomers, whose concerns he addresses on his own Internet page, www.bestyears.com.

"What gives you pleasure, concentrate on that," advised host Steve Mayfield, reporting that he himself had found unexpected happiness, through remarriage, to a longtime friend and former co-worker. "I had the rock band, the bachelor pad, the Lincoln, then I fell in love. I can't believe it," said Mayfield, a man who looked (and sounded) exactly like Steve Wyrostek.

August 28, 1998

FORAGING FRIENDS
SAVOR TASTES OF GREAT
OUTDOORS

For the Foraging Friends, together for eighteen years, the light spring rain was hardly an impediment as they set off into the woods, from Devon and Milwaukee, looking for some tasty stuff to eat.

It was as if the Chef Upstairs was freshening up the salad bar.

One man walked barefoot, but that was not a problem because the woods, unlike many restaurants, are not a "no shoes/no service" operation.

Once a month, from spring until late fall, the Foraging Friends rendezvous at noon at Heartland Cafe, an old hippie hangout in Rogers Park, then hop into Wes Wagar's cab and motor as far away as Lemont.

"Wes is our driving force," explained Bob Carlock, a longtime regular, as Wagar pointed out a stand of garlic mustard that, Wagar said, was "a weed that came over from Europe — and we do good by eating it, because it's alien, and it's crowding everything else out."

"Hey, there's a great headline," shouted Guy Garantolo, the shoeless one, nudging a visitor who had joined the group for a quick nibble.

"Eat the Aliens!"

For the dozen or more members of Foraging Friends, eating their way through woods is, at least, a hobby and, at most, a way of reassuring themselves that, if the sky did fall, they could readily survive.

With day jobs that range from waiter to academic, they love to spend an afternoon sampling greens, nibbling branches, swapping recipes and offering up the wisdom of the wild, such as Wes Wagar's observation, "Look! Violets! More Vitamin C in one leaf than in a whole orange!"

It is a time to talk of tea from raspberry bushes, of fresh clover for salads, of shepherd's purse soup, of nettles that, as one noted, "cook up like spinach, though you have to pick them with gloves, of course."

The core members of the group, who are interested in ecology, first got together "around 1979," Wagar said. Each month they place ads in alternative weeklies, inviting newcomers to join their outings.

Some stay on. Others don't.

"The thing that surprises me is that there's so much to eat out here," said Jan Boudart, who got a bachelor's degree in botany years ago and now is on the staff of Northwestern University's Medill School of Journalism.

"These are definitely edible," Boudart said, picking through a patch of wild onions, or Che-ca-gou, as natives living downtown once described them to explorers who landed to claim the land for the king of France.

"But," she went on, "you still need protein." And that means "a bit of meat," she warned, though others, their eyebrows raising, chirped in that helpings of black walnuts and seeds might do just as well.

During the wet and rainy afternoon, there were other concerns.

Taking note of the maxim, "You are what you eat," several in the crowd warned that, in the foraging game, that can mean "dead."

"Wes teaches us what's edible," said Jack Drumke, passing along an important element of the forager's creed: "Be sure, before you eat, you know what you're putting in your mouth. And that it isn't poisonous."

Several carried books with descriptions of the edible and inedible, reflecting a theme in a recent issue of *Countryside & Small Stock Journal* that "foraging for wild foods can be another arrow in the homesteader's quiver for self-reliance — and a very enjoyable one. But a good guidebook is a necessity — be very sure of your identification."

Others spoke lovingly of the late Euell Gibbons, author of *Stalking the Wild Asparagus*, a regular guest on *The Tonight Show with Johnny Carson*, a popularizer of foraging and a TV pitchperson for Grape-Nuts Flakes, of which Gibbons said, "It reminds me of wild hickory nuts."

"Yes, I've read all his books," said Garantolo, who added that he started out in mushrooms, where "you really have to watch out."

There were, in fact, a considerable number of hazards for Garantolo, who said he walks barefoot, for health reasons, as soon as the snow melts each year because "it strengthens my legs, though I carry a pair of sandals with me in case I have to go on a bus or into a restaurant or a business."

Walking a route that plunged deep into the Clayton Smith and Bunker Hill Woods, the group came across broken bottles, fake plastic flowers with sharp points, abandoned toys and crushed cans as well as nature's tangles of sticks and stones, all of which Garantolo nimbly stepped around.

They passed by a number of wind-blown plastic shopping bags, many snagged on branches. "We call them Jewel Tea tumbleweeds," said Bob Rudner who edits a Web page for the Chicago Greens, a team of grass-roots activists who hold, among other tenets, that "the Earth sustains all life forms. What we do to the web of life we do to ourselves."

Though this spring has been cold and dry, putting nature's edibles a bit behind schedule, all agreed that they loved the woods, whatever condition they were in. "(I) was interested in this for a long time. Decided it's something I wanted to learn about," said Wagar, when asked how he got into using his taxi-cab, almost two decades ago, to lead such outings.

Then he turned to Boudart for help on a positive ID of Solomon's Seal, a perennial herb of the lily family with gnarled roots. "It's important," said Boudart, "because out West some settlers, used to eating Solomon's Seal in the East, ate False Solomon's Seal." And they died.

May 2, 1997

AT LEAST ONCE A
MONTH, ANARCHISTS
REIGN AT MEETING

In a church basement, on a Sunday afternoon in New Town, a group of anarchists assemble in Heretics Hall, as they call their rented room.

"Work is Hell" suggests a placard on the literature table. On a bulletin board are two words, "Listen" and "Respect," under a picture of Emma Goldman, a hero of the anarchist movement, jailed for inciting riots.

"One of us gives a short spiel. We discuss among ourselves what's going on in the world. Then we eat," explained Mike who, while not in charge, seemed more in charge than any of the dozen others in the room.

On this day, Beth brought the salad, though a motto on the wall, carefully stitched in needlepoint, urged: "Eat the Rich."

Welcome, sort of, to the monthly meeting of Some Chicago Anarchists where the talk runs from philosophers Georg Wilhelm Frederich Hegel and Jean-Jacques Rousseau to what went wrong in tortured Spain in the 1930s.

And, of course, there is talk, some heated, of the ill-fated protest meeting of anarchists in Crane's Alley, near Haymarket Square, on May 4, 1886, an event — marked by a bomb, shootings, clubbings and dubious trials — later to be known around the world as the Haymarket Riot.

"Often, we throw reporters right out of here," Mike was saying to a visitor with a notepad, "because they never get it right."

And, said Fred, speaker of the day, "I don't want my picture taken."

Nor did anyone else. They also kept their last names private.

A century ago, militant anarchists were a potent force in Chicago, with thousands of followers and eight anarchist newspapers, one of them a daily, the *Chicagoer Arbeiter-Zeitung*, published from 1884 to 1910.

Now, Some Chicago Anarchists, as the modern-day gathering calls itself, carries on the battles, in a philosophical way, urging on the anarchist ideals of freedom from domination by others, or of others.

"I won't rule over anybody — or be ruled by anybody," said Dave, across the room, summing up an anarchist credo for a decentralized society, built around two Greek words, an archos, or "without a rule."

"Anarchism should be understood as aiming at the abolition of all forms of domination," noted one group theorist, Ron Carrier, in a recent issue of *Autonomy*, the group's monthly newsletter, on the literature desk.

That, Carrier went on, covers any form of human relations "where one decides for another, without the other's consent, how the other is to live and coerces the other into living that way."

They sense, they said, some support for their views.

Every election day, for example, Some Chicago Anarchists set up a booth in the park triangle at Lincoln and Fullerton Avenues.

"We have a sign, 'If you hate politicians, honk your horn,'" said Beth, noting that the din from passing cars is always deafening.

As part of its educational outreach program, the group, which has been meeting for about fifteen years, sponsors forums and holds picnics in the summer.

The rest of the year they meet in the basement of Second Unitarian Church, at 656 West Barry Avenue, though staffers at the church were careful to note that "we merely rent out the space, much as we do for weddings and Alcoholics Anonymous meetings."

The topic at the first meeting of the fall season was "Free People Ask, 'Who Needs the State?'" It lasted three hours.

"The whole problem," began Fred, the keynote speaker, "goes back maybe ten thousand years to the Middle East, where surplus crops were turned over to a shaman who hired warriors to guard it before it was sacrificed to the gods. The shaman, precursor to the modern-day wealthy, kept a large share for himself, living off the community's production, but not contributing."

These days, Fred said, jumping to the present, "as the Golden Rule says, 'Those who have the gold make the rules.'"

Others reflected on how modern laws often seem to be selectively enforced, targeting the poor, the weak, the vulnerable.

"Look at the IRS," one said, referring to recent Senate hearings on abuses by the Internal Revenue Service. "They're chasing people who don't have much money. They know rich people can hire lawyers and tie them up."

Another complained of "insane drug laws where a baseball player, who is doing well enough at work to earn $1.5 million a year, is arrested for possession of drugs — and prevented from working."

"My point," agreed Fred, "is that government often establishes conditions that makes government seem necessary."

"Dogs work together," he said. "They don't kill other dogs. Cooperation is how we survive. Competitiveness is not at all natural."

"Ah, it's all control issues," added Dave, speaking of problems of the modern workplace. "If the bosses let go, the jobs still get done. But people who have control don't want to give it up."

"There was a lot of support for the UPS strikers," said Elizabeth, "and that's a good sign. You see that the boss isn't always your friend."

Others noted "the constant need" of the establishment to have a "bogeyman," responsible for most of the evils of the country.

Once, it was anarchists, as faded newspaper clippings attest, including an 1886 editorial in the *Tribune* hoping that "those who sympathize with its horrible doctrines will speedily emigrate from her borders or at least never again make a sign of their sentiments."

"There's always a bogeyman," said Mike. "It used to be foreigners, then anarchists, then socialists, then communists. Now it's drug lords and gangs."

The topic for the next meeting has not yet been decided.

October 3, 1997

COURTING LAUGHS

'Twas the week before the big lawyers' Christmas show, and all through the rehearsal hall at the Sheraton Chicago Hotel and Towers there was the usual chaos. Actors flubbing lines. Dancers misstepping. Someone brushing against Mia Farrow, or a reasonable facsimile, as she tried to reach a microphone.

"I am God," shouted the show's director, E. Leonard Rubin, a lawyer with the firm of Willian, Brinks, Olds, Hofer, Gilson & Lione, as he recited an 11th commandment. "Do not bump into people as you are exiting the stage."

The Chicago Bar Association's annual "Christmas Spirits" extravaganza, this year subtitled *Beauty and the Brief*, opens Tuesday night for a six-day run at the Sheraton Chicago. It will be the sixty-ninth in an unbroken, if occasionally raggedy, line of parodies stretching back to 1924, when members of the bar began celebrating the season by mounting a drag show.

Rehearsed and staged in a two-week December blitz, such tuneful epics as "Dial M for Merger," "Dictum Tracy," "City of Angles" and "Docket to Me," have been thrown together, over the last three decades, by a small group, notably Rubin, Circuit Judge Julian J. Frazin and John E. Corkery, a professor at John Marshall Law School. Along with lawyer Phillip M. Citrin, now retired, they have acted for years as "The Four Musketeers."

For years, they have hung out together. Lunched every week. Spent six months out of each year swapping jokes and ideas. Toured the country with a bar show unit, doing mini-revues to cheer up other bar associations. Put framed pictures of each other on their pianos at home. Then, come December, they hole up in a hotel, while still practicing law by day, and, after a week of rehearsing a cast of a hundred or so, start a weeklong run. It's no piece of cake.

"It's hard enough to get two lawyers to agree. To get 106 lawyers to follow directions is virtually impossible," moaned Rubin, a trademark and copyright specialist who once studied improvisational theater at Second City under the legendary teacher Viola Spolin.

"Lawyers are not, by nature, actors," he said, during a break last week. "They're good at making themselves heard in court-rooms, but most of them have little sense of timing, timbre, projection or characterization. We have to school them in the theater arts. If they don't follow instructions, we threaten to tell their clients that they have no sense of humor."

"Those of us who came in the sixties thought that humor might be able to make some changes in society, working from inside the Establishment," recalled old-hand Citrin, referring to a time when many social institutions came under review and faced protest. Citrin's favorite role was Wiley Nelson, a shady paving contractor singing "On the Road Again." But there was also, he recalled, a practical payoff for many cast members. The show was something of "a legal meat market," he said, the younger actors often making contacts with older talent search-ers and later jumping to other law firms.

This year's show, its script constantly under revision with late-breaking quips, will have amusing things to say about courtroom TV, Britain's royal family, the men's movement, poll-sters, Ross Perot, regional transportation and a variety of local concerns, including cost hold-downs at law offices. "The heat is on at this firm," moans one song, echoing the play *Miss Saigon*.

There will be high jinks at the firm of Going, Going & Gone, suggestions for the site of a third airport, and Mary J. McNichols, head of the bar association's entertainment com-mittee, who does a good Queen Elizabeth. There also will be mention of Farrow vs. Allen, the sinking reputation of Christo-pher Columbus and the leaking of the Chicago River. That muddy matter will be addressed by Joel Daly, a WLS-TV anchor, professional country singer and lawyer, who will sing and yodel "The Wabash Waterfall," to the tune of "Wabash Cannonball." Sample lyrics:

So, listen to the splatter, the rumble and the roar
As the pumping sent a cascade through every open door.
LaSalle and Clark and Wacker, in buildings short and tall.
And the soggy scenes repeated with the Wabash waterfall.

Rather than prattle on with insider legal humor, the show's writers try to stay with material that is generally accessible, though one year a new member of the script committee came up with what he thought was a humorous look at the Illinois Code of Civil Procedure. "We didn't use it," Rubin recalled.

Tucked away in copious files kept by Judge Frazin are mementos of the show's earliest days, when it was staged at the old bar association headquarters, at 160 North LaSalle Street. A group of male lawyers, aided and abetted by a lot of whiskey, got together, carpentered some comedy and appeared, in women's clothing, doing high kicks. The set was a mock phone booth in which various characters had imaginary conversations with departed brethren, the "Christmas Spirits."

Some of the city's big legal names pitched in to help, among them Edwin C. Austin, a raucous piano player. Far from being shocked, his partners at staid Sidley & Austin "generally approved of some annual frivolity as an excellent morale-booster and a way of relieving the pressures of heavy workloads," according to an office history. Later, agreeing that all torts and no play made for dullness, a group of jurists joined in with an all-judge kazoo band.

Since then, the annual production has leaped from peak to peak, with only an occasional crash. (The worst: in 1975, when the stage slid forward, injuring eighteen people, none seriously. Lawyer Fred Lane, on stage at the time, escaped harm and nimbly picked up two new clients among the hurting.)

But this year, the show faces a new challenge. In what Jimmy Durante might describe as "a revoltin' development," it is being leaned on to turn a major profit, of about a hundred thousand dollars.

Unlike the devil-may-care accounting of spectacles past, when each show laid out about as much as it took in, dazzling crowds with laser displays, Mississippi riverboats, "Cats" costumes and other stage wonders, a Scrooge-like hand of accountability has fallen on the budget of "Christmas Spirits."

Not that there won't be lots of magic this year. There'll be a rousing finale, "A Chicagoan's Dream," built around the trees, twinkly lights and store signs of North Michigan Avenue, a play on the show-stopping number "American Dream" from, again, Miss Saigon.

But there is also a sense that this is a year for trimming back, for ordering three robotic costumes instead of eight, for holding back on expensive props and for cutting a better deal on the meal.

"We're not going back to the '20s, with two pianos and the phone booth," says business manager Dean Trafelet, a Cook County Circuit Court judge who sits in the law division, "but this year turned out to be a light show, in terms of what the creative people wanted for costumes and sets, and that's what we wanted too."

The budget will run about $500,000, with $242,000 for the show, about $160,000 for dinner for about ten thousand people, and the rest profit, well down from the $750,000 budgets of years past.

"We want to have our cake—and eat it too," noted bar association president Thomas Demetrio, a successful personal-injury attorney and partner in Corboy & Demetrio who oversaw the shifting of the show this year away from its longtime home, the Chicago Hilton and Towers, and into a better deal at the new Sheraton Chicago Hotel and Towers where, he said, "I personally tasted four different entrees and arranged the presentation of the salad."

Profit from *Beauty and the Brief*, Demetrio said, will enable the bar association to hold off a dues increase next year and will help out its $8 million budget, under some strain since the twenty-three thousand-member association moved into the bottom half of a sixteen-story, $15 million building at 312 South Plymouth Court in 1990.

But the point of the bar show is not to dwell on gloomy finances.

"It is a forum to entertain office workers, clients, family and friends in a congenial atmosphere," Demetrio said, describing an annual ritual in which the legal community gathers together, at up to eighty-five dollars a head, to schmooze, slap backs, swap small-talk and applaud colleagues who have survived a roller-coaster ride of rehearsal, stage blocking and what lawyer Cliff Berman once called the humiliating process of "begging for a key change."

Old-timers in the bar association remember days when the show was pasted together at what one called "weekly three-martini outings." Bar tabs were free for lawyers working on sketches, a perk that led, he said, to certain excesses. In 1971, after a lawsuit, women were allowed into the show. These days, starting each fall, a central committee meets one night a week in a wood-paneled boardroom atop bar association headquarters. Several couples in the group bring their children along for dinner, letting them crayon while the adults quip.

So, has the show changed? Has it softened? Have "the bean counters" taken over, as one veteran recently chided. Has *Christmas Spirits* lost its spirit?

"No," said Frazin, who is the kind of guy who, if the show

were fading, would reach for sheet music to "The Party's Over," look wistfully into the middle distance and riffle off some situationally-appropriate lyrics.

"But you don't want to talk about budgets," Frazin went on. "You want to talk about the big Michigan Avenue finale," referring to this year's show-stopper, set on the Magnificent Mile, with chorus and non-lawyer professional orchestra, led by Chicago composer and arranger Larry Novak, belting out "A Chicagoan's Dream."

Over the years, the bar show has offered a view of history, a wry compendium of the notables and events that caught the attention of Chicago. John Corkery, then a law student, recalls seeing his first show, *Tenets Anyone*, in 1966, staged at the long-gone Edgewater Beach Hotel. One high point was a depiction of U.S. Supreme Court Justice William O. Douglas, recently remarried, singing "Strangers in the Night."

In 1969, during the Chicago Seven conspiracy trial, a bar-show skit based on *Alice's Adventures in Wonderland* lampooned the judicial style of U.S. District Judge Julius J. Hoffman, who presided over the case and who attended opening night. The skit drew the ire of a *Tribune* editorial. A revised version was later attacked by *Chicago Today*.

Several years later, a parody of Frank Sinatra's "My Way," sung by a lawyer portraying Cardinal John Cody, the late Catholic archbishop of Chicago, was pummeled by WBBM news commentator John Madigan. One frequent target has been Richard Nixon, going back to 1963 when three Nixon impersonators appeared on a panel show, *To Tell the Truth*.

Many veteran showgoers still remember the late Judge Albert J. LaPlante playing Pierre, the headwaiter at the Chez Paris, in "Ex-Parte Girl" in 1953. Or lawyer Hugh Brodkey as conductor Daniel Barenboim, leading a Chicago audience in coughing and wheezing. Or such other longtime notables as Tamara Tanzillo, a lawyer for the University of Illinois in labor relations; Sonja Johnson, real estate tax lawyer with Madigan & Getzendanner; Audrey Holzer Rubin, a corporate attorney for a North Shore corporation who met her husband, "Christmas Spirits" director E. Leonard Rubin, through the show; and criminal defense attorney James Montgomery, who was city corporation counsel under Mayor Harold Washington, was the first black in the show and is still one of its few black cast members.

"It's a good way to meet a lot of other lawyers in a hurry," says E. Leonard Rubin. "It's more intimate than a cocktail party or a continuing education seminar."

The show also helps with professional skills. After a few on-stage outings, shy lawyers become extroverted. There is also a premium on quick-wittedness. Trafelet recalls a night six years ago when a twelve-volt battery that powered a prop was discovered missing forty-one minutes before it was due to be used. Lawyers were dispatched to scout the neighborhood. One came back with a battery from a show staffer's car parked in the Hilton garage. Stagehands installed it with thirty seconds to spare.

For others, the show is a big break.

"For two weeks a year, I can forget being a lawyer, a wife and a mother and pretend to be a Broadway star," says trial lawyer Joyce Staat Lewis of Clausen, Miller, Gorman, Caffrey & Witous. This year, Lewis will play Mary Ann McMorrow, the first woman justice on the Illinois Supreme Court, and will sing — what else? — "Tomorrow."

December 14, 1992

FINDING THE
HUMOR IN HAGGIS

One Scot, mounting the stage, recalled an old-time Scottish entertainer who used to play the fiddle while standing on his head — "a guaranteed success when you're wearing a kilt."

Another entertained the crowd with an amusing story involving a mouthy Scotsman, a surly innkeeper's wife and a meal of "boiled tongue."

A third quoted poet Robert Burns on the subject of haggis — that "great chieftain o' the puddin' race" — then frightened some in the hall by noting, as he raised a dagger high above the encased animal parts, that "this one's moving in some very strange ways."

Then, plunging his dirk deep into its middle, he stood aside as cooked guts spewed, steam rose in little puffs and the whole thing sank onto a ceremonial table, wounded and edible.

Well, sort of.

Yes, there were moments of great beauty at the 152nd annual dinner of the Illinois St. Andrew Society. At one point, all six hundred guests, in a joint hum, shaped a sound like the drone of a hundred bagpipes, letting it float up to chandeliers that glowed like the last gold and pink rays of a Highlands sunset, as fiddler Alasdair Fraser played a Scottish wailing song.

But, amidst the nostalgic group that gathered in the grand ballroom of the Chicago Hilton & Towers to hear of "the hills of Scotland moist with mist, heather in bloom and the skirling of pipes down the glen," there was also a good deal of humor.

Haggis Humor.

One good line came when a couple, after slipping a waiter a ten-spot for an extra haggis, "to go," left the ballroom briefly to stow the reeking treasure in the parking lot. "Now," joshed a table mate as they returned, "you'll certainly have no trouble finding your car."

Another came from featured entertainer Fraser, who told of one of his stranger gigs, an invitation to perform for a private party at the Los Angeles home of actor Charlton Heston who, Fraser reported, "decided about ten years ago that he was a Scot."

Though Heston looked good in a kilt and was credible while reciting Burns, Fraser was trying to figure out what was wrong with the picture "when the other act, a wee piper from Edinburgh, whispers to me, 'Aye, and it's something to see Moses doin' the haggis, isn't it?'"

At the Hilton, the serious purpose of the night was to raise funds for the Scottish Home in North Riverside, opened in 1910, which recently completed a $7.5 million campaign to add a twenty-two-bed unit for senior citizens suffering from dementia and Alzheimer's disease.

The home is also the site of the "Scottish American Hall of Fame," with plaques honoring successful Scottish immigrants from industrialist Andrew Carnegie to detective Allan Pinkerton, along with such Chicago-based Scots as reaper-maker Cyrus McCormick, the meat-packing Armours, poet Vachel Lindsay, and John Kinzie, "the most powerful man in Chicago from 1804 to 1812," a period, as a visitor noted, when there wasn't much competition for the title.

Another Scot remembered at the dinner was George McClellan. A Union general during the Civil War, it was McClellan, then stationed in Chicago and working on the city's harbor problems, who first called for Scottish men to celebrate St. Andrew. In 1845, McClellan gathered twenty people at the Lake House hotel on the patron saint of Scotland's day, November 30.

The next year saw the birth of the Illinois St. Andrew Society — and it has been the "Full Robbie" ever since, an annual outing to talk not only of "Robbie" Burns, but of such favored pursuits as tossing cabers, wearing tartans and doing the Highland Fling, a dance originated by kilted Scots warriors, without underwear, getting up to speed by twirling atop war shields.

On sale in an antechamber this year were such "bonnie bits o' Scotland" as tartan sashes, bow ties, lapel pins, tote bags and copies of *The Scots of Chicago: Quiet Immigrants and Their New Society*, a 185-page look at local Scots by Wayne Rethford and June Skinner Sawyers.

Golf, a Scottish invention, was brought to Chicago by a sporting Scot, Charles Blair Macdonald, the authors note. They describe the achievements of "a proud minority whose fiber has been a strong part of the American scene from pre-Revolutionary days to the present."

These are times of greater Scottish visibility, those at the dinner agreed.

A mention of Scotland's recent decision to elect its own parliament got a round of applause. So did an observation, by one of the evening's speakers, "that young people in Scotland these days are turning off TV and heading out to dance to the old tunes."

Nor were old tunes or dances in short supply on this evening.

"Oh, I love this," murmured one matron, as the Midlothian Scottish Pipe Band strode into the hall, followed by the Gillan School of Dance and the Thistle & Heather Highland Dancers.

This year's "Heather Queen" is Laura Jane Garraway, a Scotland-born sophomore at the University of Iowa. Named "Scot of the Year" was John McCormick Buchanan, senior pastor at Chicago's Fourth Presbyterian Church and former moderator of the Presbyterian Church U.S.A., who recalled happy times one summer "with his family as an exchange minister in the western Highlands."

The "Haggis Child" was Russell Carey Thompson, six, of LaGrange who, in an interview, said he was "not scared" when he was carried in, completely covered, on a sedan chair.

"Did you like your haggis?" he was asked, after dinner was over.

"Yes," he said, dutifully.

"Would you like some more?" "No," he said, firmly.

November 19, 1997

CLUB DISPENSES PLENTY
OF BON MOTS

One man, a chef, came to talk longingly of his birthplace, a tiny village in the Loire Valley where he recalled feasting on forest mushrooms each spring and fall.

Another joined six years ago at the behest of his French girlfriend. They broke up, though, as he noted ruefully, "We'll always have Paris." Others had French nannies as children. Or they spent time in France during their college years. Or they have friends — from Quebec, the Ivory Coast, Haiti or other points on the French-speaking world map — and want to share the florid language of Voltaire and Racine.

"We are not a singles club," warned James Zerwin, a Chicago forester who has spent time on the French Riviera. "But," he assured a visitor dropping in on Frogs Anonymous, a support group for local francophiles, "we do allow any kind of ridiculous behavior — from telling bad jokes to being politically incorrect — as long as you do it in French."

"Ah, Greg — bon soir!" Zerwin said, breaking off to welcome one of the group's weekly attendees, trudging up to the mezzanine of Portillo's, a restaurant on the West Ontario strip specializing in garnished chiens chauds — also known as hot dogs.

Pragmatic, in a French way, the members of Frogs Anonymous, named for lovers of a food group favored in, among other gourmet centers, Paris, chose Portillo's less for its cuisine than for its layout, specifically for a vast, usually-empty, waiterless, upper-level seating area.

There, each week, they show up to kiss cheeks, wave hands, shift tables around as they see fit, stay as long as they want, eat a lot or a little and, as one put it, "if one decides to smoke, zere is no hysteria."

Talk can "get a bit rowdy," especially when people just in from France "express astonishment," a favorite French trait, "about O. J. Simpson's trial or the troubles of President Clinton with Paula Jones," another noted, sipping on Beaujolais, just in.

But if there is one topic on which all F. A. members agree, it is this:

When it comes to French, these days it's "use it or lose it."

There was a time, as older revelers recalled, when Chicago was an all-French town. Its first settler: Jean Baptiste du Sable, a fur trader following in the wake of emissaries from Louis XIV, the Sun King of Versailles, who dreamed of forging a chain of forts and villages from Montreal to New Orleans.

Lately, ethnologists suggest, the world has been shrinking for La Francophonie, as France, its fifty former colonies and other areas, such as Quebec, are collectively known.

Though French is the language of choice for at least 126 million people, making it Number Nine in the planet's Babel, compared to Mandarin Chinese, at Number One, with 999 million speakers. But English, a rocketing Number Two, with 487 million, has been invading technology, travel, movies, rock music and the Internet, which the French call inforoute.

"We were in second semester of business French, but, in a class situation, you don't get to speak that much," explained Sheri Ard, telling how Frogs Anonymous — and a dozen other French-speaking social groups — have grown out of Alliance Francaise de Chicago, a hundred-year-old center of French culture, now housed in a Victorian townhouse at 810 North Dearborn Street.

These days, reunions francophones are held in Evanston, Naperville, Oak Park, Hyde Park, three North Side restaurants and the Ambassador West Hotel, where le groupe professionnel meets to swap tips on interesting movies, promising restaurants and job opportunities.

"We are expanding," added Sonia Aladjem, executive director of the Alliance, part of a worldwide network, supported by the French government, which owes its start here in 1897 to efforts by William Rainey Harper, first president of the University of Chicago, Charles Deering of International Harvester, and Henry Furber, president of the 1904 Olympic Games.

Next June, when workers finish converting the former Michael Reese Hospital resale shop on West Chicago Avenue, the Alliance will link its current building, via a glassed-in walkway across a back alley, to a new auditorium "where we will have movies, lectures, theater, music and exhibits," Aladjem said. Also, classroom space will double, upping enrollment in its French classes to four thousand students a year.

At Frogs Anonymous, which now has a mailing list of 630, the idea is "to forget about pronunciation and rules of grammar. Simply speak," said Zerwin.

A third of those at its gatherings are native French, a third are Americans and a third are "foreigners with a francophile bent," he noted, looking around a room that was filled with people from France, China, Mexico, Canada, Cuba and a dozen of the United States.

Many bring good news, such as chef Michael Maloiseau, formerly of the Ritz-Carlton Hotel, who spent much of the evening talking of Resto 22, a restaurant he is about to open in Ukrainian Village, which he called "a nice neighborhood, with good parking."

Others had more personal concerns. Known as a good place to meet people, Frogs Anonymous, now ten years old, has notched ten marriages. Several couples, members reported, with a certain amount of envy, have moved to France permanently.

November 28, 1997

"DEEE-FENSE!
DEEE-FENSE!"

The lights dim. The music rumbles. A hand-held spotlight picks up the team members as they run, one by one, slapping hands, through the darkened assembly hall to line up on stage.

"Now, ladies and gentlemen," yells coach Bruce Holmes, picking up the cadence of Chicago Bulls announcer Ray Clay, "please welcome — YOUR OAKTON CHESS TEAM!"

And the whole school goes wild!

Backed by such fervent pep rallies, which take place every time new members join the team, these kids, in kindergarten through fifth grade, are the campus heroes these days at Oakton Elementary School in Evanston. Defying current recreational theory, that youngsters will hate any game that doesn't involve a ball and running around, they play chess — to win.

And win they do. Last month, after some hard matches in Springfield, Oakton brought home the state championship in the primary division, kindergarten through third grade. In the elementary division, grades four and five, the team placed fourteenth, beating twenty-six other teams.

Next week, a dozen Oakton players, plus parents and supporters, will fly to Charlotte, N.C., for the 1993 National Elementary Chess Championships, starting April 23.

"These kids have a lot of guts," said Holmes, who started the chess club two years ago after his son Chris, now seven, earlier expressed interest in the game. "Playing in a chess tournament is scary, exhausting. These kids are troupers."

They also have caught the attention of Oakton's diverse student population with a message often missing from other after-school recreations: Anyone, even the small and the slow, can play. The deal, Holmes explained, is this:

"First, we teach them how the pieces move. Often, the better players teach the beginners. Then, we use a book, *Pawn to Queen*. They go through that and answer all the questions. Then we teach the technicalities, such as how to castle, so they don't get blindsided. Then we show them the tricks of the trade. What an opening's all about. What is a pin? And various mating combinations, such as two rooks against a king."

"I'm tough," Holmes said. "I've had parents say, 'You can't expect a 1st grader to learn this.' But I tell the kids: 'It's OK to make mistakes. You come back until you get it. Then we check that off. You've learned it. When you learn the basics, you qualify for the team.'"

So it was on a recent spring afternoon that forty kids sat in a classroom from 2:45 to 3:45 P.M., huddled over row after row of chess boards, working on tactics to exploit weaknesses, spring weapons, deal blows and mount attacks, the staples of chess strategy. Anyone can walk in and begin. A dozen who have completed basic training form the varsity squad.

"I like the French defense," noted Jesse Wolfson, eight, a veteran of two years' play. "You line up pieces in a row. The other player gets real irritated. He loses concentration. He makes dumb mistakes — and you kill him."

Tyler Drendel, seven, who won five of his seven games and drew one at the state championships, explained how he lost that one game. "I took a rook, but forgot about his bishop," he said ruefully. "I saw it, but forgot it."

"I don't know any of the terminology," said one watching mother, Jerry Zbiral, whose son Max Zbiral-Teller, eight, joined the Oakton chess team the moment it was formed in 1991. "My son will say: 'I won. This is how I did it. Queen b5.' I'll go: 'Yeah. Uh-huh. That's great.'"

Oakton may lack the funding available at wealthier schools in New York and California that, in many instances, employ grandmasters as on-staff chess coaches. But there is no shortage of zeal or of appreciation for the game.

"Sitting, thinking, using strategies; if students can do that for chess, they can do it for reading and math," said Oakton principal Clara Pate, explaining why she was such a strong supporter of chess. "Even better is that this whole thing has been put together, and run, by parents."

"It teaches concentration," Holmes added. "We stress reasoning. Planning ahead. Taking responsibility for what you've done. You can't blame someone else for your errors. You study your mistakes and you learn from them. And you have to be able to sit there with your butt in the chair."

In this jumpy age, that's no mean feat.

"Every other week, I get a call from some parent at another school wondering how did we do it," Holmes said. His answer, essentially, is one move at a time.

It started when son Chris, then four, watched a video called

Donald in MathMagic Land, in which chess pieces fought battles. Later, Chris saw the Teenage Mutant Ninja Turtles playing chess. "That cinched it," Holmes recalled. "He had to learn. I knew enough to show him how the pieces moved. We started playing together. The battle aspect of chess captured his imagination. He spent hours moving pieces on his own."

Holmes took out children's chess books from a local library. He took Chris to chess clubs in the area. He got him a subscription to *SchoolMates,* a magazine for the fledgling chess set. Later, trying to decide between sending Chris to Oakton or a private school, he asked Pate, during an open house, "Do you have a chess team?"

"No," she shot back, "why don't you start one?"

In fall 1991, the school put up three hundred dollars, half of the principal's discretionary fund for the year, and Holmes bought chess sets. To teach, he borrowed a large magnetic demonstration board from the chess coach at a nearby high school and started a lunchtime chess class, expecting a dozen students.

Pate walked in with seventy children, about half of whom were girls.

Parents volunteered to help supervise. At first, Holmes said, different students were assigned to come on different days. "But eventually we had to give that up," he said. "It was so hard to turn kids away at the door."

Kids taught each other. Holmes moved from board to board, giving pointers. "One day," Holmes said, "I looked around and realized I had fifty kids quietly playing chess. No, that's a lie. It was never quiet. But they were playing chess."

When twenty-five children had been taught the basics,

Holmes held the team's first induction. "For the ceremony, I called up the Bulls and found out what music they use and I taped it," he said.

In the dark, with a wavering spotlight, "each child's name was roared out in the best imitation of the Bulls announcer I could muster," Holmes said. "Each kid wore the team T-shirt and was awarded a medal. I think that sealed it for the school. Chess became part of the culture of Oakton. Being on the team was hot stuff."

To sharpen the team's players, Holmes imported a Chicago chess master for several sessions. Brian Schuman, who plays out of the No Exit Cafe in Rogers Park, worked through nuances of such chess ploys as opposition, attacking overworked pieces and maneuvering a pawn across a near-empty board to regain a queen. "That's how you learn chess," Schuman said in an interview. "You learn to think a certain way, to look for things."

In recent weeks, preparing for Charlotte has raised another challenge: money. The team needs six thousand dollars for travel expenses. It has raised most of it by selling chocolate and, to put it bluntly, by hustling. Under a banner that reads, "Help send Oakton School to the national championships. Play a chess champion — if you dare," Oakton moppets have been playing chess for money, two dollars a game, against all comers.

Victims have included patrons of a Barnes & Noble bookstore and a Video Adventure outlet, and students at Northwestern University, where many, to their embarrassment, have lost badly. "I guess I had a long game," NU freshman Scott Beauchamp told a reporter after Chris Holmes whipped him in twenty minutes. "The guy beside me got beat in four moves." But, Beauchamp said, "it's OK. I can still take him in arm wrestling."

Can Oakton take the nationals? Or, as a Bulls fan might put it, do a one-peat? It's possible, though not probable, coach Holmes suggested.

"Illinois is one of the better chess states in the country, behind New York and California but ahead of everyplace else."

Meanwhile, he's trying to keep his team loose.

"I want them to go in, have a good time, and see what happens," he said. "I'd like to take some of the pressure off them, but these kids are competitive. I don't have to tell them anything. They'll do their best."

April 16, 1993

LAUNDROMATS TAKE CLEAN
TO NEW EXTREMES

It was at the third stop on "The Coin Laundry Tour of the Decade" that Jack Blanton, in from Florida where he runs The Laundry Room near Tampa, nearly lost it.

"Honey, did you see this?" he shouted to his wife, Robin, at The Blue Kangaroo, 2509 West 47th Street, Chicago, calling her over to the "Express Laundry Center" where high-speed units, their round windows filled with roiling suds, were whamming through several loads of soiled undies.

Almost twice as fast as conventional washday weapons, the machines, signs noted, were also automatically injecting the soap, bleach and softener, for only twenty-five cents more.

"Great for bachelors. They don't need to think," marveled another pro, who was among 250 members of the Coin Laundry Association who spent a day checking out local places of interest to them.

The outing hit ten operations, from Berwyn's Laundry World to the Scrub-A-Dub at 3333 West Fullerton Avenue, Chicago, and was part of the CLA's four-day national convention in Chicago, a time to share nuances that are little noted nor long remembered by amateurs in the laundry field.

These are heady days for the nation's thirty thousand coin laundries, 80 percent of them owned by small entrepreneurs. Revenues last year edged toward $5 billion — a lot of quarters.

It is also a time when coin laundries are working hard to reverse what they consider an out-of-date image, that of a dimly lit, vaguely threatening, back-street operation set up in a space that, in better times, might have housed a failing bowling alley.

"Yes, there is a trend to brighter, cleaner, larger coin laundries," reported David DeMarch of BDS Laundry Systems in St. Paul, this year's chairman of the twenty-two hundred-member CLA, which is based in Downers Grove. DeMarch rode on one of the six buses in the tour's flotilla.

The smart operator, other association staffers noted, has an eye for flow, a sense of how to have clothes go smoothly from washers to dryers to folding tables.

They try to avoid narrow aisles that force customers to

"move carts, laundry baskets and their bodies up against the machines to let others pass by."

They try to have enough dryers to prevent bottlenecks, as well as spacious folding areas so that "carts full of wet clothes don't hit people." They also provide child play areas so that kids "aren't climbing into carts, on top of the washers and generally being a nuisance."

These days, as others on the tour noted, operators also have been throwing in everything but the kitchen sink to put more fun, or at least more convenience, into what association surveys call "the Number Two Most Hated Household Task — after cleaning toilets."

The modern laundromat may well have a coffee bar, wrapping service, fax machines, Internet access, tanning beds, shoe parlor and, in college towns, study pits with sofas and lamps.

Two graduate students in Ohio have started a chain they call Laundry 101. Another multi-unit operation, Harvey Washbangers, is spreading through the South. Many have bars and food service.

Where laundry is done "has always been a meeting place," noted Brian Wallace, the CLA's director of communications, summing up a history that begins by banks of rivers and now continues at such wet-and-wild spots as Wrigleyville's SaGa Launder Bar, at 3435 North Southport Avenue.

There, launderers can eat, drink and keep an eye on an overhead numbers system, which flashes them when to switch from washer to dryer. "Our motto is 'Meet, Eat, Drink and Do Laundry,'" noted owner Sam Aiello, who said he named the place for "myself and my wife, Gloria."

"Basically, you're looking for people with dirty clothes who don't have a washer and dryer," Wallace said, when a visitor asked how one would go about setting up a successful modern-day coin laundry operation. For best results, he added, take an area with many renters.

Nationally, indications are that coin laundries will continue to get hotter.

In a service-oriented economy, many customers now use laundries for drop-offs, which, tour members noted, are a strong profit center. The wash is done by attendants, who are there anyway.

Also, in a world where mothers often have less time for laundry, others noted, it often falls to coin-laundry attendants to instruct young launderers, just starting out, in such delicate ways of the world as presorting colors and whites, stain-spotting and appropriate load levels.

Many on the association's tour came with specific agendas, making notes of what might work back home.

"Beautiful. Really nice," murmured Bob Fransen, owner of nine coin laundries in east central Minnesota, as he entered Laundry World, at 6947 West Cermak Road, Berwyn. He particularly liked the no-slip tiles on the outside sidewalk. Others pointed to wash units set in a trough so that water spills went under the machines into a drain, leaving the floors dry.

At Wash Around the Clock, in the Kedzie Plaza shopping center, near 47th Street and Kedzie Avenue, conventioneers inspected a snack bar and poked behind machines to look, approvingly, on a maze of pipes and wires feeding in a coin laundry's three major requirements: water, electricity and gas.

"We came specifically to look at debit cards," said Chris Gamble, part of a team from Atlanta's Bustin Suds interested in Chicago's newest laundromat, Su Nueva Lavanderia 2, which opens Friday at 4030 South Western Avenue. There, customers are steered by attendants toward machines that dispense cards much like those issued by the Chicago Transit Authority.

"It's the thing of the future," murmured Lucy Nikolsky, representing Aladdin Laundromat in Poughkeepsie, N.Y. Others in the crowd agreed that a coinless coin laundry, without bags of quarters to dispense and track, would be easier on both management and customers.

Just last month, reported Bob Matthews, national sales manager for ESD MoneyCard Systems, "a woman in Watts, in Los Angeles, told me that 'I guess this means they won't be taking my money any more.'" Was she being hassled by street hoods, Matthews then asked her?

"No," the woman replied. "It's my husband and my sons. They raid my change bottle."

July 10, 1998

ALL THE NEW
THINKING ABOUT
THE ARTS

PORTRAIT OF THE
ARTIST — WHITE COATS,
BUT NO CHISELS

When Cynthia Plaster Caster appeared as a guest lecturer at the School of the Art Institute, some in the school's crowded auditorium were reminded of a discussion long ago between sculptor Lorado Taft and Chicago socialite Bertha Palmer.

It had to do with the nature of art.

"Art is anything that the average person cannot do well," Taft suggested, to which Palmer tartly retorted, "Well, speaking of art, my husband can spit over a boxcar."

That can be chancy, especially in a windy city.

Yet, as no one in the audience needed to be reminded, it has always been the duty of art — and artists — to explore complicated issues, to confront taboos, to jump-start the senses and to search relentlessly for distinctive materials to express their personal visions.

As posters set up around the art school noted, "Cynthia Plaster Caster is a sculptor who lives in Chicago. Since the 1960s, she has cast in plaster the male genitalia of her musical idols. Some of her models have included Jimi Hendrix, members of the Lovin' Spoonful, Savoy Brown, Led Zeppelin and the Mekons."

These days — despite plenty of skeptics and shrill objections against federal funding for their labors — artists have been using varied materials to make their points.

But few artists have so identified with one medium as to make it their last name — as Plaster Caster has done.

According to anthroponomasticists, which are people who study names and how they fit into society as a whole, this sort of thing used to happen a lot at the dawn of time, when an archer became Archer, a smith became Smith and a mason, Mason. Now, it's rare.

But what was even more interesting to a non-artistic person at the Plaster Caster lecture was how much this fifty-year-old artist has used art to shape her life over the past thirty years. Art, plus street-smarts, linguistics, a sense of sociology and a recognition of modern-day realities.

In her work, for example, Plaster Caster found it useful to look official.

She often wore a lab coat.

Unlike some sculptors who, according to legend, at least, simply can look at a block of marble, knock off the unnecessary bits and bring forth a marvel, Plaster Caster's efforts have required all these non-studio skills to produce some forty white-plaster moldings, two of which, when she held them over her head, appeared to be rather beautiful, at least from the twenty-sixth row.

She did not, she admitted, start out to be an artist. In fact, her goal in the 1960s, she said, was "to meet a rock star and get married."

The twinning of personal goals and artistic aims is, of course, nothing new in the art world, as anyone who hangs out in the Art Institute knows. Take Paul Gauguin, who got bored trading on the Paris Stock Exchange, dumped everything and sailed off to the South Seas to paint female natives, many of them wearing less than was required by big-city dress codes.

Similarly, in her hankering for rock stars, Plaster Caster "found listening to records less than satisfying." Not much better was pleading for autographs, especially when normal ways of meeting such people ("hanging out in the alley behind the theater") had been overwhelmed by "the invasion" of mop-topped Brits whose mobs of fans led to tightened security.

Thus it came to be that — in defiance of orders from "my mother, The Warden" never to enter a man's hotel room — she found herself going to where bands were staying, using back stairways to make her way "up twenty floors," hiding in broom closets, knocking on doors of stars, seeking a moment.

Often, propelled by hotel detectives, she found herself "on an elevator — headed down." Nor were band members overly willing to admit a person they did not know and could not relate to.

Her first breakthrough, she said, came when she joined a fan club that arranged up-close meetings with rock groups before concerts. Members of many British groups, she noticed, spoke to one another in a kind of rhyming cockney.

Picking up key words, she learned how to phrase a hand-written note, in hip insider lingo, that would elicit a room number. Then, in 1966 — "and this is where the art comes in," she explained — she was majoring in art at the University of

Illinois-Chicago Circle and got a "really boring assignment," to make a plaster cast of "something solid."

Voila — as Gauguin might have said.

"I'm shy," she confessed, but her idea was that, if she could get into the hotel room of a rock star and present her artistic vision with enough sincerity, it would lead to intimacy and, as her introducer at the School of the Art Institute lecture put it, help "to demystify the untouchable legacy of musical genius as a learning experience for herself, and to explore the weaknesses of these icons."

On the one hand, some might call it looking for love in all the wrong places.

On the other hand, what artist, at some time or other, hasn't?

Her early efforts, Plaster Caster conceded, were, in an artistic sense, disastrous. Once, in a Holiday Inn, her plaster went lumpy and failed to harden. Much of the material, dumped down a hotel toilet, solidified there. Other times, the plaster would be frigid, turning off the model.

Later, more successfully, she turned to substances called alginates, used in dental molds, helped with a coating of warm wax. She also learned to affect an official demeanor, showing up for castings wearing her lab coat and carrying a box that included, for no particular reason, aluminum foil and a ruler.

Back in her North Side studio, Plaster Towers, she finished off "my babies," as she calls them, putting a serial number and name on each base.

Yes, all present at her lecture seemed to agree, it's art. Done by an artist.

"We are elated to have you here," began Valerie Cassel, an organizer of the school's series of public programs, which this fall have been featuring "artists explaining the interaction between portraiture and contemporary experience." Another speaker called Plaster Caster "a legendary artist" whose skill is "capturing the fleeting moment in permanent material."

The students had questions.

"Why plaster?" one asked.

"I love the statuary-ness of it," she said. "It has an ancient timeless sense."

Another wanted to know whether she had ever considered sculpting female private parts. "A friend of mine tried it and got a yeast infection," she said, advising against it.

"Did you ever use a chisel?"

"No."

Finally, someone put forth the ultimate question. In personal terms, what had it all been for? Had it ever worked out? Had Plaster Caster ever had a long-term relationship with a moldee?

"No," she said, sadly.

December 7, 1997

BETTING ON BUTTER,
ART GALLERY SPREADS IT
ON THICK

Modern artists have used everything from Plexiglas to cannon-balls to express their personal visions. Now, an art gallery on the Near West Side, known simply as Margin, at 1306 North Cleaver Street, has mounted an exhibition devoted entirely to butter. The show is cool.

It has to be.

Or it would melt.

"I've been leaving a window open," reported Nathan Mason, the owner of the four-room gallery, formerly a basement apartment, and curator of "Butter."

In it, some thirty-five local artists offer everything from a clay rendering of a butter pat, stuck to a ceiling, to a butter replica of an outreaching hand, titled *Butter Fingers*, to a wall mounting that Mason described as "a fun little Wisconsin piece."

That is a butter carton artfully folded to make its Indian maiden logo look sexier.

In one back room, two artists, in *Target Practice*, invite visitors to use a Super Soaker spray gun filled with molten butter to slather portraits on a wall.

Others did a photo montage centering on an "L" stop, buttering their work, then microwaving it, then repeating the process several times to get a nicely blurred effect.

"I was surprised, when exploring the idea for the show, by the number of people who told me, 'I've had a butter piece on my brain for years,'" said Mason, leading a visitor on a tour.

"I like the idea that the show has to be cold," one artist added later. "It's like (TV late-night host) David Letterman keeping the temperature in his studio so low. Standing in this tiny apartment, freezing, makes you a little more clear-headed."

Though "Butter" appears to be the city's first all-butter outing, butter, it seems, is not unknown in other parts of the country as an arts medium.

Several years ago at the New York State Fair, sculptor Sharon BuMann took seven hundred pounds of butter and made a life-

size figure of Santa Claus, eating milk and cookies, with butter children peeking around a corner, and kittens tangling with mounds of yellow yarn.

Long before that, the talk of Dallas, at the State Fair of Texas, was a butter sculpture of a milkmaid and dairy cow, an achievement that later led fair authorities to convert an empty radio broadcasting studio into a refrigerated butter-sculpting space.

Recently in Des Moines, artist Norma "Duffy" Lyon, known in Iowa arts circles as "the butter lady," used three hundred pounds of butter to greasily replicate *American Gothic*, Grant Wood's famed portrait of a stern-faced man holding a pitchfork next to a tight-lipped woman.

At Margin, to an outsider, the most accessible work was a bust of Richard Nixon, molded from three pounds of unsalted butter, available for thirty dollars.

"I do political figures," said artist Adam Pincus, in a phone interview from his studio at 3-D Politics, a North Side firm that produces plaster figures of Nixon, as well as President Clinton, Vice President Al Gore, Mayor Richard Daley and other politicians, for sale in gift shops.

All his heads, Pincus said, would also be available in butter.

"What," asked the interviewer, "would one do with them?"

"Eat them," suggested Pincus, indicating that such sculptures would be dandy for dinner parties, where one could say, for example, "Would you please pass the Daley?"

Or, as Mason suggested, they can be kept in a refrigerator, "as conversation pieces."

"In your refrigerator," Pincus reported, "the figures will last indefinitely. After a while, you might not want to eat them. But they will last indefinitely."

The actual longevity of butter art, it seems, depends on the sensitivities of owners, often their sense of smell. Indeed, at Margin, barely two weeks into its show, an astute nose could already detect the first whiff of decay.

February 17, 1999

FAUX ETHNIC DISHES
FEED STUDENTS' MINDS

"It's chicken and dumplings. Whenever we have relatives over, my mom makes it. It's Irish," said Nicole O'Hara, explaining her contribution to an eighty-foot table, the greatest local replica of food since artist Judy Chicago stunned the city with her "Dinner Party" in 1981.

For the past month, the show, which has seventy-eight ceramic sculptures of meals from forty countries, all designed and executed by sixth graders, has been the talk of the main-floor corridor at Bell Elementary School, at 3730 North Oakley Avenue, in the West Lakeview neighborhood.

"My clay sculpture is a plate of crab, with small carrot flowers," said Victor Huang, describing an offering from China. "My dad used to own a restaurant. This was the most expensive, best-tasting meal there was. It was a tradition on special occasions. I love it."

Andy Poswal chose potato porridge, he said, because "my mom made a lot of it in South Africa when we had a barbecue or had people over. Sometimes, I helped make it."

"I chose to make African stew and fu-fu (uncooked dough balls) because it is part of my heritage," said Arit Nsemo, whose father is from Nigeria. "It can get messy, but it's good."

And so it went, as far as the eye could see: rows of exotic foods, formal settings and place cards at a fantasy dinner for School Board officials, City Hall bigwigs and such hot-ticket invitees as Mr. and Mrs. Michael Jordan, TV host Bob Sirott, and Leonardo DiCaprio and guest.

The "International Banquet 1999," which ended last week (when artists got to take their work home) has been a chance for the school to celebrate its ethnic diversity — and to offer a common project to students who, through no fault of their own, often go separate ways.

Bell Elementary, noted principal Robert Guercio, was named for Alexander Graham Bell, a teacher of the deaf who, while looking for a way to transmit the human voice by electric current, invented the telephone in 1876. The school now serves three constituencies.

It has a program for hearing-impaired students who rely on sign language, a center for academically gifted students and public school classes for children of the community.

What brings everybody together, quite often, is art.

"I can't say enough about the art teacher. She's amazing," said Guercio, speaking of Phyllis Burstein, who is on staff both at Bell and at the Art Institute of Chicago, where she teaches art education techniques and other subjects.

At Bell, Burstein's role is to think of art projects that will enrich understanding of topics studied in other classes. The challenge, noted Guercio, is to encourage artistic outpourings on a common theme, among students whose intellects vary widely.

The results are often striking.

Last year, white cranes shaped from papier-mache hung in school hallways. That was part of a schoolwide study of Japan, with an emphasis on a sister city of Chicago, Hiroshima, where paper cranes were folded for peace after its atomic bombing during World War II.

At other times, Bell students have erected totem poles while studying native cultures. Figurines of animals, now mounted in a glass case outside a classroom, were part of an art project tying in with biology that undertook to study creatures of the wild at rest.

"Art is a great equalizer," Burstein noted. "Some kids here are doing college level work. Some of the deaf kids are struggling with language. In the art room, everyone can succeed."

Unlike Judy Chicago's show, built around ceramic table settings chronicling contributions made by women to Western civilization, the great-eats project came about because home cooking is often one of the few remaining traces of ethnic background, Burstein said.

Helped by a grant from the Oppenheimer Family Foundation, "the kids were told to make, out of clay, a meal that . . . was meaningful to them," Burstein said. "Our concept was about meals, how they are important in family life. And their stories were just great."

"My great-grandmother told my grandmother how to make this. And my grandmother made it for me," said George Kanoon, telling of an Assyrian meal of ground lamb and grape leaves.

The route was not always easy.

"My plate broke twice," said Sunia Khatri, explaining nuances of shaping a dish to hold chapitis, a favorite of her Pakistani family. But, she added, she really liked the project "because everybody could show their heritage, how different they are."

One American dish, of T-bone steak and potato wedges, was chosen by Matthew Arndt because, he said, "my stepfather barbecues while everyone else has fun talking and playing games." The meal was memorable, Arndt added, because "one time my stepfather almost blew up the propane tank."

May 7, 1999

WORKING-CLASS ARTISTS
DO A LITTLE PR

Clearly, the longtime home of artist Carlos Cortez and his wife, Mariana, on a leafy side street near Logan Square, is a good place to talk about labor and art.

Years ago, it was a butcher shop. Later, the building was converted to housing by a family from Eastern Europe, becoming a New World base for twenty-one hardworking immigrants. These days, its ambiance comes from the art on the walls and the labor-friendly mottos on the refrigerator.

"To me, art and labor go together — good," said host Cortez, seventy-six, as he welcomed the organizers of this year's Chicago Labor and Arts Festival into a living room lined with his own works, strong portraits of determined faces, caught in sketches, posters and prints.

Indeed, the purpose of the gathering was to talk up the annual month-long fest, a showcase for artists celebrating joys and struggles of working-class people. It was a night for poets, for painters, for talk of labor organizer and folksinger Joe Hill, and for homage to Thomas McGrath, a North Dakota farm boy who won a Rhodes scholarship to Oxford, then found his way back to the Midwest to become a fiery poet and activist.

It also was a chance to talk with members of Chicago's activist arts community about ways in which the arts can serve as a force for social improvement, helping those who feel left out, deprived and, in many cases, invisible, in a time of unparalleled economic prosperity.

"A community can't be healthy unless its individuals are healthy. As with disease, if one person has a communicable disease, everybody is at risk," noted one guest, Diana Berek, the curator of the festival's opening event, "Just Health Care? Get a Life!"

"The people of the working class helped to build the infrastructure of this society, and now we're unable to get simple health care, in the nation that is the most advanced, the wealthiest in the world," added Berek, spelling out this year's theme, the crisis in health care.

How can artists help?

One way is by shaping complex issues into more easily understood messages.

For example, several guests mentioned a pair of cartoonists, known as Carol*Simpson, whose works are seen in union newspapers. One cartoon, on display Sunday, will show a man at a hospital desk, murmuring, "I can't make the co-pay. Can I give an organ instead?"

Artist Pat Olsen often depicts workers in moments with emotional resonance, such as *Locked Out*, her study of backs of workers at a plant which has barred them. "It shows underlying pain people can relate to," said Berek, "even if they haven't been in that exact situation."

Others mentioned a project by the Chicago Coalition for the Homeless and painting students from the College of DuPage who illustrated poems by homeless urban poets.

"Place," observed Lew Rosenbaum, a festival organizer, "is more than just a house. It's a place in society. When you feel you have no place, you are alienated from that society."

But as artist Chris Drew noted, an important aspect of working-class art is reaching out — to people who never go to art galleries. Drew is into T-shirts.

"Our galleries are the people who wear them," he said, noting that T-shirt art, unlike, say, that of the Impressionists, "goes to the people — which is the essence of community art."

Some two hundred pieces, "some worn, some not," will be on display starting September 24 in the tribal hall of the American Indian Center, Drew said. Some reflect history, turning points in the labor movement, for example. Others make points quickly grasped through cartoons.

"Cultural images go well," Drew added, "because often people wear T-shirts to express themselves — as African-American, Latino, Native American."

The essence of such populist art is to "simplify and clarify" because, as Drew noted, "obviously, nobody's going to stand and stare at a T-shirt for a long time."

Also to be heard during the month will be singers, musicians, muralists, collagists, film and video makers and, of course, poets, three of whom gave readings at the Cortez home.

One, Cathleen Schandelmeier, read a moving work about her father, a trimmer of cow hoofs, who died of liver cancer after his lack of health insurance delayed his access to medical treatment.

Later, Reginald Gibbons, before reading from his newly

published homage to Thomas McGrath, reissued a call to arms by McGrath, who once proclaimed: "There is tactical poetry, which is meant to mobilize people and get something done. And strategic poetry, which is meant to raise public consciousness over the long run. And great poetry — which is both."

September 1, 1999

THE VIEWS FROM
THE BOAT

Most architects would like to blow up the work of most other architects. So it was with some trepidation that two hundred building buffs boarded the SS *Fort Dearborn* for a two-hour, box-lunch cruise along the Chicago River led by Helmut Jahn, Stanley Tigerman and Thomas Beeby.

Would their guides, each a leading shaper of the Chicago skyline, fall into fisticuffs? Would the fiery Tigerman toss the acerbic Beeby overboard?

Might Beeby, in turn, whip out a pen and splatter ink on one of the dapper Jahn's trademark white linen suits? Would the waters of the Chicago River, which turn green each St. Patrick's Day, run red from the bloody melee?

None of this occurred. By mid-afternoon, when the ship returned its guests to a riverside dock below the looming Merchandise Mart, there were only slight complaints, mostly about the torrid weather.

It had been obvious from the outset that this would be a day of high heat but little humility.

Tigerman, of Tigerman McCurry, had arrived at the ship dock first, in a lightly crumpled searsucker suit, a pink shirt with a white collar, a mostly yellow tie covered with dots, and highly polished brown loafers.

Jahn, of Murphy/Jahn, both hands thrust into his pockets, showed up in a white linen suit, black tie and short-sleeved, black-checked shirt, with sunglasses on a safety chain dangling against his chest.

"He's wearing white deck shoes," said columnist Henry Hansen, tracking details for *Chicago* magazine.

Beeby, of Hammond Beeby and Babka, the last to arrive, was dressed in a look that former Vice President Walter Mondale once described as "full Norwegian": blue blazer, gray slacks, white shirt, black shoes and a darkly striped tie.

As the ship pulled out, all three quickly removed their jackets.

"Welcome to the Amazon," quipped moderator Ross Miller, of the Chicago Institute for Architecture and Urbanism, a privately funded, not-for-profit organization dedicated to reinvigorating the American city.

"I don't have to introduce any of these characters," he said, wiping his brow and using a hand microphone to introduce them to the crowd, which paid fifty dollars a head and included architects, stockbrokers, interior designers, several caterers, a major banker, book authors and a scattering of lawyers.

"We'll start out by dumping on Chris," said Tigerman, referring to one crowd member, Christopher Kennedy, vice president for marketing of a Kennedy family enterprise, the Merchandise Mart.

As the ship passed under its first bridge, Tigerman launched a vigorous attack against the Kennedy-owned Holiday Inn Mart Plaza and Apparel Center, 350 North Orleans Street, calling it "a barren fortress with a stumpy park" that "made no contribution" to the area.

Moving downstream, talk turned to buildings on the east side of the river.

Jahn said he felt that the old Kemper Insurance Building on South Wacker Drive "showed a certain attention to detail and simplicity of form that many buildings of the nineties fail to achieve."

Beeby liked the "brittle, neo-classical ornamentation of the Lyric Opera House," which was "not one of the great theaters of the world, but fairly impressive."

Tigerman, in turn, said he was drawn to the older bridge towers because they reminded him, in their ornateness, of the gates of Old Jerusalem. Downtown Chicago needs more such defining entry points, he said, noting that inbound travelers using the Kennedy Expressway are abruptly dumped into the River North area.

Similarly, motorists on the Eisenhower Expressway, driving underneath a post office, are denied the sweeping entry views of the central city available to those approaching, say, Philadelphia or New York.

"Now, I think we ought to talk nasty about Helmut, our very dear friend, because neither Beeby nor I have any buildings on the river," said Tigerman, whose downtown contributions include the Hard Rock Cafe, a parking garage inspired by a Rolls Royce, and the dog-eared Anti-Cruelty Society building. Beeby, whose work stretches from the oft-revamped penthouse of the Drake Tower to the Harold Washington Public Library, agreed.

The problem was that nobody could think of anything demolishing to say.

Tigerman and Beeby liked all the Jahn buildings they could see from the ship, notably the sinuous Northwestern Atrium Center, which Tigerman praised for its "rigor." So they decided instead to talk about everybody else.

Passing the Sears Tower, designed by Skidmore, Owings and Merrill, Tigerman complained that its plaza looked as if it had been designed by Adolf Hitler's architect, Albert Speer.

All three architects hated the stolid Presidential Towers of Solomon Cordwell Buenz and Associates, looming to the west, lacking in detail, a development that Jahn called "not only an architectural disaster but a financial disaster," noting that "there sometimes seems to be a synergy between the two, in this case rightly so."

They also dismissed the barge-like *Sun-Times* building, which, Tigerman recalled, was designed by Naess & Murphy, a predecessor to Jahn's firm.

"Perhaps Helmut will help us to rationalize this building," Tigerman said.

"I'd like to put a new building there," retorted Jahn quietly.

The Illinois Center complex drew mixed reviews. Though there were no specific complaints about buildings, Beeby said their placement contributed to "the Houstonization of the city. There is no sense of place. Buildings are just plunked down."

Tigerman noted that the center's traffic flow seemed to be inward, away from nearby streets and plazas. Instead of invigorating Michigan Avenue or the river's edge, "you never see people outside it," he said.

They liked Lake Point Tower, which, Jahn said, "couldn't be done today, given the economy of the times. No apartment building in the past ten years has had any kind of opulence. Only office buildings, built by high-profile developers for high-level tenants, have had that."

Passing the eighty-two-story Amoco Building, whose stony simplicity was admired, the three discreetly omitted mentioning the disastrous technical problem that forced the building's owners to replace its outer marble sheathing at a cost in excess of a hundred million dollars. But they dumped on its neighbor, Two Prudential Plaza, a soaring tower commonly known as "Two Pru," which Jahn called "a total misunderstanding of what a spire should be."

They also threw bricks at the Stouffer Riviere Hotel ("no clue to Chicago traditions," snapped Tigerman) and the R.R. Donnelley Center, a building of such severity that Tigerman called it "fascist."

All three had praise for the curving, green-glass building, known by its address, that hugs a bend in the river at 333 Wacker Drive. "What makes it beautiful is the synergy between its form and its facade," Jahn noted.

They also liked River City, which Tigerman described as "this eccentric project of Bertrand Goldberg," calling Goldberg a "crusty, interesting architect" who uses cement and curves, "which he feels are more human."

Moving through the South Loop, its riverbanks ripe with trees, bushes and, in some places, dumped office furniture, Beeby was excited by the tangle of emerging residential projects, filling in land now abandoned by railroads that, in urban planner Daniel Burnham's day, had refused to consolidate their Chicago operations.

"It's amazing," said Jahn, "in one of the great cities of the world, how much spare land there is."

Beeby paid tribute to architect Harry Weese, "the Darth Vader to Ludwig Mies van der Rohe, an amazingly innovative man of courage, who proposed novel plans for the lakefront and the river, who always seemed to be doing the opposite of whatever Mies wanted to do."

He pointed out some of Weese's "attempts to recolonize the river as a housing area," notably putting apartments into a cold storage warehouse with walls so thick that workers had to blast window openings from outside and inside at the same time.

The three also liked the renovation of what is now the headquarters of Helene Curtis Inc. "Good railings," Tigerman observed, pointing out an employee cafeteria with what looked like loge seats hanging over the river.

Next to that, Beeby noted less happily, was a municipal parking garage built in the 1950s that illustrated "the city's approach to the river at the time — as a toilet." All three liked Marina City, though Jahn lamented its decline, and they praised the IBM building and the new NBC Tower.

"I love Chicago. It's so overt," said moderator Miller, as the ship headed in. "This city," he added, "resists formal order with its entrepreneurial energy," a kind of archi-speak phrasing that seemed to point to the city's continuing capacity for surprise.

But just so things didn't get too out of hand, the ship's sound system wafted music into the air during most of the tour. What was it? "Mozart," said a deckhand. "We always play Mozart. It's soothing."

June 21, 1993

FRAGMENTS GAIN
NEW LIFE IN HANDS OF
MOSAIC ARTIST

"Crazy! Nuts! My wife don't talk to me," said Seymour Adelman, seventy-six, of West Rogers Park, a retired office-furniture restorer, describing his second life, as an artist. Adelman is, by his own admission, somewhat obsessed.

"Come downstairs. Look. I got hundreds of them," he said, leading a visitor down a flight of winding stairs into a bungalow basement full of tools, bathroom tiles, shards of glass, scraps of wood, broken mirrors — and stacks of colorful mosaics.

For twenty-seven years, ever since he got turned on by a small home improvement chore — laying tiles on a hallway floor — Adelman has been squirreling himself away in his below-ground atelier.

How much time has he spent down there?

"Who knows?" he said. "It's like making love. If you look at the clock, you might as well forget it." It could be, he admits when pressed, up to fifty thousand hours, so far.

The result, in a genre known as Outsider Art, is a trove of works, ranging in content from ancient Navajo patterns to cityscapes to portraits of almost every celebrity of the Twentieth Century, from Michael Jordan to senior federal court judge Abraham Lincoln Marovitz.

"Here are the Marx Brothers, done in porcelain. That's George Halas. I did a glass window of Jane Addams. And another one of Golda Meir. Wait, let me turn some more lights on. This is Charlie Chaplin, life-size," he said, pulling out a portrait of the Little Tramp made, he estimated, out of approximately forty-five thousand chips of colored ceramic materials.

Like other notable outsider artists, from Grandma Moses who did rural landscapes to Howard Finster who does messages from God, Adelman has had little formal training, has few preconceived ideas about what art should say and works outside the mainstream.

That is to say, his is not the kind of stuff that hangs in formal exhibitions on museum walls, or gets picked up by art galleries where wealthy patrons gather on Friday evenings to sip wine and nibble nougats at the weekly openings.

On the other hand, many Chicagoans — and art-noticers as far away as the Middle East — may well have walked by an Adelman and appreciated his artwork, if not his name.

Adelman's mosaics are on view on walls of schools, hospitals, theaters, apartment buildings, playgrounds, corporate headquarters, senior centers and homes in Chicago, New York, Paris and Israel, where he has placed four pieces at the Weizmann Institute of Science.

There are, as yet, no Adelmans in the Art Institute of Chicago, but he has cracked his way into academia.

"Sure, I know him. He's a real character. He came in off the street, up to my office and gave them to us," Rolf A. Weil, former head of Roosevelt University, recalled Tuesday when asked about the two large Adelmans, portraits of Franklin and Eleanor Roosevelt, which were affixed to a stairway wall above the main lobby during Weil's period as the school's president.

"People like that are interesting — and there certainly are lots of them in this city," said Weil, recalling the day that Adelman, who had no ties to Roosevelt, made his gift in 1973.

Anonymity, of course, was not exactly Adelman's dream.

"I never did artwork in my life until I was forty-six," said Adelman, who took it up after he injured his back at his previous trade, furniture restoring. One year, he did three thousand chairs at the Harris Bank, refinishing, lubricating and replacing casters, where necessary.

After his injury, he went on, "I had to redo a floor at home. I was too cheap to hire anybody. So I got some tile from a friend of mine, a salesman at a lumber yard. The thing came out so beautiful, that's how I got hung up on it."

He started out placing works on walls and windows. "I let him put whatever he wants wherever he wants," said his wife, Shirley.

"Here's Geronimo," Adelman said, standing in a back bedroom. "It's made out of bathroom tile, but it's realism. You can't tell it from a photograph if you stand back far enough."

Later, using materials cadged from scrap yards or donated by dealers, he spread out, offering his pieces as gifts to people and institutions he felt should have them. Sometimes, he got paid, or helped by sponsors. Often, he didn't.

Fame, he felt, would come from his distinctive style.

"I don't sign my work. I don't bother," he said. "When you

see a Picasso without a signature, you know it's Picasso. When you see an Adelman, you know it's an Adelman. My work is totally recognizable." Maybe — and maybe not.

"I was in a garage repair shop getting my brakes fixed," he said, recalling a recent painful incident. "I got to talking to a woman who was getting her brakes fixed too. She said she'd been to Israel a couple of months before.

"I said, 'Did you, by chance, go to the Weizmann Institute? Did you see murals there?' She said, 'I did. And they were so beautiful that I asked the guide who made them. And the guide said, "Ah, some poor schnook who lives in Chicago and makes them in a basement."' "

October 21, 1997

MITTENS KNIT
A TRIBUTE TO THE 43
FORGOTTEN

It was perhaps Chicago's creepiest disaster, the Big Heat of July 1995, that hastened the deaths of more than 550 people when temperatures of more than 100 degrees turned homes into ovens.

But unlike a fire or a plane crash, which offer quickly visible signs of calamity, it was not until the burials of victims that the magnitude of the misfortune hit the city and the world.

One startling image, photographed and telecast from a cemetery in Homewood, was an open mass grave, 160 feet long, filling up with the plain wooden coffins of forty-three people who had died alone, walled off from help, their bodies later unclaimed by relatives or friends.

No one who knew them showed up at the services. There was no grieving. No weeping. Instead of names, each box was marked with a case number assigned by investigators from the Cook County public administrator's office, should family members show up later. Few did.

"These weren't homeless people. The average age was sixty-seven. The youngest was forty. There were more men than women. Many lived in neighborhoods along the lake," noted artist Nancy Gildart, forty-one, who lives in Homewood and is studying at the School of the Art Institute of Chicago.

Struck by what she felt was the awful anonymity of the end of lives sincerely led, Gildart had an "urge to remember these people as individuals," she said, showing a visitor around her exhibit, now on display in the school's gallery at 847 West Jackson Boulevard.

Part of a show, by the graduating class in the school's bachelor of fine arts program, Gildart's piece is titled *Remembering the Unremembered, Part 1*.

It involves mittens.

Each pair has been knitted by hand, by Gildart, and labeled with the name, address and birth date of a heat victim, along with a photo of the outside of the building in which he or she died. The mittens are lined up in rows on a living-room floor.

Gildart herself sits on a chair in front of a homey-looking fireplace, knitting the last of the forty-three pairs.

To Gildart, her contribution is an act of mourning, honoring, nurturing and helping.

"Ultimately," Gildart said, "these mittens will be given to a homeless shelter, in honor of the unremembered, for children who need protection" from a different aspect of Chicago's often-threatening climate — the cold.

"It is ironic," she added, "to knit for dead people, especially people who died from the heat." But, as she noted in an artist's statement on her World Wide Web page (gildart.com.), "the time it takes to knit one pair is about the time it would take to attend a funeral and burial service."

"A number of our advanced students this year have been engaged in making art that interfaces with social issues," said Anne Wilson, chairwoman of the fiber department at the school, which holds graduation exercises Saturday.

Gildart's art, she added, "uses the familiar vehicle of a well-made mitten to speak of issues of loss and mourning, scenes that are universal among us."

"I believe my job as an artist is to make people think about things they hadn't thought about. Or see things in a different way," said Gildart, who was born in Albion, Mich., the child of a newspaper writer, and trained as a librarian at the University of Chicago.

After college, she worked for Kraft Foods Inc. in marketing research and acquisitions.

In 1993, she lost a good friend to AIDS. Before he died, he told her, "It doesn't matter how long you live. It does matter what you do." She quit her job and enrolled in art school.

She began thinking of grief and loss after her parents died and "my sister and I spent two months cleaning out the house." To evoke their personalities and presence, she made a memory tableau out of clothing, tools and other objects they had often used.

Her current work, expanding her thoughts on grief to a public arena, has drawn praise.

"This is a unique thing Nancy has done," noted Elaine Egdorf, president of the Homewood Historical Society, who often leads tours through Homewood Memorial Gardens. Egdorf also supports what might become "Remembering the Unremembered, Part 2."

That is a plan by Gildart to plant a garden at the cemetery

as a permanent memorial to the victims of Chicago's heat disaster.

"My plan includes daylilies that would bloom in mid-July and a circular hedge of forty-three red-twig dogwoods," she said. "These plants would eventually grow together for support and become a community. It would be a place to meditate and remember."

May 22, 1998

CLASS VIEWS
CIRCUS AS ART

Evanston has never been much of a circus town, but that may be changing. What it takes, says teacher Sylvia Hernandez, is less fear, more trust.

She knows. She's been there.

For years, before she "retired from Ringling" in 1990, one of her jobs was to stand on the end of a teeter-totter and, when two people jumped on the other end, flip backward, spin through the air and land on a pole.

"Yeah, that was me — up into the chair," she said recently while sitting outside after class at the Actors Gymnasium. "It didn't take a lot of thought, but basically my greatest job skill was trust."

Her parents were the ones who jumped.

It was her brother who always held the pole.

"If you don't trust the people that are going to support you, spot you or stand under your web," she said, speaking of a wide range of skills she is now teaching to Evanston residents, "you won't be able to do it."

And fear?

"People come in here afraid of heights. Of falling down. Of muscle aches. Or that they won't have the strength for it," she said, speaking of classes in circus arts for adults she teaches at the Noyes Cultural Arts Center in a suburb better known for leafy streets and comfy homes.

The classes, a visitor noted, are packed.

One night this week, for example, a half-dozen people tottered around the gym on stilts, adhering to barked advice from instructor Chuck Stubbings.

The use of stilts, unicycles, tightropes or other balance apparatus requires continual motion, Stubbings said, without going into vestibular sensing, angular velocity, rotational inertia or muscle extension — nuances of physics and biology that have long interested circus theorists.

"If you stop moving, you fall," he warned, moving to the bottom line.

"Confidence comes with practice," he added, telling students of Chinese walkers he had recently seen who were sufficiently adept to do backward flips on stilts then dive through fiery hoops.

With trapeze, suggested Hernandez, turning to a subject students will take up later in the semester, "the swing has its own rhythm. You have to get your body to move with that rhythm, not against it."

The ones in the Actors Gymnasium, about twenty feet off the floor, come equipped with safety harnesses to prevent mat splats.

Founded in 1995, the operation is part of Chicago's Lookingglass Theatre, a troupe formed, as one co-founder puts it, "in reaction against the kitchen-drama realism theater that's been dominant in the past few years."

Anyone can sign up for the ten-week circus classes for adults, which cost $150 and teach warmup exercises, trapeze, teeterboard, juggling, unicycling, acrobatics, tumbling and standing on shoulders.

In addition, the gym provides certification workshops for the Society of American Fight Directors, training actors in the use of stage weapons, principally guns and axes, as well as theatrical martial arts.

"I don't go see a show unless I know there's going to be a lot of movement. And that's what we provide for audiences," said Hernandez, lauding what she called "new and inventive ways" of using such physical skills on stage. Several gym students, she said, have already gone on to stage roles, using job skills they picked up in circus class.

Others, says Hernandez, "have a lot of potential."

Even those who don't go on to the big top, or the big stage, gain a new appreciation for performers, she added, just as a novice taking music lessons later gasps at seeing a symphony orchestra.

This week's class started with stretching, a hush broken only by cracking sounds from bending knees.

Later, students took to the Spanish Web, a twirling rope with a loop, like a noose, to hold a wrist or an ankle.

"I've seen it done a hundred thousand times, but I never knew it hurt so much," said Laurie Flanigan, an actress rubbing a sore arm after coming down.

"Don't come down on your knees like that," teacher Stubbings warned a student in a far corner as he collapsed from a headstand with a thud.

In class, the teachers are careful to keep close, leading participants step by step. They start low, or slow, then "get confidence," Hernandez said. "You have to trust that, if you go, someone will catch you."

"Point your toes, Naomi," Hernandez shouted, as the class glided around the room, skipping sideways before moving into a lunge-and-roll.

"The farther you lunge, the better," said Stubbings, before telling Solange Khoury, an occupational therapist, the secret of a good cartwheel: "Point your toe. Draw an imaginary line in front. Plant your hands there."

"To have fun," Khoury said, when asked why she had signed up for the class, a thought echoed by Karen Lisondra, a senior in film studies at Northwestern University, and Josh Byer, a men's clothing salesman.

Although many students are actors expanding their bag-of-tricks, many are not-in-the-business "adults fulfilling childhood dreams" or simply people "looking for a different kind of workout," Hernandez said.

Some come to circus class twice a week. But those looking for instruction in being shot from a cannon, performing with tigers, or mounting a family pyramid on a high wire, have to go away to graduate school.

September 12, 1997

STRING FEVER

It's like a movie. You go into this dim old building on South Michigan Avenue, make your way through a maze of marble-floored corridors, edge by the crowds of music students waiting for elevators, cross a ramp by the fourth-floor courtyard, find a stairwell, go down two flights and — presto! — you're back in the Eighteenth Century, in a long workroom with a dozen craftsmen hunched over benches shaping rare woods into violins, violas and, over there, cellos.

Except for the roar of elevated trains past the far windows, it hardly seems like Chicago. There is a sense of time past, of being strangely out of place. You are waved in by a man with flowing brown shoulder-length hair who dresses and walks like a European dandy at his day job. At first, you suspect who he might be, but it soon becomes clear, from his Chicago accent, that this is not Antonio Stradivari. No, this is William Harris Lee, thirty-six, raised in South Shore, graduate of Lane Technical High School, proprietor of what he says may now be the largest old-line instrument workshop in the world.

It is a place of gouging, scraping, filing, planing, sanding, drilling and, often, a floor covered with wood shavings. There is carving, molding, gluing and varnishing, all of it carried out under a skylight painted black so that artisans can focus desk lamps, picking up nuances of wood grain much the way that workers did three centuries ago in the Amati and Stradivari workshops of Cremona, Italy, using the slanting rays of the afternoon sun.

Temperature is important. Winter air seeping in has been known to congeal glue. So is humidity, which, in summer, can cause an instrument to sound muted, just a shade, but enough to alarm a maker or a musician. Wood needs to be dry, to avoid rot, but not too dry, which can lead to cracking. Then there are the special resins, secret varnishes, subtleties of design, even (or so it is rumored of Stradivari) the application of certain cat fluids, all calculated to produce an instrument that, as someone once said, "smolders with caged emotion even when lying in its case."

Some claim the secret of the Strads, which now are worth

$750,000 to $2.4 million, was the varnish. Nonsense, says Lee, who notes that every other year somebody claims to have broken the master violin-maker's secret code. "Some of the best Strads," he adds, "have no varnish left on them."

What Lee has done, however, is to set up a workshop that functions in much the same way as the great shops of Cremona, where the violin evolved during the Renaissance from earlier bowed instruments such as the medieval fiddle.

"People said this could never be done here," he says. "I get a real charge out of the fact that we have done it. We've got our instruments into major orchestras. People are amazed when they come in and see what we do."

So, what does William Harris Lee & Company do?

The firm turns out about forty instruments a month. Hanging in rows above its workbenches, in various phases, are dozens of violins, which sell for $2,000 to $15,000; violas worth $3,000 to $16,000 apiece; and cellos, instruments that can take two hundred or more hours to complete, at $4,500 to $25,000.

Clients range from beginners to members of the symphony orchestras of Berlin, London, Milwaukee, Fort Worth, Florida and Chicago, where eight musicians in the string section of the Chicago Symphony Orchestra use Lee instruments.

"What Bill Lee has done that is quite outstanding is to develop a system to make instruments in quantity that are of good musical and structural quality," says New York violin maker and restorer William Monical, past president of the American Federation of Violin & Bow Makers, a group for the nation's hundred or so classical violin makers.

"They aren't latter-day Strads, nor are they the kind of instrument you'd buy in Hawaii, like a ukelele," Monical adds. They are, he observes, better than the commercially-made instruments from Europe and Asia, though less expensive than one might expect to pay for an instrument custom-crafted by a master. The world's top violinists may have a dozen or more instruments, some passed down from past virtuosos, others made by elite craftsmen who may produce only one or two a year.

How did Lee get into this line of work? He grew up in a family that, he said, was "strong on the work ethic." In high school, where he played the clarinet in the school orchestra, he apprenticed with a family friend, Manfred Rienl, who had a violin shop at 92nd Street and South Commercial Avenue. "I loved the work he did, though he kept trying to talk me out of it, telling me I should become an auto mechanic," Lee recalls. "But I loved violins, particularly taking them apart and putting them back together."

It has been thirteen years since Lee opened his own firm, in the Fine Arts Building, 410 South Michigan Avenue, using space filled at the turn of the century by the Studebaker family as a warehouse for the carriage business that preceded its shift into the manufacture of automobiles.

Next door to the Auditorium Theatre and down the street from the Art Institute of Chicago, the building was recycled, when the Studebakers pulled out, into Chicago's answer to Carnegie Hall, a gathering place for artistic interests, a warren for musicians, artists, writers, ballet schools, pocket orchestras, the likes of sculptor Lorado Taft, poet Harriet Monroe, architect Howard Van Doren Shaw and, more recently, cartoonist Lynda Barry.

"It takes hours of manual work" to make an instrument. "There aren't a lot of shortcuts you can take by using a machine," Lee says. He employs nineteen people. Nine are Cambodian refugees, hired through church-run job placement services in Chicago. None of the refugees had woodworking experience, but, Lee says, "they had a good work ethic." One previously was a Buddhist monk. They were taught by older workers with years of experience in the field.

"We are the only place in the U.S., if not the world, that teaches the traditional handworking techniques of violinmaking, much the same way as the European workshops of the Seventeenth and Eighteenth Centuries did."

"So, now, explain what goes on here," a visitor asks, during a tour.

It is, Lee notes, a typical afternoon in the workshop. Two people are applying antique varnish to a viola. Another uses a finger plane to shape the back of a violin. Michael Darnton, a maker and restorer, polishes another violin and, later, shapes a cello neck. Music from a CD player fills the air, cellist Emanuel Feuermann performing Don Quixote by Richard Strauss.

"Other than strings, which started out being made of lamb gut and now are often synthetic, there really haven't been a lot of changes in violins over the years," Lee said. What makes a fine violin? "Woods. How they are cut, and aged. The time spent shaping the instrument. And the judgment of the maker."

Poplar and willow work well for violas and cellos, a discovery made inadvertently in Cremona, a Northern Italian town on the banks of the Po River southeast of Milan. During the explosion of new arts and interests that became known as the Renaissance, the local shipbuilding trades bought up all the available hardwoods in the area. For violas and cellos, the burgeoning musical instrument-making trade had to make do with the softer woods, which happily turned out to have a darker, richer sound that people liked.

Violins traditionally have been fashioned from maple, a harder wood, and often from European maple, which has a tighter grain than its American cousin and produces a better sound. According to acoustic formulas passed down for centuries, and in gradations measured at some points by tenths of a millimeter, soundboards are carved, leaving a thickness where tension plays on the wood, a thinness where it doesn't. An inlay, called purfling, is set around the edge of the soundboard. A bass bar, to provide the support, is mounted. Neck blocks are cut and shaped. Strings, hitched to tuning pegs and a tailpiece, stretch over a bridge, which transmits vibrations to the front soundboard, inside sound post and back, producing beautiful throaty tones.

"Setting a neck into an instrument is extremely hard," Lee said. "You're dealing with different planes. The angles have to be right each way so the tension on the strings is perfect. If it's off to one side, bringing the instrument up to pitch will be difficult. You'll get a real flabby sound."

For cellos, the dimensions of the neck are important. If a neck is too thick, a cellist's fingers lose action. Too thin, and the fingers bounce up. Viola players are equally demanding. Once reserved for people who couldn't get jobs playing violin, viola playing has blossomed in recent years, Lee notes. Repertoire has expanded and modern players want an instrument, he says, "with faster response and a real viola sound."

What dumb things do people ask him at cocktail parties?

"One is about whatever new 'secret' of Stradivari has just been on television," he says. "Another is whether or not violins are somehow made by machines, not painstakingly carved in pieces by hand, as they are. A third? That all violin makers are eighty-year-old people with white hair. They aren't."

Lee operates out of a small office filled with photographs of customers, notably violinist Benny Kim, and, in a corner, a stack of back copies of *The Strad*, a trade magazine from London that features articles on such matters as "wood-bending techniques" and color fold-outs of violins in the news.

There isn't much time to read. Lee spends most of his days talking with clients, or overseeing minute production details. "It's a good shop," says Chicago cellist Dennis Connor, who bought an instrument there two years ago for five thousand dollars and later took it in for minor bridge adjustments. "They're really interested in making sure the instrument is serviced properly."

"I play two instruments, an old Italian, and one of Bill's," says Florence Schwartz, a violinist with the Chicago Symphony Orchestra. "I bought it two summers ago, mostly to play at Ravinia, because the older instrument is real temperamental when you go back and forth from air conditioning into humidity. Bill's plays real well. It has a great sound. I got a lot of compliments. It looks good too, not like a new fiddle. I practice on it at home, take it on tour all over the world—what else can I tell you?"

A violin, like a child, is born with a personality. Some are hot. Some are brilliant, or soft, or harsh. Tone quality can be changed, by adjusting the soundpost or string setup. Lee asks musician friends and associates to "test drive" his new instruments to get a sense of their characteristics.

But matching an instrument to a buyer is a complex process, Lee explains. It takes much fiddling, and, if you need something to do it with, see Lee's brother upstairs. He makes bows.

October 7, 1997

FOR THE CSO, IT'S
MAHLER ONSTAGE AND
PING-PONG BACKSTAGE

Onstage, under the merciless glare of a conductor, facing a hushed audience of two thousand knowing ears, the pressure is relentless for each member of a symphony orchestra. In the upper registers of the musical world, the thrust for precision can be draining.

"Will I come in on time? Will I play a C sharp instead of C natural? Your mind has to be there all the time," said Chicago Symphony Orchestra violist Richard Ferrin.

Added a seatmate, "I sweat, after all these years, before certain passages. You're keyed up. If you miss it, you know it."

Small wonder, then, when the applause dies down, after conductor Daniel Barenboim hustles offstage and CSO musicians take a break, that some of them look for something to help unwind.

Given the solemn nature of much classical music, one might assume its players would turn to reading, meditation, phone calls to loved ones — or the settling of upcoming scores.

Hardly. Unbeknownst to audiences, CSO members, like their cultural counterparts across the country, have long huddled backstage for furious games of pinochle, chess, bridge and poker, as concertgoers drift off at intermission to restrooms or conversation or drinks. But more recently, the CSO, perhaps befitting its lofty status, has taken this tradition into even more adventurous terrain.

CSO members have been sprinting offstage to play, would you believe, table tennis.

Often in formal dress, they have been smashing tiny celluloid balls around during the brief breaks, a form of exercise that, many of them say, diverts the mind and refreshes a body that, as every musician learns in musician school, "is the other half of your instrument."

That little-known diversion has come to play a role in a dream of certain orchestra members, admittedly one far below such big-ticket items as acoustics, stage views and improved seating for its audiences.

Even as the CSO gave its final performances before departing for an eleven-day trip to Germany, many of the CSO's string players, plus a significant number in brass, have been quietly rooting for what, to them, would be a major improvement when the orchestra's Symphony Center, renovated at a cost of $105 million, grandly reopens October 4.

They want a permanent roost for their Ping-Pong table.

It would be an allotted space, in the musicians lounge, for the large green instrument, divided into halves by a net, that they have come to turn to when Mahler or other job challenges threaten to burn them out.

They were talking about it — and getting a bit misty — the other day before they trooped onstage at Medinah Temple, their temporary home, to perform one of their final concerts of the downtown season.

Table tennis at the CSO, it appears, has many of the touches of a secret underground cult. It is unknown to the general public, even to many devoted fans of the CSO, who little suspect that at intermission some orchestra members are rushing downstairs because of the table's "first come, first served" rule.

"It's a frightening sight," admitted one longtime player, violist Maxwell Raimi, "to see musicians, carrying priceless instruments, sprinting to get there first."

Known for an ability to hit edges, Raimi likes to tell of the intermission when bass player Michael Hovnanian ("He's our Dennis Rodman") shredded a sleeve on his tails diving for a floor shot.

During the renovation, players made do with a temporary setup at Medinah.

In late June, they will shift to Ravinia, the CSO's summer home, where players use a table under the main pavilion stage, in a space soundproofed to muffle "pings, pongs and screams," as one player puts it.

"I can't imagine another orchestra where the level of Ping-Pong is so high," reported cellist Jonathan Pegis. "We have so many styles."

Trumpeter Mark Ridenour, one player reported, is "a specialist in underspin — touch it and it goes right into the net." Bassist Stephen Lester "is into scoops." And Ferrin, said one longtime opponent, "has this serve that comes off the table like a dead fish. It just lies there — and spins.

"It's like going after a ball of phlegm."

At other orchestras around the country, card games, TV and

the occasional shoulder massage are popular ways for high-level musicians to unwind. But some, on hearing of the CSO's thrust, seemed a little jealous.

"We don't have room for a Ping-Pong table," observed Karl Reichert, a staffer at the Minnesota Orchestra, "but we do have a massage therapist who comes in for all the concerts and does five-minute massages for the musicians. It's something the musicians worked out with management to deal with tension, repetitive motion and stress."

The Portland-based Oregon Symphony also has a massage therapist. This one, though, volunteers her services in return for the privilege of sitting backstage during concerts, noted Carrie Kikel, the symphony's public relations director. Television, she added, is another popular stress-reliever for the Oregon performers, reporting that, "If there's a basketball game on anywhere in the world, it's on the television set."

"The big thing at Tanglewood is chess," said a staffer at the summer home of the Boston Symphony Orchestra, though BSO conductor Seiji Ozawa has been known to demolish opponents at table tennis, once flattening a half-dozen Chicagoans during a party at Hugh Hefner's Playboy Mansion. But no, the staffer added, BSO members do not have their own Ping-Pong table.

So, what is it about table tennis that turned on music-makers in Chicago?

"Music is very tense onstage. You have to concentrate for two hours or more. Ping-Pong is wonderful for the eyes. It ups your coordination — and it's very relaxing," explained Ferrin, noting that contributors to the CSO table tennis players fund include principal horn Dale Clevenger, assistant principal trumpet William Scarlett and substitute violist Lisa Rensberger.

"It's analogous to musicmaking," piped in Raimi, explaining the appeal of the game to string players with a ferocious sweep of a paddle and proclaiming that "the forehand is an up-bow. A backhand, a down-bow."

According to Ferrin, table tennis at the CSO started in 1985 when David Chickering, now playing with an orchestra in New Zealand, donated a table. To show approval, Sir Georg, and later Daniel Barenboim, chipped in funds for paddles. James Levine, then conducting at Ravinia, donated a hundred balls.

"You know who was a great Ping-Pong player? Jascha Heifetz," Ferrin said, recalling a magical day in 1966 when "I played doubles with Jascha and his son, Jay, at his home in Los Angeles."

"Also, Nathan Milstein," he added, talking of another violinist quick with paddle, though not as adept as Sir Georg Solti, who once came backstage at the CSO and, with conductorial flourishes, whomped everybody.

June 6, 1997

CHICAGO:
LAND OF BOOKS
AND WRITERS

HOMETOWN HUG
FOR HEMINGWAY

Hemingway?

Forgotten?

Not in Paris. Even now, some seventy years after papa hit his literary stride, writers still hang out at the Dome, the Select, La Closerie and other Ernest haunts, scribbling into black notebooks, trying to turn tangled thoughts into his kind of simple, direct sentences.

And certainly not in Oak Park, where the birthday of a lad who grew up in that village to become a Nobel laureate for literature was celebrated over the weekend with fervor and a writing class.

And not at Oak Park-River Forest High School, where "not a kid goes through here who doesn't read Hemingway at some point," as school superintendent Donald Offermann ringingly assured Hem fans sitting in the room where the master once studied literature and debating.

But there were signs of a certain, um, softness creeping into the annual celebration of a man who, in that same room, after falling wounded in Italy, brought back a show-and-tell bag with army pants cut by shrapnel and splotched with the dark stains of his own blood.

This year, for example, they were serving lemonade, not martinis, on the front porch of Hemingway's boyhood home, at 339 North Oak Park Avenue.

Lemonade!

Lemonade, to honor the man who liberated the Ritz bar in Paris in 1944 by clambering onto the hotel's roof, firing a burst from his Sten gun, bringing down a clothesline and taking two prisoners, a pair of elderly German orderlies left behind on laundry detail.

Lemonade, for a writer who once kicked a pet lion out of another Paris bar after the beast urinated on his shoes and, as Hemingway later shaped the tale, "failed to adequately apologize."

This year in Oak Park, there was no running of the papier-mache bulls through the streets of downtown, with people falling down, getting "gored," a longtime hit of a Fiesta de

Hemingway (based on Hem's Spanish adventures). That was totally scrapped.

Organizers were quick to explain that what they had in mind was not some vegetarian substitute, like a Running of the Tofu Cubes, but something that would cost less and, well, get back to basics.

What the Ernest Hemingway Foundation of Oak Park, which runs a museum, and the Oak Park Public Library, where he hung out, planned for his birthday Sunday (he would have been ninety seven) was a full-weekend celebration of "his powerful, style-forming mastery of the art of modern narration," in the words of the selection committee when Hemingway received the Nobel Prize for Literature in 1954.

That meant a two-hour class at the library, led by writing teacher Molly Daniels Ramanujan, a primer for aspiring novelists who themselves might one day burst out of town to conquer literary worlds.

There was a walking tour of notable Hem sites that ended in the Hemingway Room of Oak Park-River Forest High School where aficionados read aloud his short story, Hills Like White Elephants.

An exhibit, "How Hemingway Wrote," opened at the Hemingway Museum, at 200 North Oak Park Avenue. A book of essays, Ernest Hemingway: The Oak Park Legacy, went on sale in local stores for $19.50.

"Without conflicts, there are no stories. Conflicts open doors. We become aware and see things we would not otherwise see," Daniels Ramanujan reminded the writers group, which included, among others, a community organizer, a clothier, a social worker, a preservationist, a real estate agent and a number of historians.

"What I like about Hemingway stories is that one-eighth is revealed, and seven-eighths is not," noted Evangeline Fotias, a teacher at Morton West High School. "It's up to the reader to interpret his stories," she said. "You have to pick up on the subtle meanings."

Her own students, she said, enjoy Hemingway, but "need a little help" with his ideas and themes. Explained, Hemingway's stories "blow them away," she added. Others quoted Hemingway on writing.

"He said, 'Just do it. Write about your own experiences. Don't follow advice you don't agree with,'" said Gerard, a telephone maintenance man from Lemont who asked that his last name not be used.

"Hemingway wrote about 450 words a day," added Daniels Ramanujan. "If you write two typed pages a day, you'll be keeping up with Hemingway. People used to say that writers are born, not made. But we all have light, energy, genius. We can learn tactics.

"Everybody has at least one book in them."

There also is no shortage of shorter works, said another participant in the weekend Hemingway festival, Etta Worthington, an editor of the *River Oak Review*, a local literary magazine.

More than 250 writers submitted stories in a recent contest organized by the review, she said, though many of them reflected a common plot line, "principal characters bumping off ex-spouses."

As various contributors to *Ernest Hemingway: The Oak Park Legacy* noted, Hemingway did not have an easy childhood in the leafy suburb, growing up in a household ruled by a domineering and obsessive mother, a major source of later confusion, anxiety and irreverence.

His mother dressed him as a girl for his first three years, passing him off as a twin to his older sister, Marcelline. The two slept in the same bedroom in twin white cribs, had dolls that were just alike and played with similar china tea sets. Later, the mother held back Marcelline so the two could enter grade school together.

His tense, henpecked father often fled to the rural outdoors where, one contributor said, "a sense of freedom could be exercised." It was a family with great gifts, but also tension and depression.

His father, a doctor, gave him his first gun when Hemingway was ten and shot himself when Hemingway was twenty-nine. Later, in the hallway of his home in Ketchum, Idaho, using his favorite custom-made, twelve-gauge double-barreled shotgun, Hemingway did the same thing.

"We make much of him with our students, but not too much I hope," said Offermann, speaking in the Hemingway room, an Oxford-style classroom, built in about 1910, which boasts a brick fireplace, oak paneling and leaded windows. "He grew up in a community that valued education highly," Offermann noted, though "some feel his attitudes towards women wouldn't square with today's realities."

These days, Offermann added, the Hemingway Room is rotated among the school's thirty-two English teachers, "so every student spends at least one week a year studying in the same room where Ernest Hemingway sat" during the last year of his formal education.

He never went to college.

Still, there is no fall-off of visitors who make their way to Oak Park to see firsthand where the legends began.

Many come from abroad, said Hemingway Foundation archivist Barbara Ballinger. "They come to the museum, as if to a shrine," she said, recounting recent visits by a family from Japan, who brought in a book on Hemingway in Japanese, and a young man from France who asked museum officials to stamp two novels to mark his visit to Oak Park.

In much the same way that a vacationer in Sarasota might hit the beach, Jenny Alderson, seventeen, a high school senior from Wichita, had her own agenda when she came to spend time with her aunt in Oak Park.

"This might sound weird," she said, writing down tips around a big table at the Oak Park library, "but I'm writing a novel."

December 7, 1997

IRISH AUTHOR'S FANS
GATHER TO CELEBRATE
ULYSSES, OTHER TALES

And, yes, night came to Wrigleyville. And, yes, there was a crowd at a theater on North Southport for Bloomsday, the sixteenth day of June, when James Joyce, Ireland's great writer, is celebrated around the globe.

And, yes, there were a dozen readers, including a computer programmer, a T'ai Chi instructor and a customer service representative for the gum company from which that increasingly well-off neighborhood pulls its name.

And, yes, the final moments were given over to Molly Bloom and her passionate reveries, the ones that lead to her promise, "yes, yes, yes."

And no, Molly didn't go into the raunchier bits of her famed soliloquy — the ones having to do with sailors — possibly in deference to a community that is now largely built around the consumption of coffee.

One doesn't, of course, have to be Irish, or wanton, to love Joyce.

Nor need one fully understand a writer whose complexities, according to late-breaking thought, were a precursor of much modern communication.

Joyce's writings, as an Internet contributor recently noted on a James Joyce home page, "contain multiple links to both internal and external documents." Joyce, it appears, wrote in a sort of literary hypertext, long before personal computers and coded words made jumping from theme to theme possible with the tap of a key.

Others simply think he's sexy.

"On June 16, 1904," host Steve Diedrich began, as an audience filled the 320-seat Mercury Theater, "Joyce went out walking for the first time with a woman named Nora Barnacle. Shortly after, they eloped to Europe."

The literary child of that first date, as none present needed reminding, was *Ulysses*, Joyce's reshaping of Homeric myth, in a third of a million words, with all the events taking place on one single day in Dublin.

"The hero," Diedrich went on, setting up the evening's eleven readings, "is named Bloom. June 16 has come to be known as Bloomsday. All over the world Joyceans gather together and celebrate the novel. In New York, they are reading the whole book. We are much less ambitious."

On the other hand, there was, in Chicago this Bloomsday, no shortage of credentials. Some there were Irish. Some passionate. Some both.

One reader was Rory Childers, now a professor of medicine at the University of Chicago. It was his grandfather, caught up in the Irish troubles of the 1920s, who instructed a British firing squad, in his final words, "Take a step closer, lads. It'll be easier for you."

"Was that really true?" an audience member asked at intermission, after Childers completed reading a passage, "In the kitchen at 7 Eccles Street."

"Yes, it's true, but hasn't much to do with Joyce," he said, turning the talk back to what he called "a staggering book, for so many reasons."

So complex is *Ulysses*, he suggested, that "a close reading takes a good year. It's very complicated — not an easy read. Joyce knew that when he said, 'I'm going to keep the Ph.D-ites busy for two hundred years.'"

And that, as any perusal of posted lists of scholarly Joyce conferences will attest, remains certainly true.

Last January, for example, hundreds of Joyce analysts gathered in Florida for a three-day conference, dubbed "Miami J'yce." Last week, hundreds more met at the University of Toronto, under the banner of the International James Joyce Foundation, to discuss "Historical Joyce/Hysterical Joyce."

All this week in Dublin, scholars are gathering for readings and lectures, dressing up in Edwardian garb and doing walkabouts on a shoreline near Dublin which, as one in the Wrigleyville audience whispered to a companion Monday night, "looks just like Diversey Harbor."

In Chicago, the Bloomsday readings began a decade ago, at the Red Lion Pub on North Lincoln Avenue, a gathering generated by Mary Nell Murphy, who met her husband, she noted, at a James Joyce discussion group, though "we didn't fall in love until half way through *Finnegan's Wake*."

Other local Bloomsdays have been at the Newberry Library, where Diedrich teaches Joyce. "I took a class at the Newberry. I knew I'd never read it myself," noted Kelly Kleiman, a consultant for non-profit organizations, who read a passage titled "Gerty MacDowell and the fireworks."

"I took a class several years ago and really enjoyed it," said Molly Zolnay, one of a trio of students in the Mercury's crowded lobby at halftime. "It touches a lot of people because it's about a whole bunch of people — on one day. Like *Under Milkwood*," she said, comparing Joyce to another writer whose words sound better aloud, Dylan Thomas.

"Intoxicating language," Mike Kurshinsky averred nearby. "It's my birthday," added Jennifer Farrell, who said she liked *Ulysses* because "it's a classical theme. It continues," through the ages.

This year's event, one organizer noted, far surpassed last year's, when foul weather and a Bulls final championship game pretty much limited the Bloomsday group to "the readers and the people who drove us."

"Thank you for coming," said host Diedrich, at evening's end. "We had a great time. Read your Joyce and we'll see you next year."

June 18, 1997

BROOKER WINNERS
DON'T GO BY THE BOOK
WHEN COLLECTING

One winner found a treasure in a bin at the Hyde Park Cooperative Society's annual used-book sale, paying a quarter for a treatise on logic printed in Paris at the height of the French Revolution.

Another, who collects art books, keeps track of museum-shop sales in distant cities and follows up on promising leads from friends.

Others, turned on by such Hyde Park literary landmarks as Powell's Bookstore and O'Gara & Wilson, have trekked to other secondhand book emporiums as far afield as Ann Arbor, Michigan, and California.

Serious book collecting, as aficionados aver, is a matter of making choices, of setting principles, of displaying taste — and showing brio.

It is just that "vivacity, or spirit," as dictionaries translate the term, that turns on judges in a peculiarly Hyde Park battle for the annual T. Kimball Brooker Prizes for Undergraduate Book Collecting.

"The key question is coherence versus accumulation," Brooker judge Alice Schreyer was saying the other day, sitting in a book-lined room in the University of Chicago Library, 100 East 57th Street. She was chatting with a group of people who have judged or won Brookers in its eight years of existence.

In other words, said Schreyer, who is curator of the library's special collections, "what we look for is some unifying theme, some principle of organizing. It's not just a great number of books."

Anybody, other judges noted, can take a Visa card, march into Seminary Cooperative Bookstore, a Hyde Park haunt, and buy an aisle. But as judge Edward Rosenheim, professor emeritus in English language and literature, explained, a Brooker candidate must "make a case that the books form a collection in a way that confers specialness."

The art is in the linkages.

"Shaping a collecting theme and pursuing it through book sales, used-book stores, even dumpsters — that's what's exciting," Schreyer said.

Book collecting, however curious it might seem to some as the object of a cash prize, is also oddly personal.

"'Would you come see my books?' is a very intimate invitation. So much is revealed," said John Saumarez Smith, a legendary London bookseller whom bibliophiles love to quote.

As with any passion, sport or art, the big question in book collecting is how to do it well. The Brooker contest, its organizers hope, offers case-history suggestions to the fledgling and the floundering.

This year, from the hundred or so who took entry forms, the holdings of the twelve finalists were examined by the five judges. The awards — with one thousand dollars for a senior, five hundred dollars for a sophomore — will given out May 28 at the University of Chicago's Honors Assembly.

And the winners will be — drumroll!!! — senior Benjamin Lord for his collection of art books on abstract expressionism and sophomore Nathan Mauk, who impressed the judges with the thrust of his assembled volumes on cognitive psychology, analytic philosophy and the nature of meaning.

It would be stretching matters to say that Lord and Mauk were carried through the streets of Hyde Park on the shoulders of classmates when the news of their victories became known on the South Side campus.

But both allowed that the money will come in handy for more book buying and that they were happy that books from their collections will be on display in a glass case in the library's main lobby.

In an interview, Mauk said his winning "came as a surprise — because I think my collection is very incoherent." Lord, who split for Paris the day his exams ended, said Tuesday by phone that he had spent the day roaming Left Bank bookstalls and seen "an interesting book on Max Ernst."

That, for Schreyer, brought up an important point — that many private collections, lovingly shaped, later form important parts of libraries, bringing in broadsides, music scores and other material associated with a theme "that otherwise never would have survived."

"What was really exciting was watching my collection grow," noted Nathanael Crawford, last year's senior winner for his gathering of thirty winners of the Newbery Award, a children's literature prize, and an essay on the increasingly challenging themes of the genre.

As a child, "I was homesick and my mother read me *The Door in the Wall*, by Marguerite de Angeli," Crawford said, referring to the 1950 winner and the genesis of his interest in the award, named for British bookseller John Newbery and given by the nation's children's librarians each year.

The Brooker Prizes, in turn, are funded by a longtime Chicago bibliophile who received a similar prize when he was an undergraduate at Yale, university officials said. The competition is not without risk.

In his dorm room, Mauk said, he keeps almost a thousand books, "a collection that is ever expanding, threatening the people downstairs."

And what, for the judges, is most difficult?

"Roommates," said Rosenheim, recalling one visit to a finalist whose room sharer interrupted the interview to feed his pet snake.

Another time, while out viewing holdings on a student's farm near Kankakee, two Brooker inspectors were held at bay by the family's judge-hating dog.

May 14, 1997

WHERE OLD BOOKS GO
TO BE READ AGAIN

Throwing out a book, to many readers, is akin to dumping kittens by the side of a road, an act reserved for the heartless and, possibly, criminal.

Book owners have been known to comb their collections and, with moaning and whining, to cull one, possibly two, they could live without. The problem, even for the marginally obsessed, is what to do next.

It is not, they say, like throwing out a lamp.

Enter the Book Orphanage.

Though it isn't called that, the city's only home for unwanted books, at 5801 North Pulaski Road, inside the iron gates of North Park Village, is a place where a tome, facing a date with the Great Shredder, can get a sporting chance to show its spine and to find somebody new to love it.

Packed with everything from steamy romance novels to weighty works by Saul Bellow, the Book & Magazine Exchange, as the converted house trailer is formally known, is part of a recycling center at the village, a former sanitarium that is now a nature preserve and a city-run home for senior citizens.

The center also takes in plastic containers, paper, bottles and cans, but it's the books that bring in the crowds — from as far away as Elgin.

"As far as I know, we're the only operation like this in the area," says center manager Ted Zielinski, explaining the ground rules.

Basically, it's like this. The book trailer is open every day of the year, from 8 A.M. to 5 P.M. Book owners bring in books they no longer want. People who want books, take them away, for free. The limit is five.

As book-owners aver, there is something about a book, a kind of printed soul, that hangs on long after its words have been absorbed. As with a friend, one is reluctant to tell a book, once chosen, to later go away, a phenomenon that many in the used-book game have come to recognize.

"We've had people give us books and tell us, 'It's okay if you throw them away, but I couldn't do it myself,'" notes Dan Crawford, manager of the Newberry Library Book Festival, which sets out bins with some 150,000 pre-owned books for a major exchange of titles each year in late July.

"Your books are an extension of yourself, your education, your parents, the things you grew up with. They reflect what's good in your life," adds Paula Katz, a volunteer for the past thirty-nine years at the Brandeis Book Sale, which opens a nine-day run Saturday at Old Orchard Shopping Center in Skokie.

Last week, Katz was helping a friend, moving into smaller digs, pack up twenty-one boxes of books for this year's assembly of four hundred thousand books. It was not easy, she said, because "every time I put a book down, she picked it up."

And that, suggests manager Zielinski, is exactly how it should be.

"Anything in print is valuable," he said. "People took time to write, to edit and to print it. They used resources, paper and ink. And if we can squeeze a few more readers out of it, that's good."

A former printer laid off when his employer closed down, Zielinski began five years ago as a volunteer at the recycling site, an outpost of the Resource Center, a non-profit environmental education organization at 222 East 135th Place. Quickly promoted to manager, he now oversees half a dozen others who come in to help every day with its varied operations.

All are energy efficient. One grinder, for example, powered by a bicycle ridden by Zielinski, turns plastic containers into chips to be converted into boards to line compost heaps to provide fertilizer for a garden.

"This place wouldn't go without him. Hardest worker I've ever seen," a man was shouting the day a visitor dropped in to look for a book (and went away with five copies of National Geographic magazine).

"Give that man a 50 percent pay raise," retorted Zielinski, referring to Lyle "Steve" Wilson, a retired Army sergeant who acquired his nickname as a teenaged football player because "it sounded tougher."

Wilson currently serves as the center's unpaid "librarian," a title he likes, even though his books go out and don't come back.

"People used to come and throw their books on the floor," he said. Two years ago, "I came over, made shelves, and now I take care of it."

At any moment, Wilson has about two thousand books in residence, placed on shelves in no discernible system. He once tried to put them in order, but people mixed them up too much while trying to figure out what to take.

"It's not like a library. I come in here having no idea of what I'm looking for," browser Mike Egan was saying, as he looked over the stock.

"If someone reads a book, it's still good for someone else," added Tom Stefanski, leaving with *A Survival Guide for Teenagers and Stepfamilies*.

The limit is five, but Wilson has been known to waive the restrictions, as when an attractive woman of a certain age recently wanted to carry off a larger-than-allowed number of romance novels. Permission was granted.

The cutoff, Wilson noted, is to prevent commercial book-nappers from carrying off the better volumes to sell at flea markets or fairs. "That's not what we're all about," said Zielinski. "The books are here to be passed on, especially to people who can't afford to pay anything at all."

June 11, 1997

A SANCTUARY WHERE
WRITERS CAN THINK AND
BE CREATIVE

Artistic life demands a certain saintly single-mindedness, and some claim it was easier when Gustave Flaubert shut himself in his room for five years, drumming out sentences on a table to get his rhythms right, producing two pages of *Madame Bovary* in a good week and telling his mistress to go away.

Today, faced with jangling interruptions from friends, relatives, hucksters and people phoning from noisy bars looking for somebody named Raoul, even hardened recluses have a tough time keeping their work on track. That is why writers and other creative persons react so strongly when the talk turns to artist colonies where telephones — and other modern clutter — are kept under strict controls. In a recent listing of such American colonies, *Coda*, a literary newsletter, glowingly called them, "On Cloud Nine: 21 Heavens."

One of these "retreats of peace and natural beauty" is Ragdale, an old estate in Lake Forest that is celebrating ten years as "a sanctuary for artists, writers and scholars" by opening an exhibition of ten resident artists at Fairweather-Hardin Gallery, 101 East Ontario Street, followed by a considerable amount of music, readings and dinner at the nearby Arts Club of Chicago.

It is also a time to honor the idea of arts colonies everywhere.

"Many people can work ten times as well in a place like this because they are not interrupted. They have protected time and space," says Alice Ryerson Hayes, who began the Ragdale encampment in 1976. It is in a home built in 1897 by her grandfather, Howard Van Doren Shaw, an architect who designed Lake Forest's Market Square, one of the nation's first shopping centers, and the Art Institute's Goodman Theater. In the last decade, one thousand artists and writers, in their own private ways, have retreated behind rows of trees at 1260 North Green Bay Road for periods of from one week to two months to work in ten guest rooms, walk acres of tall prairie grass or relax on screened porches amidst comfy chairs, hammocks, books and stacks of aged *New Yorker* magazines.

Better-known counterparts exist in the East, such as Yaddo

at Saratoga Springs, N.Y., whose guest list has included Carson McCullers, Philip Roth, Saul Bellow, Truman Capote, Leonard Bernstein, John Cheever and Aaron Copland (though not all at once) and New Hampshire's MacDowell Colony, where Thornton Wilder wrote *Our Town*. Colonies also have been set up by a lake in the Adirondacks, at a restored Victorian military base on Puget Sound, on a 150-acre patch of the Berkshires, in a nature sanctuary in southern California, near a small town in Vermont, in the mountains of Wyoming and on the 600-acre estate of Edna St. Vincent Millay in upstate New York.

Ragdale also has had successes, such as Joan Chase, author of *During the Reign of the Queen of Persia*, cartoonist Nicole Hollander, short-story writer Bette Howland, whose *Things to Come and Go* received a 1984 MacArthur Fellow Award, and poet Denise Levertov. All worked at Ragdale. So have hundreds of other creators, lesser known, perhaps yet to be honored.

From the beginning, Howard Van Doren Shaw's home was open to the arts. An outdoor theater, with Japanese lanterns strung in the trees, was set up in the back garden. Poet Vachel Lindsay came to visit. Editor Harriet Monroe once dropped by with William Butler Yeats. Carl Sandburg came out from Chicago for a meal. The busy Mrs. Shaw, a playwright, poet and society woman, produced a "vegetable" play for children, adult romps such as *The Heir to Manville Grange* and *Dream Flower*, poems for Monroe's *Poetry* magazine and three children, Evelyn, who later married *Tribune* cartoonist John T. McCutcheon; Sylvia, a sculptress, later Mrs. Clay Judson; and Frances, Mrs. John Lord King. Alice Ryerson Hayes is Sylvia's daughter.

According to historians, the main house with its oak-paneled living room and cozy fireplace chimney corners was built "when the auto was a newfangled contraption and Green Bay Road a peaceful byway where chickens scratched for grain." Later, there was time for rafting on the Skokie River, lazing under the spreading elms and playing in "The Lincoln Cabin," brought from the Chicago fair of 1933 along with Sally Rand's bathroom. In the back fields, neighborhood children gathered every fall to toast marshmallows before a huge bonfire, the kind seen in McCutcheon's cartoon "Injun Summer."

Turning the Shaw estate into an artist colony raised some Lake Forest eyebrows. Some Forest homeowners feared that fields and streams would be polluted by carousing bohemians. But, unlike one colony where the manager's wife recently ran off with a painter, Ragdale has been crushingly quiet. Indeed, complaints about noise run the other way. Sometimes stereo music drifts in from neighboring estates. Except for one incident, in which a young black writer walking back from town was stopped by police and, some felt, rudely questioned, problems are rare. Says resident manager Evadene Judge: "Three-quarters of our 'incidents' involve knocking on doors during the day."

Still, at Ragdale, not every moment is serious. Len Aronson, a WMAQ-Channel 5 producer and fledgling playwright, spent two weeks at Ragdale last year, working on *Dicks*, a play about undercover Chicago detectives, with Robert Benjamin, a former Channel 5 staffer who is now press secretary to gubernatorial hopeful Adlai Stevenson. "To me," says Aronson, "the best part was being in this gathering of kindred spirits, shamelessly coming forward to join in an intellectual experience. There was wonderful companionship — among people who openly wanted to be creative. We had a lot of fun."

Many evenings, guests read material aloud. Sometimes, they listen to special visitors, such as poet Gwendolyn Brooks, hear tapes by in-residence composers, play a game of "Dictionary," read plays or simply sit around and talk. They seldom watch television. Each October, a "really pagan" bonfire takes place, with pipers, marshmallows, chili and mulled wine. Other outings are made to Ravinia, Wrigley Field, movies, plays and local displays of fireworks. One night, on a break from writing his novel, Lloyd Sachs, a former contributor to the *Reader*, led an expedition to Libertyville with a Ragdale bowling team, a playwright, a sex-therapist author, a short-story writer and a neon artist.

Not everyone adjusts to silence. At Yaddo, a stone mansion with a portcullis, baronial dining room and ornate carvings throughout, several writers have complained of ghosts appearing in their bedrooms. At another colony, a writer was thrown out after his wife arrived for a weekend visit, found him reading in bed with a poetess and broke her jaw. But most artists learn to stay quietly in their rooms and work.

At Ragdale, many writers are compulsively neat. They shuffle their furniture, push chairs near, or away from, the windows and align their papers, books, pencils and, these days, computers. One writer hangs a piece of stained glass in her window and each morning fills a vase with fresh flowers. Before departing, guests leave notes in a book kept in each bedroom. "I love that this room is not full of anonymity, like hotel rooms, but holds the feeling that others were here," wrote one. "Sit at this desk after midnight, and watch for the moon through the trees," urged another.

A poet said:

> Finally
> I'm here
> a year's anticipation
> rising hopes
> fears rise too
> questions to myself
> and others
> waiting work
> scattered pieces of my life
> to rearrange.

Like all colonies, Ragdale faces problems in fundraising. Retreats must be exclusive, with standards to separate the artistic wheat from the general public chaff. For corporations, donating to secluded colonies is less appealing than giving funds to such public ventures as orchestras, operas and theater companies. "Colonies are an eclectic little group," says Alice Ryerson Hayes. "Some may be used by as few as a hundred people a year, but each colony is immensely valuable to the arts."

Ragdale, not as wealthy as Yaddo or MacDowell, is better off than many facilities where artists must provide their own food, share housekeeping duties, work to raise funds or, in one case, bring their own gas lamps. Its budget is $150,000 a year, with $20,000 coming in from its fees of ten dollars a day, the rest from fundraising and a small endowment. The heaviest demand is during academic breaks, in summer and January. April is the slowest month. Last year, 392 persons requested application forms, 155 applied for space and 110 came to stay.

Visitors make their own breakfasts and lunches and wash the dishes afterward. About 6 P.M., they gather for a communal dinner that can run to stuffed lobster, steaks, Szechuan specialties and strawberry mousse. Or, they can pick through the kitchen's well-stocked refrigerators, find a corner and keep to themselves. Talking and mixing are not compulsory. Nor are credentials. "People don't have to be professional artists to come here," says Evadene Judge. "They have to be people on their way up who show commitment to their work."

Often, the mix is eclectic. In residence during one recent period were a divorced female novelist from New York, a female teacher spending her summer writing short stories, a male poet taking a break from his job as a cab dispatcher, a female fabric artist, a male composer for piano and South American flute, a female poet interested in "planetary energy alignments," a female critic finishing off a book and a journalist polishing up his memoirs.

Many form fast friendships. A folksinger and a filmmaker who met at Ragdale later collaborated on a movie. Two writers, who found they were good critics of each other's work, kept in touch back in New York. Several other writers formed their own workshop. But not everyone sees the charm. "Everyone's so happy! So sappy! They all love this place! Doesn't anything go wrong?" snapped one non-artistic visitor, after scanning the guest registers.

Actually, not much, notes Ron Wray, a resident poet and director of the Ragdale Foundation. And, he adds, "We have no plans for change."

In many ways, Ragdale is a tribute to the skills of its builder. "You get a feeling that something passed from the man to the house," says Molly Ramanujan, a teacher of fiction writing at the University of Chicago who has led workshops at Ragdale. "There's something creative in the air."

Alice Ryerson Hayes says her grandfather "named the house he built with as unpretentious a name as he could find because it was a house for children and artists, not a place for the stuffy or the grand."

That tradition, happily, continues. This year, the Ragdale Foundation turned over its houses and gardens to the City of Lake Forest. "Writers and artists will continue to have a place here for a long time to come," says Hayes. Backing those hopes, her twelve children and grandchildren, arriving at O'Hare Airport for a recent family reunion, all wore T-shirts proclaiming, "Ragdale lives!" That, its guest artists avow, would be heavenly.

On that topic, writer Woody Allen once observed that it is not a matter of whether heaven exists, but how far is it from downtown and when do you get your laundry back? At Ragdale, the answers are "thirty-one miles" and "in about an hour." As a further service to its artists, a washing machine and dryer, both free, have been installed, just off the kitchen.

September 17, 1986

HE CHOOSES HIS
WORDS WISELY

A thoughtful poet and host, John Frederick Nims welcomed a visitor to his Lake Shore Drive apartment, offering him hot coffee — and a fresh simile.

He was struck once, Nims recalled, by the idea that an ambulance coming down a street looked, to him, just like a lighted Christmas tree. "But I never did anything with it," he said. "You can have it if you want."

Known as "a master of a deceptively difficult form whose essence is the wedding of terseness and wit," it was Nims, now eighty-three, who once wrote, in a two-line poem, "Lunch with An Old Flame" that it was

> A pity: the midnight linen, passion's map,
> Shrunk to this pallor of napkins in our lap.

Much of creating poetry has to do with "how words feel in the mouth," observed Nims, who will offer a public reading Wednesday at 6 P.M. in the ballroom of the School of the Art Institute, at 112 South Michigan Avenue. Nims has picked samples from each of his seven most productive decades.

He is, critics agree, pretty good at it, what with writing nine books of poetry, notably *The Six-Cornered Snowflake*, *Zany in Denim* and *Flesh and Bone*, compiling the *Harper Anthology of Poetry*, editing *Poetry* magazine and teaching at the University of Illinois-Chicago.

Yet what, the visitor wanted to know, are a poet's real job skills? How does a poet see the ongoing scuffle that daily affronts all human eyes? Unlike those stuck in prosaic jobs, how does a poet plan his day?

After a long silence, Nims began by noting that he first had become interested in poetry "when I was very young, almost as soon as I could talk." His father, a rural mailman near Muskegon, Mich., used to quote Tennyson. "I didn't know what it meant, but, gee, it sounded nice," he said. "In those days, it all had a regular rhythm and it all rhymed."

Even now, years later, he still agrees with Robert Frost's view that "free verse is like playing tennis with the net down."

"Poems are not made of ideas. They are made of words," Nims went on. Indeed, what he does most days, he suggested, is play with words, judging how they go together, how they sound, if they are appropriate. "Poets like the physical quality of words, not just what they mean," he said, "much like a pianist who says certain kinds of music flow under the fingers."

Most mornings, Nims watches dawn rise, often rosy-fingered, over Lake Michigan from the window of his work-room, a den with grass-mat wall coverings, an ample cot for naps and shelves of books. Following Henry James' advice, Nims, a courtly, social man, tries to be "one of those on whom nothing is lost." His own advice to student poets: "Notice things — and read a lot."

He does that each afternoon when he repairs to a coffee house, taking work in progress. These days, it's translations, a project he started a year ago after a party at the Art Institute where he watched, as another poet once put it, "the women come and go talking of Michelangelo."

As a poet, Michelangelo "liked tough forms — sonnets and madrigals — just as he liked working in hard stone," Nims reports. He translates two a day into English, on schedule for a reading at the big Michelangelo show coming in May at the Art Institute. Among modern poets, "I know quite a few who are good," though Nims declines to name names, "but I can't think of anyone great."

Nor, he has concluded, despite his years of leading poetry workshops, is it really a teachable art form. Picking out "what a thing is like or not like — you can't teach that," he said, suggesting that poets, in their youth, usually fall into a have-it or don't-have-it category.

Sometimes, rough-stone beginnings take years to polish. Recently, for example, an image from the Bible caught his ear, causing him to wonder:

> Why are the 10 no-nos hard to keep?
> The Lord's my shepherd, but I am not a sheep.

He's still working on it.

February 14, 1997

LEADERS OF THE
GREAT PARADES

A MOGUL TALKS ABOUT
HIS FAMILY DYNASTY

Seated at a paper-cluttered desk on the thirtieth floor of a Loop bank building, eyes squinting, head tilted for better hearing, A. (for Abram) N. (for Nicholas) Pritzker seems like a Chicago version of "the two thousand-year-old man," the Mel Brooks creation who has been everywhere, met everyone, done everything.

"A lot of people say I brag a lot," he says with a twinkle, "but what the hell, I got a lot to brag about."

Much of it is about his family. Unlike most moguls, who collect photographs of presidents and other notables shaking hands, usually with them, A. N. Pritzker's office walls are lined with family pictures and mementos. He is a patriarch, and, indeed, in an era when American family dynasties are producing more lemons than Mellons, he is quite possibly the greatest patriarch in the country.

Along with his kids, this elderly man, who works in shirt-sleeves, owns or controls the world's Hyatt hotels, Braniff Airlines, *McCall's* magazine, Hammond organs, Levitz furniture, casinos, a law firm, insurance firms, travel agencies, cable TV systems and companies that make everything from railway box-cars to aluminum forgings for missiles.

A. N., as he is called by more people than he can remember, turns ninety on January 6. But on December 8, jumping the gun, more than a thousand supporters of Israel bonds will pack into a ballroom at the Hyatt Regency Chicago to honor a person whom their Chicago area board of governors describes as the head "of one of the great mercantile families of the world, a man of enormous talents, a conglomerate of goodness, who has never forgotten his people and his roots."

One highlight will be the presentation, by Meir Rosenne, Israel's ambassador to the U.S., of the "Israel Prime Minister's Medal." But the evening also will be, in many ways, a time to sum up a life built from material usually reserved for the fictions of a TV miniseries.

It is an American saga, started in 1881 when A. N.'s father, Nicholas Pritzker, arrived in Chicago from a Jewish ghetto near

Kiev, a Russian immigrant so poor he was taken in by Michael Reese Hospital on the day it opened, treated for a cold and given an overcoat that cost the hospital nine dollars.

"Best investment they ever made," says A. N. "I paid them back for that coat — about a million times."

These days, a century-plus later, the Pritzker descendants operate a bewildering network of manufacturing companies (most under the umbrella of the family-owned Marmon Group), enough ventures, interests and investments to bedazzle outsiders and, according to one recent count of their holdings, own 266 companies and subsidiaries.

Forbes magazine puts the family's worth at $1.5 billion. The Pritzker name adorns such good works as the Pritzker Center for Disturbed Children, the Pritzker Youth Foundation and the Pritzker School of Medicine at the University of Chicago (for which A. N. wrote a $12 million check). Ten years ago, A. N., a World War I Navy petty officer, logged another achievement. At eighty, he became the oldest man ever catapulted off the deck of an American aircraft carrier.

"It's a funny feeling," he says, recalling his flight from the U.S.S. *Kitty Hawk*. "They push the button, or whatever they do, you shoot forward and it takes all the air out of you." It was, he adds, like getting "a prolonged kick in the ass."

So what's life like these days?

Asked that in an interview, A. N. Pritzker shrugs, makes a face, sticks out his tongue and sums it all up in a word: "Feh!" (Translation: Lousy.)

"I'm mad at my sons," he says, "but there's nothing I can do about it. They can't bring me in any more. I can't sit and talk to ten people on a deal. I can't see. I can't hear. All this happened in the last year, but what am I going to do? I might as well shoot myself. I can't sit home. I can't even play solitaire. I can't see the cards.

"I have two sons who are about as brilliant as anybody in the world. They've learned pretty well. They think I ought to retire and I think they're right," he says, though his mind is sharp enough to remember deals made forty years ago and he still keeps close daily tabs on the business news generated by sons Jay, sixty-two, and Robert, fifty-eight. (A third son, Donald, then thirty-nine, died of a heart attack in 1972.)

"We have the Hyatts, about 140 of them," he says, "and we're on a big search for smaller towns. We've got all the big ones, New York, Washington, all that. Bob, my second son, runs almost everything we got except the hotels.

My older son Jay gets the places and Bob runs them. Bob does about $300 million a year, very successful. He's got factories, about 150, in every country in the world. I don't know how the hell he can keep track of where the factories are, let alone anything else."

His older brother, Harry, who died in 1957, was a criminal lawyer and raconteur who once wanted to go into vaudeville. (His father wouldn't let him.) Unlike Harry, who had little connection with the mainstream of family business, younger brother Jack, who died in 1979, was a real estate whiz, a master of intricacies of leases and titles. It was A. N., the middle child, who was the deal-maker. He also set the family tone of secrecy.

"We don't believe in public business," he once said. "Any public corporation that seeks vast expansion has a conflict with shareholders, who follow the daily market and are not thinking of future gains and tax benefits. We take a book loss on a building or a hotel, but how do you keep the shareholders fully informed of what you're doing? You can kill a deal revealing information."

Beyond that, he distrusts reporters. "All they want to do is sell newspapers," he grumps. "They don't care what damage they do and the stuff they find interesting just embarrasses somebody." Members of the Pritzker family show up at charity events (and often run them), as does A. N., with his second wife, Lorraine, whom he married in 1972. (His first wife, Fanny, whom he married in 1921, died in 1970.) Pictures show up on the social pages, but interviews about business matters are rare.

In his own role, which he calls "the negotiator," he has played a central, but little publicized, part in Chicago's business life for over fifty years. Trained as a lawyer (Harvard, class of '20), he was an early backer of real estate developer Arthur Rubloff. He was a close friend of the late Chicago Bears owner George Halas (and once tried to buy the team with former quarterback Sid Luckman).

He was a major force behind the 1980 ouster of First National Bank of Chicago chairman Robert Abboud, a pal of accountant Arthur Andersen ("wonderful man") and the first employer of lawyer and later U.S. Supreme Court Justice Arthur Goldberg, a man he recalls as "bright, but very arrogant. He didn't want to know you unless you were important."

Most, if not all, American fortunes come with problems, particularly in Chicago where, during the city's tumultuous building period, connections between the business community, public officials and the crime syndicate were often subjects of speculation. Some, for example, wonder about relationships between Pritzker interests and Sidney R. Korshak, a highly successful labor lawyer and business adviser who has been identified by federal, state and local law officials as an important link between organized crime and legitimate business.

A. N. Pritzker doesn't duck questions on that — or other matters:

— On attorney Korshak: "You know something? I like him. I met him when he was attorney for Goldblatt's (department store) in 1920. He represents some of the best firms in the country, all perfectly legit. I don't know a single gangster he represents. I don't think he has to. The *New York Times* wrote a whole article about how he represented us. He never represented us — ever. We couldn't understand what the hell they were talking about. I called up his brother Marshall, a pal of mine, and said, 'Where the hell do they get this stuff?' I've known Sid for sixty years. He's done favors, but I've never used him because I'm afraid (of his reputation)."

— On whether he's dealt with the mob: "Yes, once, when I was in the practice of law. I had a fellow with me, Stanford Clinton, a trial lawyer. After I stopped the practice of law, he stayed on with the firm. We gave him office space. He was representing Jimmy Hoffa. I met Hoffa a few times and found him completely responsible. I'm not saying he never had anything to do with the gangs. Of course he did. But as far as I was concerned,

Hoffa was 100 percent and because of him we became involved (with the Teamsters).

"The Teamsters had a place in Lake Tahoe that went bankrupt three times in four years. It was a gambling joint and it was closed. You know what that's worth? Nothing! We told them, 'We'll pay you what you paid, that's $19.5 million, if you put in another $3 million to get the place going again.' We gave them a note for the whole amount, about $22 million, at 8 percent, a fair rate of interest. That's the only deal we had with them. Would you say we did anything wrong?"

—On the 1981 skywalk collapse at the Kansas City Hyatt Regency: "It was a terrible thing, but that building is owned by the card guy, you know, Donald Hall (chief executive officer of Hallmark Cards, Inc.) I think he's the sweetest guy I know. But he built that building. We just manage it. We had nothing to do with construction. We're responsible because we're managing it, but I don't how the hell we can discharge our responsibility if we had no right to examine it (while it was being built)."

—On financier Henry Crown, board chairman of Material Services Corp.: "Let me tell you about him. Forty years ago, I bought Meyer Material Co. He called up and said, 'Did you buy that?' I said, 'Yeah.' He said, 'You ought to know friends don't compete with friends.' Bang went the phone. For forty years, he's refused to talk to me."

—On *Playboy's* Hugh Hefner, partner in a soured Atlantic City casino deal: "Met him years ago. He wanted to borrow money. I offered some, but as compensation I wanted an option on part of his magazine. He didn't want that. In Atlantic City, let's say we're kissed out. We have almost nothing to do with that. My sons are not keen about the gambling business. They never were. Now, his daughter (Christie), she's a doll."

—On relations with the First National Bank of Chicago: "We've been fifty-five years at the First. We were practically running that bank. Ours is the only family in America I ever heard of where every member was up to the statutory limit (for loans). That's the kind of relationship we had. I had my big fight with (former chairman) Bob Abboud (over the method of sale of a hundred million dollar New Jersey amusement park) and we forced his ouster. Then he came out with unfortunate statements (about the stability of the bank). He should have kept his big mouth shut, but he was thrown out and he wanted to get even. That wasn't any way to do things. Anyway, we've become friendly again, though he doesn't run over and kiss me anymore. He always used to kiss me."

— On Chicago's 1987 mayoral election: "I don't know who to vote for. I'll have to run myself so I'll have somebody to vote for."

— On mayoral candidate Jane Byrne: "As far as I'm concerned, I would take potluck with any person on the street rather than her. Her main financial adviser, Charles Swibel, I've known thirty years. I wouldn't trust Swibel ever. Not only that, when (son) Jay was on the Chicago School Finance Authority and wouldn't vote for her (budget) proposal, she sent policemen to check every Hyatt hotel. Then she denied she knew about it. Can you picture fifty men going out on a mission from City Hall and the mayor doesn't know?"

— On former schools superintendent Ruth Love: "Ah, she's a pain in the rear end. She has an argument — and she sues." Pritzker offers no judgment on her battles to settle her contract; he just dislikes litigation. "I'm against it," he says. "I believe you can settle everything better than you can litigate. It's just a means of putting pressure on people. It's outrageous the number of lawsuits."

— On his longstanding commitment to Israel: "First of all, I'm Jewish. There's no question about that. Being Jewish, I'm naturally sympathetic to the Jews. I think they're entitled to an opportunity. I criticize Israel because they are too religious. I think it's outrageous. The Orthodox want to run the whole affair. I don't believe in their principles. Me, I'm as irreligious as anybody you ever met. I've been a member of my temple for thirty-five or forty years and I've been there twice."

Which temple is that?

"Christine," he says, calling to his secretary in the outer office. "What temple do I belong to?"

"Emanuel," she replies.

"What's his name, the rabbi?"

"Schaalman," she says.

"The rabbi is a close pal," he explains, "but I have a lousy memory for names. Everywhere I go, people say 'hello.' I say 'hello,' but I don't know who they are. Christine has to remember these things for me."

The Pritzker family buys $500,000 worth of Israel bonds each year and, besides their other philanthropies, also makes donations to universities and institutions in Israel. "I get thirty letters a day asking for money," moans A. N. One appeal that hit home came five years ago, from his old neighborhood, Wicker Park. "A girl calls up and says, 'I'm the principal of the school you graduated from in 1910,'" A. N. recalls. "'I know you're lying,' I say. 'My principal would be 114 today and dead fifty years.' But she came down, we had lunch and she told me what was going on out there. It was terrible, murders with butcher knives, dangerous streets, thieves, drug dealing."

Now A. N. takes over the school when it closes at 2:30 P.M., pays (at a cost of $40,000 a year) for courses in everything from computers to cooking, photography, band and sports and, on his private seven-seater plane, takes students along on trips to New York, Washington, Boston and Philadelphia. "It's quite an experience for them," he says. "They've never been out of Chicago, let alone on a plane." In five years, the school crime rate has dropped 90 percent.

Otherwise, these days, complains A. N. Pritzker, "I don't know of a thing to do. I'm too old." He lives on the twenty-ninth floor of a Gold Coast building, in an apartment with a startling view up Lake Shore Drive. He bought it two years ago from the late gadget king Samuel Popeil. He does minor legal work for friends, such as selling a house for the widow of a co-owner of the old Chez Paree nightclub, a former client. He is working on his autobiography, with the help of author-historian Herman Kogan.

"I'm half finished," he says, "but we're not letting out a copy. My father wrote one when he was seventy and called it *Three Score After Ten*. Mine is ten times as big. He passed his out. He didn't care who got it. Mine is strictly for the family." How's that going? "It's a pain," he says, then he points to exactly where.

November 24, 1985

CZECHS AND BALANCES

"The beautiful thing about life is that it always brings surprises," Václav Havel, the world's hippest head of state, mused
the other day as he slid onto a soft sofa in his suite at the Ritz-
Carlton Hotel and chatted about his life, his hard times, his philosophy and the challenges of his current role—president of
the Czech Republic.

Havel was nursing a bad back, but showed no signs of strain.
He sipped a glass of Heineken beer and smoked three Camel
cigarettes. He'd been up late the night before, after a long flight
from Prague and a trip to Rosa's Blues Lounge that was as private as it could be riding in a limousine and accompanied by a
squad of nervous Secret Service agents.

"Breakfast of Champions?" asked a reporter.

"Czech medicine," Havel murmured, a slight smile raising
the sandy moustache that covers his upper lip.

He is, on one level, a very serious man, prone to giving
speeches about "the theme of civilization as a context for contemporary politics," as he defined his intellectual thrust in one
recent address.

He is also, according to one of his Chicago buddies, a lousy
dancer.

"We were listening to Magic Slim and the Teardrops and
somebody came over from the bar and asked him to dance,"
said Jan Novak, an Oak Park writer who met Havel when Novak
helped with the *Valmont* screenplay for director Milos Forman, a
friend of Havel's since both were children in Prague.

It had been Novak's suggestion that Havel take an informal
late-night tour of Berwyn "for head cheese and other Czech
foods," drive to Oak Park to see Ernest Hemingway's childhood
home, then stop at Rosa's, 3420 West Belmont Avenue.

The president's plane, battling headwinds, was two hours
late into Chicago, scrubbing all stops but Rosa's, where the
group settled in for two hours to listen and dance, while Secret
Service agents lined the bar, many with fingers in ears to block
out the sounds of the blues.

"It was good to see a president dance," Novak said smiling.

Havel, playing with a gold lighter, dapper in a pin-striped

blue suit with maroon tie and matching breast-pocket hand-
kerchief, chose his words carefully.

"I have always been happy when I felt I was succeeding in my
efforts. I have had depression when I did not have that feeling,"
he said. "The truth is that being president carries a greater mea-
sure of responsibility.

"Even before I was president, I gave a great deal of thought
to the broad aspect of things. The same has remained true during my presidency. That is why my speeches may go beyond the
usual television statements. I was not surprised when communism fell. The communists thought they understood everything, that they could tell what would happen."

Life, he noted, doesn't work out that way.

"We have made a great deal of headway," Havel said. "We
have had free elections twice. We have established basic demo-
cratic institutions, with checks and balances, though there
is room for improvement in the area of political culture." But,
he noted, "we are in a special situation. Communism, as Milan
Kundera once wrote, is a regime of forgetting. With freedom,
our society has begun to rediscover itself, its history. The
continuation of this is important. It helps with our self-
identification."

He talked of the Czech Republic's hopes of joining NATO:
"Because of the values we share, we feel part of the West." Of
Russia: "Efforts should be made to establish friendly relations,
but Russia should not have the right to advise where nations
should belong." And he talked of his country's difficult past,
including a current controversy over whether to open the files
of Czech citizens who may have cooperated with Communist
security oppressors.

"It's not right to say, 'Let's forget the past.' We need to know
history. It would not be healthy to forget. But I'm not going to
indulge in needless witch hunts," Havel said, though there
were times, he admitted, when his own oppression led him to
believe that his life was in danger.

Once, he was taken to prison in handcuffs, while suffering
from pneumonia. Another time he was sent to work as a laborer
in a beer factory. He was jailed twice more, then later allowed to
serve as a stagehand in a theater, though forbidden to write. His
plays and essays, many of them filled with humorous parables
of life under communism, were banned, though he was allowed to receive royalties from their performances abroad.

"It's true," he said, "that I might have been in danger in

prison — my health. But I took it as a matter of fate. What will happen, will happen."

He never thought of leaving the country.

"In fact," he went on, "emigration was offered to me a number of times by the Communist authorities. There were efforts to blackmail me to leave. They said my relations would be jailed. But I felt had to stay at home. I had started something and had to continue. I believe one does not flee from a battle he has begun. But I'm not in any way angry with those who did leave the country. It's a matter of individual choice."

Havel has a strong sense of personal theater. There is a story that, while working in the beer factory, he was permitted to use his foreign currency earnings at a state store which sold only luxury items. He bought a Mercedes-Benz. "It's true," he said. "Conditions were strange."

Now fifty-eight, Havel, whose father and uncle ran a film studio, started publishing articles in literary and theater magazines at the age of nineteen. His first play, *The Garden Party*, was produced in 1963, followed by *The Memorandum* in 1965 and *The Increased Difficulty of Concentration* in 1968, the year Soviet troops put an end to the regeneration process known as the Prague Spring. He wrote essays, helped organize committees for the defense of the unjustly prosecuted and, after the collapse of the communist regime, was twice elected president of the Czechoslovak Republic.

In January 1993, he was elected as the first president of the Czech Republic. One of his missions is to reconnect Czech expatriates with their homeland, as he made clear here at a black-tie dinner sponsored by his host in Chicago, the Mid-America Committee, a group of business executives who promote stronger trade and cultural ties with foreign countries.

"As a political or cultural figure, Havel has no Western equivalent. He is the nation's philosopher-king," observed a recent assessment in *Esquire*. "Because Stalinism forced him to live so rough for so long, in and out of prison for twenty years, there's a strong, dirty, rock and roll streak running down his back. He exists somewhere in the broad ground defined by Elie Wiesel, Thomas Jefferson and Keith Richards."

Havel also has become a good friend of the Dalai Lama, one of the first official guests he invited to Prague after he first took office.

"It was a most interesting visit," Havel recalled. "Probably I was the first head of state to receive him, though afterwards others did. Some in my country thought it might hurt our trade ties with China, but that didn't prove to be the case. We talked of spiritual matters, the condition of civilization and Tibet and I took part in a meditation."

In his speeches Havel has leaned heavily toward a rediscovery of a more spiritual world, at a time when, as he put it, "the abyss between the external and the internal, the objective and the subjective, the technical and the moral, the universal and the unique constantly grows deeper."

Once, writing about his childhood, Havel said he always felt like an outsider, like "a heavy little boy."

"Sometimes, at the very bottom of my soul, this feeling remains present," he said. "I take it as a challenge, a driving force to continue. I should add that I don't understand why I find myself in this most expensive suite in a Chicago hotel with a fine view of Lake Michigan. I feel I don't deserve it. On the other hand, I understand there is a point to why I am here."

October 7, 1994

LADY THATCHER SETS
DOWN HER RECORD

The first issue, as Margaret Thatcher waved a reporter into her suite at the Park Hyatt Hotel, was the seating. "Supposing I sit here. Where would you like to interview? I think opposite is easier. Elizabeth, you come here. Mr. Anderson can be there," she said, waving her press aide, Elizabeth Buchanan, down onto the sofa, fixing a steely gaze on her guest and eyeing him toward a chair.

She was, as they say, very much in command, with a busy schedule. She'd flown in the night before from Toronto and went directly to a North Michigan Avenue bookstore. Huge crowds. Heavy security. Spent two hours at a round table autographing copies of her 914-page tome, *The Downing Street Years*. Later, a sixty-minute radio show.

When told that she had an ability like Elizabeth Taylor to create excitement—referring to her appearance at Stuart Brent Books, where the crowd had included everyone from Chicago social figures to a rowdy Irish youth who was removed by security staffers — and that few ex-prime ministers, other than Winston Churchill, could draw such a crowd, she said:

"Yes, well, the years one's written about were exciting years. Years when the West did something. Unlike Bosnia," Thatcher snapped, with a stare that could reduce a person to ash.

Dressed in a purple suit, with a string of big pearls, holding a cup of black coffee, Thatcher, sixty-eight, has not slowed a whit since the day when, as her book tells it, she walked out of 10 Downing Street for the last time and her personal aide "wiped a trace of mascara off my cheek, evidence of a tear which I had been unable to check."

When asked if sexism played a role in her ouster, referring to the Cabinet revolt that led to her resignation as prime minister on November 28, 1990, she responded: "I don't think so. It was (my) personality — firm, determined, purposeful. I just think some of them just couldn't take it."

Nor had she suffered any sort of narcissistic injury, as many leaders do when the rough-and-tumble of politics catches up with them. "There's no point in looking back and having re-grets," she said. "I'd been there eleven and a half years, three years longer than an American president can stay in office. I obviously had to go sometime."

What dismayed her was the timing.

The revolt, she said, "came while I was away, signing a disarmament treaty (in Paris). In the middle of a Gulf War." She had managed "to get high interest rates down and I wanted to see that through."

She had wanted several more years to work a suitable successor up the ranks. What really hurt, she noted, were the "weasel words" of friends and allies covering up "their betrayal as frank advice and concern for my fate" in winning a leadership struggle.

Eyebrows have been raised by some critics of her memoirs, but Thatcher said she had not spent time brooding.

"It happened. So be it. And it gave me the chance to write down the record of those years while they're still vividly alive in my memory. The events. The difficulties of decision. The agony of the Falklands (war with Argentina). Being absolutely on the spot in Aspen when Saddam Hussein went into the Gulf," she said. "If I hadn't been there, the whole future might have been different."

In August 1990, Thatcher and President Bush were in Colorado to address the annual Aspen Institute Conference. Just after the Iraqi invasion of Kuwait, they met on a ranch.

"Fortunately," she writes, "the president began by asking me what I thought. I told him my conclusions in the clearest and most straightforward terms." Mostly, she says, he followed them.

She "always liked George Bush," she said, taking a sip of coffee. She later hectored him about "going wobbly" on sanctions against Iraq. Jimmy Carter was likable but limited, with a slim grasp of economics. Ronald Reagan, of course, was a paragon of virtue though, as she put it delicately the night before to WGN Radio host Milt Rosenberg, "He was not a detail man."

"It is not the faint hearts who make history or get things done. It is the great hearts," she had added. Or, as she said in her book, "Above all, I knew that I was talking to someone who instinctively felt and thought as I did."

In February 1981, Thatcher was the first foreign head of government invited to Washington by Reagan after he took office.

Their first outing, as leaders of the Western World, came in July, in Canada, when chiefs of the seven biggest industrial nations gathered at Chateau Montebello, a luxurious log hotel near Ottawa. Reagan was still recovering from an assassination attempt four months earlier.

As former *London Times* staffer Geoffrey Smith noted in his book, *Reagan and Thatcher*, Reagan spent much of the meetings doodling circles on a pad, filling them in with faces and adding cowboy hats.

The two met privately, providing Thatcher with "my most useful discussion at Ottawa." Over the next eight years, they talked often by phone. Among their accomplishments, she suggested, was the collapse of Soviet-backed communism. The factors? "One, the determination of the West, of Ronald Reagan and myself, to have superior military forces and the latest technology. They couldn't keep up. Two, a determination to fight the battle of ideas every way we could — and we did. Three, the coming on of a new generation of politicians in the Soviet Union who looked at communism through different eyes. And four, the many people who worked from within."

Thatcher declined to discuss President Clinton.

"Look, that's not the purpose of this interview," she said. Nor Hillary. "Mrs. Clinton is not elected," she added. "What advice? I have no advice to give to a spouse of an elected president. You can, if you like, read my book, about Denis."

That would be her husband, now Sir Denis, whom she married in 1951. They have a twin son and daughter, Mark and Carol, born in 1953.

"(Denis) would have stayed in the army after the second World War," Thatcher writes, "but the unexpected death of his father left him no option but to return to the family business, a paint and chemicals company. I am glad he did. His industrial experience was invaluable to me. He was also a crack accountant. He could sense and see trouble long before anyone else."

Nor, she added, could she have made it through "the lonely job" of prime minister without him.

During the long hours at 10 Downing Street, he was a rock and refuge.

"Denis and I decided that we would not have any living-in domestic help," she writes. "No housekeeper could possibly have coped with the irregular hours. When I had no other engagement, I would go up to (our top-floor) flat for a quick lunch of salad and poached egg on toast. But usually it was ten or eleven o'clock at night before I would go to the kitchen and prepare something. We knew every way in which eggs and cheese could be served. There was always something to cut at in the fridge, while Denis poured me a nightcap."

No longer prime minister, does she have more time for herself?

"Good heavens, no!" she said.

From an office in Belgrave Square, with a staff of seven, Thatcher keeps track of world events, prepares for speeches and raises funds for the Margaret Thatcher Foundation, currently funding forty young people from Eastern European countries for short courses in the workings of a free-market economy. "I'm not going to give you a figure," she said, cutting off questions on the foundation's size, "except to tell you that we need more."

She is concerned about the future.

"Europe," she said, "will remain a controversial problem. I'm very fearful that people may think, in the aftermath of the Cold War, that everything's secure. That's not the consequence. Peace has not broken out. The collapse of great empires means a dangerous situation. We must not let our guard down."

She is at work on her second book — about her early days.

Will it be easier? "No," she said, "it's not just getting it all down. It's editing it so it tells the story in a readable and accurate way."

Meantime, she's having a terrific time pushing *The Downing Street Years*.

"She loved doing *Larry King Live*. Had a great time. She loves speaking to people," said Buchanan, the press secretary.

"Tour's been fabulous. Interviews wonderful. Fantastic speeches. As Thatcher says, 'I don't mind if they stand up when I enter,' Buchanan says. 'It's if they stand up when I finish.'"

One problem, on the road, is keeping on top of things, to the extent that Thatcher likes.

"When something happens," Buchanan explained, "the world's press camps outside her door. So, she has to have something to say."

As the interview ended, Thatcher checked her watch. She gave instructions to the photographer. "Don't shoot me that way. There's not enough light in front."

She shook hands with her guest, with a motion that pulled

him past her toward an outside hallway door. Then she disappeared into an adjoining room.

"Any news? Any news?" she was last heard demanding of an aide, who was inside, watching CNN.

November 28, 1993

"AM I HAPPY?
YES, I'M HAPPY!"

On a dark and stormy afternoon some years ago, a reporter motored north to a wealthy enclave in Evanston to interview W. Clement Stone, an apostle of positive mental attitude. Turning into Stone's estate, he saw an elderly gardener raking piles of wet leaves in the cold November rain. To be friendly, the reporter rolled down his window and shouted: "Hi!"

"Terrific day! Terrific day!" replied the gardener. "Isn't this a great day?" Later, the butler said much the same thing.

Last month, another reporter (this one) motored farther north, to a modern two-story office building on a side street in Lake Forest. The mission: To see if W. Clement Stone, who will turn eighty-five in May, has had any second thoughts about an ebullient philosophy of life that he invented when he was a penniless lad trying to harness his personal anxieties so he could sell insurance policies to total strangers.

The last decade or so has not been easy for Stone. His name has been linked with politics, notably for his contribution of $7.2 million to political campaigns, mostly Richard Nixon's, between 1968 and 1972. Nixon, whose ambitions Stone backed with expectation of becoming ambassador to the Court of St. James, resigned in disgrace, favors unreturned.

Stone's daughter Donna, founder of the National Committee for Prevention of Child Abuse, died of cancer in 1985. His eldest son, Clement, once heir apparent, died last September of heart disease, three months after his third marriage. In 1982, recognizing his age, Stone turned over operating command of his Combined International Corporation insurance companies to younger insurance mogul Patrick J. Ryan. The move was applauded, but, as founder of an empire, Stone had enough second thoughts to hold up the deal for several hours on transition day.

So, these days, is W. Clement Stone happy? In a word, actually a great many words, yes.

"Greetings!" he shouts, rising from a desk filled with three ashtrays, two in-boxes and enough knick-knacks to stock gift shops from Highwood to Waukegan. In shirtsleeves, he wears a leopard bow tie and a mustache that, in a thin curious way, in two directions at once, points toward each strap of his leopard suspenders. "I am riding a permanent continuous wave of good fortune," he booms, knocking out an answer to a reporter's first question. "How are you?"

Lighting a cigar, he blows a cloud of smoke, obscuring an oil painting on the wall behind him, *The Prayer at Valley Forge*. Like a train pulling slowly out of a station, W. Clement Stone begins.

"There are two principles never taught — you never learned them — that every man, woman and child should apply. One . . ."

"No, wait, I already got the books," says the reporter, holding up copies of *Success Through A Positive Mental Attitude* and *The Success System That Never Fails*. "Your secretary . . ."

Stone flicks off the interruption. "Yeah, but the books don't indicate this," he continues. "This is, uh, my new discovery, two principles never taught . . ."

"Not in these books?"

"No!" yells Stone, full speed ahead. "Two principles to achieve any goal whatsoever provided that the goal doesn't violate universal law, the laws of God or the rights of your fellow man . . ."

His philosophy, Stone admits, is built on the rock provided by Emile Coue, a French-born psychotherapist thought by many to be the inventor of the modern platitude. Known for his suggestion that "every day in every way I'm getting better and better," Coue felt that maxims, repeated in a "confident voice," implant in the subconscious "a mechanism for eliminating ideas which cause distress and disease." Not everyone disagrees, notably former *Saturday Review* editor Norman Cousins, who overcame a crippling degeneration of connective tissue with, among other weapons, humor and later wrote about tapping into the "drugstore of the mind."

In his own writings, Stone likes to quote Lord Byron:

> A small drop of ink,
> falling like dew upon a thought, produces
> that which makes thousands, perhaps
> millions, think.

Born in Chicago in 1902, young Clement was two when his father died. At six, he was selling the *Chicago Examiner* on South Side streets while his mother worked as a dressmaker. At thirteen, he had his own newsstand and spent his spare time reading Horatio Alger stories about impoverished kids with pluck. His favorite: *Robert Cloverdale's Struggle*.

"It wasn't easy," Stone recalls, "especially with the older kids taking over the busy corners and threatening me with clenched fists." Stone learned not to quit. Thrown out of Hoelle's restaurant, near 31st and Cottage Grove, after selling three papers, he returned, sold another one, got kicked out, came back again and, to customer applause, was allowed to stay and sold the rest of his bundle. He also learned to smoke, a lifelong habit.

"Tobacco was costly," he recalls. "I used to roll coffee grounds in cigarette paper." His mother prayed, then dispatched him to the Spaulding Institute, a parochial boarding school in Nauvoo, Ill., for two years.

When Stone was sixteen, his mother pawned two diamonds and moved to Detroit to open an insurance agency. Boarding with friends, Stone entered Senn High School, but the following summer, he joined his mother and, setting out on his own insurance career, began making cold calls in Detroit's Dime Bank Building. He learned "How to Neutralize Timidity and Fear," "How to Get a Person to Listen to You" and "Play to Win," lessons included in his later books.

In gist, it worked like this. To rev himself up, Stone would stand outside a frosted glass door, shout "Do it now! Do it now!" at himself, then plunge in on an unsuspecting prospect. "I found if I spoke loudly and rapidly, kept a smile on my face and used modulation, I no longer had butterflies in my stomach," he says. He ignored eye contact. "I pointed to the policy or sales literature and looked at it as I gave my sales talk. Because I looked where I was pointing, the prospect looked, too. If, out of the corner of my eye, I saw a prospect shake his head, I paid no attention. Often, he would become interested and I would close the sale."

Dropping out of high school (he later took courses at Northwestern University), Stone plunged into insurance sales. At twenty, he took a hundred dollars in savings and set up his own agency in Chicago. By 1930, he had a thousand agents peddling accident and health insurance policies across the country.

"I trained them like actors," he says. "What to say, how to say it, how to hold a policy, when to turn it over. It's impossible to fail if you follow this step-by-step set-up." The method often proves startling to outsiders who, lost on some hotel mezzanine, inadvertently enter meeting rooms filled with Stone people chanting, "Am I happy? Yes, I'm happy."

The approach apparently works. In 1986, Combined reported assets of $3.3 billion, but Stone's scrapbooks also bulge with good-works clippings, many concerning the Chicago Boys Clubs, an interest for twenty-eight years. His motivational theories have been put to work in prisons, hospitals, schools and through such measures as "Endow a Dream," a program of fifty thousand dollar grants to such persons as West Side educator Marva Collins. Estimates of the amounts given by Stone and his wife, Jessie, over the years are upwards of $150 million.

Not all his ventures have been successful. In the late '60s, called in by the late George Halas, Stone coached the Bears in football with a positive mental attitude. It was not enough. In the season that followed, they lost more games than they won. Still, Stone decries the fact that any nation's cultural life — its plays, operas, novels, music — is based largely on melancholia, a view reflected in a country and western song, "She Got the Mine, I got the Shaft." To Stone, that's a bad attitude.

At nearly eighty-five, at a time when many persons rail, moan or complain about, as poet Dylan Thomas once put it, the task of going "gently into that good night," would he admit to any disappointment ever? "Well," he says, relighting his cigar, "with my concept that every adversity contains the seed of an equivalent or greater benefit, it's hard to think of one."

Richard Nixon?

Not at all, says Stone. "He's highly esteemed worldwide. Besides that, every American should get on their knees at night and thank God for Richard Nixon. Watergate was a wonderful thing. Without it, an attorney general wouldn't have the guts today to make charges against a senator or a president."

The deaths of two children? (A third child, Norman, a psychologist, lives in San Francisco.) Painful matters, but not without redeeming joy. "Donna had the knack of attracting quality people. She was president of our foundation and her name will go into history for her work with our committee on child abuse," Stone says. "Clem was born with a heart condition. The doctors doubted he would live. We thank the Lord we had him for fifty-eight years," he adds, speaking of his late son, whose Lake Forest mansion is now up for sale for $3.2 million.

"People ask me, 'Why do you work so hard, get involved with organizations all over the world, try to make more millions,'" Stone says. "My goal is to change the world, to make life better for future generations." But what about the meaning of life, the secret of success, the two principles that were never taught, the rules you were going to tell about that were not in your books?

"It's amazing, the power of the subconscious," Stone continues. "Well, let me give you a little background. The human computer operates through repetition, but great achievers carry it a step further. One, they keep the goal before them. Two, they take naps . . ."

"Naps?"

"Naps!"

Stone describes a Texas inventor who keeps a reclining "nap chair" in his "luxurious office" and has come up with ideas for six hundred patents, including a powder from steer skin that stops bleeding from shaving cuts. He says that Kansas psychiatrist Dr. Karl Menninger, ninety-three, excuses himself several times a day to nap and finds it useful in producing fresh ideas.

Stone himself, "no matter how late I get in," ends each day with "forty-five minutes for what I call creative thinking time.

"Sit in a room with lots of light," Stone explains. "Allow no interruptions. Take a pad. Draw a line down the center. Take a half an hour or more. Write down a goal which seems impossible to others. Concentrate. Put down ideas, negative or positive. The subconscious will come up with an answer." That said, Stone took questions from the floor.

Is his mustache real?

"Years ago, I went out with two salesmen to New Jersey and we entered into a mustache growing competition. When I came home with mine, Mrs. Stone asked me to take it off. I did, but my lip puffed up. She said grow it back. I did. And I shaped it, just to be different." Now, he notes, with a wink, "a kiss without a moustache is like an egg without salt."

Does he see dangers in great wealth?

"In the study of cycles, you find many successful individuals, corporations, even nations, eventually go out of business. Many people have problems in later life. Their morals get into trouble. They can have anything they want. But if they're not working, what they want may be out of line."

Can such wealth have negative effects on children?

Wealthy parents, he advises, "should take time to listen. A girl may have a problem. If her mother and father are too busy, the poor kid may really suffer. At the dinner table, everybody should ask questions, tell about the pleasant things they did. That way the family gets closer and closer."

His recipe for good health?

"I get up at 5:45 A.M. and start with bran cereal, orange juice, decaffeinated coffee, toasted bagels with apple butter and perhaps a grapefruit because Pam, my daughter-in-law, sent us the Fruit-of-the-Month Club. I get to work around nine, try to leave by five. I skip lunch, but occasionally I slip out for a hot dog at Fluky's."

These days, besides the Lake Forest quarters, Stone keeps three offices downtown, at Combined International's headquarters, 123 North Wacker, the W. Clement and Jessie V. Stone Foundation, 111 East Wacker, and W. Clement Stone Enterprises, 401 North Wabash, his publishing arm. Despite a weakness for ice cream, Stone's weight is "144 stripped," 45 pounds less than eight years ago.

"Mrs. Stone and I go to many parties," he says. "Our company has meetings around the country for achievers. We go dancing. I find it very healthy."

A natty dresser, with suspenders and bow ties galore, his wardrobe is spare. He has, he says, six suits, four overcoats, two sets of tails, two tuxedos and seven pairs of shoes. But he still has copies of the fifty Horatio Alger books he read long ago at Green's Resort Farm, a Michigan summer retreat where he was sent as a child.

"I knew then," he says, "that I would be a success and marry the most beautiful woman, which I did."

A picture of Jessie Stone, at nineteen, hangs in an alcove of his Lake Forest office, along with photos of Richard Nixon, Sen. Strom Thurmond (R-South Carolina) and Ronald Reagan. He keeps other treasures at home, shelves of awards and "a terrific library" of three thousand books. (His favorite novel: *The Magnificent Obsession* by Lloyd C. Douglas, an Indiana-born minister who moved to Montreal, became a writer, quit the ministry and moved to Los Angeles where he typed out religious works in a knotty-pine study.)

Does he ever consider retiring, puttering, reading, just goofing around? "Oh, no," says Stone, aghast. Nor does he have any intention of, um, popping off. "It is my intention to live past 110," he notes. "If you're around, we could have another interview."

The reporter promises to keep it in mind.

February 8, 1987

AUCTIONEER TO
HOST THE LAST BASH
AT BUTLER'S DIGS

It's been a long time now, and not many remember how it was in the old days, when the money was flowing freely and Oak Brook's Michael Butler, polo player and real estate developer and impresario of the hit musical *Hair*, threw dinner parties on summer nights with candle-lit tables stretching far out into the meadow.

But the auctioneer remembers.

"We'll have a huge tent over there," he said, pointing to a patch of the lawn by the road. "We'll have a canopy out from the main house. We'll have a caterer by the flagpole, though I may have to pop for the champagne and food myself. The court won't go for it."

It will be, in a sense, one last party. On Saturday, starting at noon. At 19 Natoma Drive in Oak Brook, the only old home-stead left in a new subdivision of chateau-style mansions. A white farmhouse, a little tattered now, but filled with a lifetime of possessions: rugs, boots, paintings, silver, masks, cushions. Open, this last time, to everyone.

It's being called "the most famous personal liquidation in Chicago history." Catalogs have gone out to thirty-seven hundred dealers across the U.S. and in London and Paris. Others will be drawn by newspaper advertising. Many will come because of curiosity. How often, after all, does an era end?

"Our strategy will be to mix it up," said Wallace Lieberman, president of Capital Liquidators, Inc., whose subsidiary, Shires Ltd., of Northbrook, is handling matters for the host, the U.S. Bankruptcy Court. "We don't know how the weather will be — rainy, hot, steamy. If someone's here to spend two hundred thousand dollars on a painting, we don't want them uncomfortable. We'll get the expensive part over quickly. Then we'll sell to the curiosity seekers.

"There will be lots of stuff from ten dollars to one hundred dollars. Pillows. Canes. Brocaded bell-pulls. They don't ring anything, like in *Upstairs, Downstairs*. But for, say, seventy-five dollars, you could get a muffineer. You know, to bring the muffins out on."

These are sour times for Michael Butler, sixty-four, the very tall, very thin and formerly very rich oldest son of the late Paul Butler, the founding father of upscale Oak Brook and once the head of the Butler Co., an enterprise that has had far-flung interests in real estate, paper, aviation, recreation, banking, electronics, ranching and utilities.

Last month, trying to reorganize his own finances and settle more than $3 million in claims brought by creditors, Michael Butler was ordered to liquidate his personal belongings, valued at between $400,000 and $750,000.

"I'll tell you the kind of guy Michael is," someone was saying the other day, standing in Michael Butler's bedroom during a private tour for two appraisers, an auditor and a reporter. "He goes ahead and (when he's out with friends) signs everything. Everyone thought he was a multimillionaire, that money was not a problem."

For a long time, it wasn't. Lanky, with a shy grin that peeked out from under a moustache, Michael Butler backed nightclubs, discotheques, restaurants, roller-skating rinks, reggae bands, real estate adventures, polo matches and Broadway shows. He was a man who, as they say, sunk many wells.

He hit big on one, *Hair*, a flower-power musical he discovered in a seedy off-Broadway theater in 1968 and converted into a success on stages around the world (total gross: eighty million dollars) and later into a movie, which flopped.

In 1981, at the age of eighty-nine, his father was killed, struck by a car as he crossed a country road at dusk, walking home from a girlfriend's cottage in the nearby woods to get a camera to record her birthday party. Two weeks ago, Michael Butler abruptly crossed that road himself, moving into an adjoining cottage, also a Butler property, leaving almost everything he owns in the main house for whatever the bidding on June 22 will bring.

"Let me walk you through, to give you a feel for the place," Wally Lieberman said to a reporter as they arrived at the front door. An amiable man, Lieberman has handled similar situations for creditors of such troubled local entities as Scandinavian Design, Kraml Dairy and the Chateau Louise resort. The main house, encumbered with liens, is not part of the sale. Lieberman hopes that, after the auction, not much will be left inside.

"It's OK. Let him in. He's with me," Lieberman said to an armed guard checking a clipboard as he began a tour in the front hall beside two paintings, *Adoration of the Magi*, by "a follower of Tintoretto," and *St. Michael Slaying the Dragon*, a depiction of a winged knight wearing an orange dress, standing with one foot on the chest of a horned satyr.

"This was the family room," he continued, moving toward an area with a suede-covered beanbag chair, a wall of bookcases and, on the floor, a pile of rug-like Arabian saddle bags with pockets deep enough to transport the belongings of a group of nomads on a trip across the Sahara.

"I told Michael he could come back for the liquor," Lieberman added, pointing to a cart with partly-used bottles of Scotch. "He's going to have a little party here next week. Also, he's allowed to take certain things that are personal property. About twenty-five hundred dollars worth. Pots and pans. Clothing. Riding boots. He has big feet. Size 14. Who else is going to fit his shoes?"

This is to be a sale, Lieberman said, that will have something for everyone. In the kitchen, "we will sell the trash compactor, refrigerator, though probably not the built-in ovens." There are two dozen rugs, worth up to twenty thousand dollars each. "We're laying them out on the porch now to give them an airing." There were chalices, vases and pre-Columbian art, much of it genuine.

"This was Michael's office. He was allowed to take his desk," Lieberman said as the group entered a paneled room with a dozen pairs of riding boots mounted on a wall and, on a bench, a buffing machine. "Too bad you weren't here earlier. Michael had all his pictures out. Jill St. John. Girlfriends. Elegant photographs. No value, except for the one with Prince Charles."

Elsewhere, there are polo mallets, some rickety with age, a drum made of zebra skin, a carved head that once served as an African grave decoration. On a veranda wall are six framed pictures of Mick Jagger. There is a table with a marble top, "probably designed by Mies van der Rohe, circa 1927." An eagle-feather headdress presented to Butler by Tommy Smothers the night *Hair* opened in Los Angeles. A sky-blue robe, with stars and half-moons, the kind of garment that Merlin the Magician might have ordered for his college graduation.

A Mongolian ceiling hanging, looking like fifty sheared horse tails, made of yak hair. Record albums by Bob Marley &

The Wailers. Three dozen back issues of the *National Geographic*. A stuffed leather rhinoceros. A stuffed leather duck. A portrait of Butler with his second wife, Robin. A poster listing "20 Good Things about Teddy Bears" (Among them: "They Never Borrow Money.")

Two Peruvian silver quail. A silver sauce boat. A brass-bound mahogany cooler from the time of George III. A string of graduated sleigh bells, mounted on a leather strap. An antique letter box with leather interior, possibly French. A mahogany hunt table. A ceremonial knife with fur-covered handle. Two Mexican lectern stands. Thirteen cut crystal champagne glasses. And a "false face society mask," attributed to "the Iroquois tribe."

"Michael is very interested in American Indians," Lieberman said, explaining one category of art objects. "He and Jack Kennedy were good friends. Kennedy was going to appoint him commissioner of Indian affairs in January 1964. But, after November, it never happened.

"And that's the Dalai Lama's robe," Lieberman added, pointing to a stiff dress hanging on a second floor wall over a stairway.

How does one plan a sale of such stuff? Contacted by the committee of Butler's creditors, Lieberman began with an initial inspection December 19. With help from researchers, notably Barbara Schnitzer of Fine Arts Appraisals, he prepared a description of each item. A court order for the sale, which will cost about seventy-five thousand dollars to mount and advertise, was signed in mid-May.

It will be, he hopes, a day of decorum and taste.

"We're not here to emasculate Michael," Lieberman said. "We're trying to do this with due respect to Michael — and to the situation. We don't want a circus. I'm very fond of Michael. He's a charming individual."

Mingling with the crowd, which is expected to reach fifteen hundred and spend $500,000 to $1 million, might be Butler himself. "Yeah, I'm planning to be there," he said in a phone interview. "I'm doing anything I can to help.

"It's strange, like facing surgery," he added, explaining that he had intended to cut back on his possessions, though not necessarily right now, nor so abruptly.

"Twenty years ago," he said, "I had five houses, one with fifteen bedrooms, but I found that possessions are a responsibility. I wanted to live more simply. After all, I built my life on non-materialism, on *Hair*.

"I am living in what used to be the cottage of my family's butler and housekeeper. The place has wonderful memories. Better, in fact, than the main house.

"I went through serious depression when this first hit. I still have my down moments. But I feel that regret for the past and fear of the future are the worst. 'Live for the present,' I say. 'Go for it.'"

June 12, 1991

CHICAGO LIFESTYLES
OF THE NOT-SO-RICH,
NOT-SO-FAMOUS

CICERO COPS ON
CRASH COURSE

The topic for the night, in an upstairs conference room at Cicero's Town Hall, was "the traffic accident." Or, as the class quickly learned to say, "el accidente de tráfico."

Clutching their copies of "Spanish for Law Enforcement Personnel," a dozen Cicero police officers, cued by their teacher, offered up appropriate sentences: "necesita ayuda?" ("Need help?")

But the idea behind this animated form of language training was not to rely on any book. Or worry about grammar, verb endings or accent. It was to jump in and be understood.

Unlike what goes on in traditional language classes, the instructor leapt around like a flamenco dancer, waving his hands, snapping fingers, encouraging students to mimic.

For seven weeks now, in an effort to reach out to a population that has become increasingly Hispanic, Cicero's oft-besieged town government has been working with a new tool, language lessons taught by local disciples of John Rassias, a professor at Dartmouth College in New Hampshire, who in recent years has become a guru of quick foreign-language study.

Favored by the Peace Corps for its trainees and by clients as diverse as the New York City Transit Police and the Drake Hotel in Chicago, the Rassias method, says one teacher, is "simple, quick and straightforward so you can hit the bricks — and start speaking."

"We try to teach in a way that is unexpected. Like real life, you don't know what's going to happen next," said Michael Intoccia, the man in charge of the Cicero course, which was organized by Harold Washington College. Intoccia directs the Rassias Language Institute at the college, with courses in everything from Gaelic to intermediate Dutch.

Already, several Cicero patrol officers noted, the training has been useful.

"I had a couple of domestics (calls) I used it on. It's helping, definitely," said John Soria, recalling households in disorder where being able to quickly understand what was going on helped defuse situations that often spell big trouble for police.

"I've had traffic stops. I know how to ask for a license in Spanish and tell what the violation is. It helps a lot," added Fred Garza, as the group ran drills during a two-hour session under the watchful eye of town president Betty Loren-Maltese, who was auditing that evening.

"I thought it was important if they just knew the basics, how to communicate. It saves a lot of police time and it makes residents more secure if they feel they are getting their points across," said Loren-Maltese, conceding that her own Spanish, learned in elementary school, had dwindled to reciting numbers and saying, "Have a nice day."

The Spanish lessons have been hailed as a small but important step for Cicero, which last month swore in its fourth police chief in a year marked by a series of scandals, charges of political maneuvering and legal battles with fired police officers.

"It's a good sign, a start," said Rev. James Kastigar, pastor of St. Anthony of Padua Catholic Church, 1510 South 49th Court, in Cicero, adding that it was "silly" in a community with many immigrants from Mexico, "how few officers knew how to speak Spanish."

"We're happy," said Dolores Ponce-de-Leon of the Interfaith Leadership Project of Cicero, Berwyn & Stickney, a group that often speaks for Cicero's Hispanic population. "It is very important for us that they not only try to hire Latino officers but try to train the police officers they do have in language skills, especially Spanish," she added.

Much of the effort in the Rassias Method is memorizing lines and being able, like actors, to speak convincingly, which is why the course's fourteen evenings often look like acting school. In times of crisis, teachers note, no one has time to consult a dictionary.

"Horrible things happen because people can't understand what's going on," said Rassias, in a phone interview. He recalled a case in New York in which a witness, shouting in Spanish, was unable to communicate to police that a murderer, who later escaped, was hiding nearby.

Many times, Rassias added, "words precede violence. If you can use the right words, you can prevent a lot of trouble, especially where a word in English is unknowingly taken as a threat."

A Fulbright scholar with a doctorate from a French university, Rassias first developed courses for Peace Corps volunteers in the 1960s, making his classes a kind of living theater where, as he put it, "emotion and rhythm and movement make people remember things."

Since then, teachers have used his methods with hotel staffs, computer executives transferred to Europe, Japanese students visiting the United States and immigration officers patrolling the U.S. border with the French-speaking province of Quebec.

"The other night," said Officer Larry Dominick, speaking of how matters are progressing in Cicero, "somebody knocks on the window of my squad car and asks if I speak Spanish. I say, 'Sí.' She comes out with a sentence two minutes long. And I say, 'So, your car got towed.'"

December 17, 1998

CAN'T GO HOME AGAIN?
TRY THE BUS

Not until the big chartered bus from Skokie wheeled around a corner and turned onto Douglas Boulevard did the crowd aboard come alive.

"Oh, my God," shouted one rider, "I'll start crying."

"They used to call this 'the Lake Shore Drive of Lawndale,'" recalled the tour guide, as thoughts of old times clouded the windows.

"Hey, there's the JPI," said one man, pointing to a battered building, once the Jewish Peoples Institute. There, young people would come, some by electric train, from as far away as Elgin hoping for a shiddach — "a romantic meeting," said another man, translating the Yiddish for a visitor.

"They had roof dances under the stars," added the guide, before directing the attention of the crowd to Temple Judea, which he described as "a synagogue so Reform that many, when passing, would spit on the ground three times."

"Hey, there's Herzl," yelled another rider, as he spotted a pillared edifice that once housed Herzl High School, named for Theodor Herzl, the founder of political Zionism, at Douglas and Ridgeway Avenue.

Others had here-and-now requests. "Can you go more slowly?" And, "Can you go around the block?"

Starting out from the Devonshire Cultural Center at 4400 Greenwood Street in Skokie on a recent sunny morning, the excursion was billed as a chance (for twenty-five dollars, lunch extra) to "travel back in time to carefree childhood days."

Or, as the brochure put it, "when was the last time you saw Lawndale, Humboldt Park, Marshall High School or Maxwell Street?"

The five-hour trip sold out quickly.

"Let the Skokie Park District whisk you back in time as Dr. Irving Cutler, a local historian, guides us through the old Jewish neighborhoods," the pitch went. "Ride in comfort through memories of youth and lunch at Manny's."

Also, the brochure suggested, "this would be the perfect time to take your adult children to see where you grew up."

Some did. Yet, for most of the forty aboard, the point was more personal.

It was a day to talk of a time, notably in the 1930s, when some 40 percent of all the Jewish families in the Chicago area lived on the city's West Side, the entry point for a tide of immigration, much from Eastern Europe.

"All traffic stopped on the High Holidays" of Rosh Hashanah and Yom Kippur, remembered Cutler, a former professor at Chicago State University who has written extensively on local settlement patterns and now, he said, "leads ethnic tours as a retirement hobby."

In Douglas Park, "you could rent a rowboat for a quarter. The Orthodox were camped out in one part, the Zionists in another, singing and dancing," he said over the microphone, as many heads nodded in agreement. "Before air conditioning, you took a pillow and you slept in the park."

Over there was the Douglas Park Auditorium, "where a young actor named Bernie Schwartz got his start — before he became known as Tony Curtis."

And beyond that was Little Jack's, known for its cheesecake. And Silverstein's Deli, now a vacant lot with a whiskey billboard. And Circle Theater, where the Marx Brothers and Mae West performed.

And Marshall High.

"Yeah!" shouted one Marshall grad as the bus swung by, adding, "They're holding their centennial this June, and, hey, the place doesn't look bad."

One can't go home again, as author Thomas Wolfe wrote, a warning that had little to do with geographical distance. Indeed, most of those who signed up for the ride gave current addresses that are within twenty-five miles of what, in their youth and before, was known as "the Great West Side."

Yet few had ever returned to visit. It is an area that, though hit hard by the riots of 1968, is "starting to come back," Cutler said, pointing out new housing, rehabbed facilities and buildings recycled after the area's Jewish population moved, for the most part, to the suburbs after World War II.

Historical nuggets were scattered throughout the trip.

"The first Jewish religious service in Chicago," it was noted, was held above what is now Monk's Pub, at Lake and Wells Streets. "This was Schmatte Row," said Cutler, as the bus moved west past the Lake Street bridge. "That's rags, offered an interpreter.

There was talk of early Jewish settlers. Of Simon Florsheim, who was into shoes. Of three clothiers named Hart, Schaffner and Marx, who combined their talents. Of the Mandel Brothers and the Marx Brothers, merchants and maniacs, respectively. Of "Kingfish" Levinsky, "the great boxer" named for his family's fresh fish stand on Maxwell Street.

"When you sit in the pews in the beautiful old synagogues of the West Side, it's a wonderful feeling," said Esther Rappaport, as the group got off the bus to ponder a building that is now in use by another religious persuasion, but where the Star of David can still be seen on floor tiles.

"They should really have more tours like this," said Donna Meyers. "It's very interesting, even though I'm not Jewish. You get to appreciate the arts, the landmarks, the history of the city. It's very moving."

Later, as the bus wheeled back into Skokie, Cutler, who also runs tours for Czechs, Romanians and other groups interested in their old Chicago neighborhoods, was asked if any one question pops up the most.

"Yes," he said. "It's, 'How come you didn't go by my street?'"

April 23, 1997

PAINTINGS TELL TALES
OF BEVERLY LIFE

History is not all battles, blood, tumult and mayhem. Much of civilization is shaped by the everyday lives of people who settle in, work, form families, raise children, talk, gossip — and do the wash.

At least, that's the idea at the Ridge Historical Society. Artist Barbara Wynne Bansley, mother of twelve children, has opened a show featuring the lives — and houses — of twenty-two of her neighboring families on the 9300 block of South Longwood Drive in North Beverly. Two years ago, Bansley, then sixty-three, went back to school at Columbia College to learn to make paper, to paint and to tell stories. On her opening night, she let it all hang out.

Her earliest inspiration, she began, was watching her mother "do the wash every Monday." Her favorite part came when "a little bluing" was added to the wash water and "I would watch it swish around.

"It was the blue of my youth — the perfect shade of blue," Bansley said, recalling that years later, on a vacation, she was struck by a similar bluish color of water surrounding the Hawaiian Islands.

Bansley was, appropriately, dressed in blue as she led a packed house deeper into the life of her block, describing one by one the paintings — all in blue — she had done on hand-crafted pulp paper.

With a shimmery quality, the twenty-two houses looked at first like they were being seen from underwater, an unlikely prospect because one of the prime appeals of the Beverly area has always been its soaring ridges.

On the other hand, as one audience member noted, the hue seemed to reflect a mist of history, a sense of stability as time goes by.

As reflected in other exhibits in the museum, at 10621 South Seeley Avenue, the settlements that grew around each train stop on the Far South Side are places where, Bansley said, "a neighbor would give you her secret recipe for spaghetti sauce after your dog ate the Christmas steaks."

Hilly, it is a land of curving tree-lined streets, of porch flags and bicycles.

On Bansley's block, she recalled, a neighbor once sent over a three-course dinner after Bansley gave birth at home. Another was humiliated when she found she had inadvertently flown Old Glory upside down.

Other neighbors had a daughter whose suitor laid a carpet of rose petals up the front steps and into the living room where the family — quickly gathering to watch — found him on bended knee.

One family, for Bears games, set up their TV on the front lawn. Their porch, stocked with refreshments, was known as "The Skybox." Another woman, each Christmas, was the block's designated fudge maker.

During the Great Blizzard of '67, Bansley related, one neighbor went into labor. Others shoveled a three-block path through mounds of snow to the nearest plowed street so her husband could get her to the hospital.

"Yes, right, that's true," averred a member of the audience of several hundred, many of whom wore blue in honor of the artist.

There were, Bansley noted, seventy-two children on her block when she and her husband, James, moved in thirty years ago. Many are still around.

"This area," she said later, in an interview, "has always been known for stability. People are born here, raised here and children decide to stay here. I don't think it's ever really changed for us."

To fund her project, Bansley received a two thousand dollar grant from the Albert P. Weisman Memorial Scholarship Fund, named for a Chicago public relations executive who had a long-time interest in community activities.

That, plus help from the Illinois Arts Council, covered one-third of her expenses.

"Like any artist, I didn't know where I was going with this," Bansley said, "but I started with sending a letter to every home on the block telling them what I was doing." What she wanted was something about homes, community, fabric and roots. Of the thirty mothers on the block, only eight declined to share their stories.

For starters, Bansley, promising discretion, asked those willing to "describe yourself and say who you are." Few could.

Many found it easier to talk of their childhood.

"When you get married, you lose your personality and identity. You don't see yourself as a person," one told her. But in groups, the women sat around kitchen tables "with iced tea to drink and plenty of chatter about the years they had spent together," Bansley said.

Stories that emerged ranged from home birthing to "a great summer vacation" — staying home and opening up a screened-in sleeping porch.

As a visitor noted, these are times that might seem to call for harder copy, in an era when even royal families are adrift, when the night air is filled with tales of life and death in fast lanes.

Then again, perhaps not.

"It was a happy problem," said Sue Delves, president of the society, speaking of the overflow crowd at opening night. "What a nice turnout," whispered one woman, as the last seat was taken.

"No, nobody thought she was telling tales out of school," Delves said later, summing up the buzz. "And it's not just her block. There are lots of blocks like hers around here."

September 19, 1997

HOPES BLOSSOM IN
NORTH LAWNDALE

There was a time, centuries ago, when French fur trappers crossed a grassy prairie along a portage trail, later paved with asphalt and known as Ogden Avenue.

In the 1870s came Lawndale, a name for the area that real estate developers hoped would call up visions of a welcoming green landscape for families fleeing west after the Great Chicago Fire.

In recent years, North Lawndale, ravaged by urban riots and economic shifts, has been an area that outsiders regard as a hardscrabble place to grow beans, to say nothing of roses.

But nature is, if anything, resilient and, as William Shakespeare once observed, "one touch of nature makes the whole world kin." Also, as Mildred Harris, president of the 1900 South Ridgeway Block Club, was quick to point out this week, "Gardeners all get along."

Harris played the hostess when several dozen North Lawndale gardeners welcomed visitors for a show and tour to inspect thirty pocket-gardens and renatured public spaces that have sprung up in the last two years in one of the state's poorest neighborhoods.

The day's purpose, said implementers of "An Open Space Plan for North Lawndale," was to display how hard work by local residents, along with seed money from outsiders, has produced mulch happiness, starting with the floral display at 1900 South Ridgeway Avenue.

Set on two lots at one end of a row of neatly kept houses dating back seventy years or more, the big garden features a wheelchair-friendly brick pathway and raised planting beds, to help older residents — and that, in truth, was most of them — who have trouble bending over.

The big news was the vegetable patch, newly lined with untreated wood beams, brought in to replace old railroad ties that were leaking oils, said Rodney Vaughn, who, with his partner, Jamie Osborn, has formed TJ Landscaping, to help with the garden and other local projects.

At a table in the shade, candies and cooling drinks were laid

Tribune photo by James F. Quinn.

out for a crowd that included Alderman Michael Chandler (24th), Cook County Commissioner Bobbie Steele, friends from many of the fifty-four other North Lawndale block clubs, plus staffers from Openlands Project, NeighborSpace and the area's umbrella Mother Nature group, the North Lawndale Greening Committee.

Later, a City Hall staffer announced that its "Chicago Neighborhood Tours" program will offer a bus tour on August 15 of what might be called "The Gardens of Lawndale."

The blooming of the neighborhood, which on these summer days includes canna lilies, petunias, marigolds and black-eyed Susans, as well as beans, lettuce, cabbages and peppers, comes as things are starting to look up for North Lawndale, an area that lost half its population and saw five thousand homes destroyed in the last three decades.

"We want to get the green infrastructure in there at the same time that people are thinking about buildings," said Glenda

Daniel, director of urban greening at Openlands, one of two dozen groups that have pitched in to help, a list that includes the Lake Forest Garden Club, the Kenilworth Home and Garden Club and the Garden Club of Barrington.

One result, in the shadow of "L" tracks, was at 1934 South Springfield Avenue, an oasis of shrubs, flowers and trellises. Nearby, tile pools dotted a plot landscaped by Ella Williams, at 3817 West Flournoy Street, in defiance of drug dealers who, early on, threw dead cats over her fence.

One day, neighbors reported, she confronted them, shouting, "Who do you think I'm doing this for? You, because you have a right to beauty, as much as anyone else."

The trouble stopped and, astonishingly, one dealer later apologized.

Aside from occasional nocturnal raids on bean patches, gardeners reported little trouble, though greening committee president Lillian Hampton told of the "Case of the Rosebush Thief."

"He knew what he was doing because he carefully dug them out. We think he was replanting them," she said. "We spotted him one night. But he saw us — and he never came back."

On the other hand, reported 1900 block-club member Annie Anderson, a peach tree planted a decade ago by her late aunt is flourishing well enough to allow for regular peach cobbler.

"You could get disgusted just looking at this area, figuring it would all be torn down," noted Gerald Earles who, with his wife, Lorean, wore T-shirts with the logo "Slumbusters."

Some years back, on weekends, Earles said, Slumbusters and other concerned groups started doing their own cleanups, hauling away abandoned cars, rubble, trash and tree stumps. Then, two years ago, the garden project got going.

"Anytime anybody does something to make things look nice," he explained, "that's slumbusting."

July 17, 1998

AUSTIN VILLAGE SHOWS
NO PLACE LIKE HOME

One house, now restored, had been cut into seventeen apartments by a nearby college seeking student housing.

Another was inhabited by a librarian whose life had gone awry. She lived with forty-five cats and, on the third floor, a lot of birds flying free.

Not the least of the neighborhood worries was Dutch elm disease.

But through it all, as real estate agent Joe English said as he stood in a third-floor family room of a neighbor's home during the 17th Annual Austin Village House Tour, "a few people just stayed."

Roughly two decades after a group of concerned homeowners started the Austin Schock Neighborhood Association, startled is the best way to describe the reaction of visitors to its West Side splendors, once — long ago — the home turf for some of Chicago's wealthiest families.

In a ninety-five-acre enclave, in a part of the city often described as troubled, are born-again homes with shined-up ballrooms, castle turrets, corner fireplaces, claw-foot bathtubs and trimmed back yards, which, as one recently did, can accommodate a tent and wedding attended by two hundred people.

If architecture is frozen music, as a German philosopher once proclaimed, it can also be "like going back into history," as Yvonne Edwards said, standing in an Austin Village living room with a tour group.

Next door, a visitor was busily sketching a front-hall seating area, to duplicate it, she said, in her Highland Park home.

Though the Chicago area can be full of surprises, it is seldom more so than during house-tour season, a time when doors from Lake Forest to Beverly open up to people endlessly fascinated with seeing how other people live.

Many are the nooks to be crannied into, as parades of outsiders assess homes of strangers, making mental notes of restorative touches, fondling scraped stair railings and resisting the temptation to poke in drawers.

"When I moved here, it was the size of the rooms that got

me," said Ginny Jones, this year's Austin Village tour chairwoman, as a thousand outsiders moved through what architectural historians like to describe as "a spectacular collection of Victorian and Prairie School homes."

The town of Austin, annexed to Chicago in 1899, was named for Henry Austin, a salesman who went into real estate when he found he could make more money cutting up his farm and parceling out lots to commuters.

Many of its mansions, in an area just east of Oak Park, were built at the turn of the century by architect Frederick R. Schock, a local specialist in large comfy homes who was once put down (though no one can remember the exact words) by a later competitor, Frank Lloyd Wright.

"What is fascinating is to look at the style and space in which another generation lived," said James Mann, regional director of the National Trust for Historic Preservation, a government agency sufficiently impressed by the homes to list the district on the National Register of Historic Places.

"I grew up in Colorado, and it's like my neighborhood out there," noted one tour leader, Dee Edwards, talking not of mountains but atmosphere — "very friendly. The night I moved in, one of the neighbors called over and took me on a tour of their house at ten thirty at night."

One visitor noted with wonder that one house, which Schock built for his mother, Marie, in 1888, was completed at a cost of $2,935. One real estate agent on the tour, offering modern-day values for a dozen blocks of homes with wide porches and other stately touches, added that, even today, "the housing stock is comparable to Oak Park, but at least 30 percent cheaper."

"Why should we be building all those small houses in the suburbs when you have all this housing available?" wondered English, a longtime village resident.

At one point in the 1970s, he said, "there were thirteen boarded-up houses on Race (Avenue) and Midway Park. Those of us who stayed sat back and waited. It turned around. Now, very few houses around here go on the market."

As tour organizers explained, the money raised pays for a variety of good works at nearby schools, including Cinco de Mayo celebrations at May Elementary School, modem fees at Byford School, math materials for St. Paul Lutheran School and scholarships at Austin Community Academy.

No funds go to the residents, though a visitor came away

from the tour last weekend with a guilty conscience, hoping the owners are insured. It happened in the home of Jerry Ehern-berger, by day a cake baker and, at other times, national president of The Golden Glow of Christmas Past, an association of collectors of Christmas artifacts.

Even on a sunny June afternoon, his is a home that offers, to put it mildly, a thousand points of light.

And lamentably, it came to pass that, on leaving the Ehern-berger house, which was decorated with twenty- two Christmas trees, miles of lights, a blizzard of tinsel, shelves of nativity figures and ornaments from many countries, the visitor brushed a shelf — and watched in horror as an angel fell to the floor, cracking off its left wing.

June 20, 1997

A HYDE PARK DENIZEN
COMES OF AGE

Life moves at a different pace in Hyde Park, as John D. Rockefeller found out almost a century ago on a visit to the University of Chicago. Touring an institution he had bankrolled, Rockefeller was stunned to find few clocks in the home of its first president, William Harper Rainey. "Buy some more," the philanthropist whispered to Mrs. Rainey, slipping her a check for a thousand dollars.

These days, time still seems askew in this urbane enclave around the University of Chicago, with its leafy streets, grand old homes, crumbling beachfront, gargoyles, used-book stores, seedy groceries and more battered leather chairs per capita than any other neighborhood in the city. An area that reflects incessant mental struggle, Hyde Park favors sitting, thinking, talking and arguing, though most people were standing up and smiling at a party there on a recent Sunday afternoon.

In Scottish circles, the afternoon would have been called a gathering of the clan; here it drew people who shared a certain spirited, involved, committed view of life. "I'd like everyone to look around this home, at the wonderful spirit of friendship," said guest of honor Andrew Patner, a young man with a passing resemblance to actor Dustin Hoffman. He praised his parents. "They taught me and everyone around them that curiosity and generosity were two sides of one coin."

Then the talk got around to an event that, for Patner, marked a sort of coming of age in Hyde Park, the publication of his first book, *I.F. Stone: A Portrait*.

Subject and author, one guest remarked, are much alike. Both are energetic, scholarly journalists who thrive on political conflicts, social issues and intellectual exploration. Stone, at eighty, is substantially older than Patner, twenty-eight. But four years ago they spent four days in Washington, taping interview sessions in Stone's home, two restaurants, a supermarket, the Library of Congress and among eight miles of city streets. Stone talked about everything from his longtime political newsletter to his coming book on the trial of Socrates, for which he taught himself Greek. Patner used the Stone interviews for a history thesis at the University of Wisconsin, kept in touch and, while studying at the University of Chicago Law School, shaped his 175-page book.

"Young Andrew has done beautifully by the ever-young Izzy," noted author Studs Terkel, a longtime family friend.

Others agreed. "It's so wonderful when the children do well," one neighbor said. "Andrew is everybody's image of the best that comes out of Hyde Park—curious, bright, his mind going in every direction," publicist June Rosner said. Added writer Toni Schlessinger: "He has a vast-ranging mind. You can ask him about any topic, and he'll tell you who to call."

Patner admitted he had been difficult to be with during his book's gestation, but he gave credit to his parents ("They can lick anybody else's parents any time"), Irene, a musician and former dancer, and Marshall, an artist and attorney for Business and Professional People for the Public Interest, who has fought for issues ranging from tenants' rights to school lunches to lake pollution to the construction of the Sears Tower, which he once tried to block because it would interfere with TV signals from the top of the John Hancock Center.

"What's this house like when it's quiet?" someone asked Andrew's brother, Joshua, twenty-five, who had flown in from New York, where he is a fashion designer for Akari. "It's never quiet," he said.

According to Andrew, the family roots in Chicago were planted in 1892, when his great-grandmother came "from the greater Minsk metropolitan area" to see the World's Columbian Exposition. She never left. His father, nicknamed Mush, grew up in West Rogers Park and in seventh grade ran for mayor of Clinton Grammar School, with Don Rose as manager. It was the beginning of a political career for social activist Rose, who devised a rubber stamp urging students to "Push for Mush."

When Andrew was born, his parents were living in an apartment above a garage in Hyde Park. The oldest of three sons, he went to Montessori school, the nearby Ray Elementary School and Kenwood High School, sang in the Chicago Children's Choir, sold lemonade at the 57th Street Art Fair, edited his high school newspaper and worked for the national distributor of political buttons for George McGovern during the 1972 presidential campaign.

In 1977, while still in high school, he went to Washington to work for the late Rep. Ralph Metcalfe (D-Ill.). He opened mail, answered phones, wrote speeches. Later, he did his first stint at the University of Chicago, where he had spent time as a youth sneaking into the taller buildings and climbing up to see the view. The hardest to crack: Rockefeller Chapel. "There's only one door to the top, and it's usually locked."

Home was lively. "We were not political in the usual sense," Patner said. "We didn't have a lot of political magazines lying around. Everything in the family came out of intuition." Family members read, or had read to them, a lot of books. They ignored TV. Patner remembers that "years ago my father became enraged at commercial interruptions while he was watching *The African Queen*. He threw the set out of the window and totaled it."

More importantly, "we were always treated as adults," Patner recalled. "Many of my parents' friends were also my friends. Life was never divided on age lines. If you wanted to do something, you went out and did it."

As befits a community that likes to pay attention to details, that meant fighting for rights of bongo players to bongo on the Point, a beach gathering place. It meant protesting when city workers brought saws to cut down trees for road-widening behind the Museum of Science and Industry. It meant rallying to fight a landlord who threatened O'Gara & Wilson Ltd., a used-book store, with a ruinous rent increase, a cause that also enlisted area heavyweight Saul Bellow.

Several years ago, one party guest recalled, a Hyde Park couple excused themselves from an early-evening meeting because, they said, they had to go to dinner at a Hyde Park restaurant and hear jazz. Did they like jazz? "No," the wife said, "but the restaurant is having trouble over its license. We're going to lend support."

"Oh, sure," Patner said when asked about the incident. "That was Butler's. I put that together. The university was trying to put the place out of business." When the university sent someone around to check, he found six department chairs and twenty faculty members and spouses enjoying the show. Butler's later failed, Patner noted, but it was a good fight.

March 13, 1988

NEW DRIVE FOR
SOUTH SIDE Y

Hardscrabble, beaten, looted, burned, the once-bustling stretch of East 63rd Street that runs west from Jackson Park under closed "L" tracks has seen it all over the last thirty years, from riots to arson to major demolitions.

But, as urban theorists have long maintained, even heavily pounded areas of the city have a way of renewing themselves, if people come up with bright ideas — and enough energy and backing to carry them out.

Like miniature golf?

"It all started at a huddle of our staff people," Harvey "Jock" Johnson, executive director of the South Side YMCA was saying, as he told a visitor about brainstorming for ways to improve the neighborhood.

"We were wondering what we could do for families that was different. And this," he noted, speaking of a state-of-the-art eighteen-hole miniature golf course complete with trees, waterfalls and benches that opened on the YMCA's front lawn last weekend, "turned out better than any of us ever expected."

The what, when and where of the twenty thousand-square-foot operation, the only miniature golf course on the South Side, are quite simple.

Open daily, weather permitting, from 11:30 A.M. to 10 P.M. and an hour later on Saturdays and Sundays, it costs four dollars for adults and three dollars for those under nineteen. All necessary equipment — a putter and a steel-centered golf ball that does not ricochet as much — is provided.

"Get your putt in gear," is one of the course's slogans. And, staffers say, since it opened last Friday, it has been "very, very crowded."

More subtle is the why and how of it all, but such matters were hinted at by speakers at an opening day of balloons, hot dogs and hoopla.

"Our community is not so much divided as disconnected," intoned Rev. Willie T. Barrow, co-chairman of Operation PUSH, while urging higher powers to "please interest our children in some good moral sports."

Tribune photo by Charles Osgood.

"A grand occasion — part of the rebirth of the Woodlawn community," proclaimed Alderman Arenda Troutman (20th) who later led her son, Jerimiah, three, around the course in time-honored parental fashion, standing behind, leaning over and guiding shots, using skills she picked up, she said, "as a child in Ohio — where there were putt-putt courses all over."

"I'm all excited about this," noted Babette Johnson, a pre-school teacher at the YMCA who then punched in a hole-in-one and shrieked, "I'm going to call my father! He's been playing golf since I was born!"

Behind her, Bria Gooch, three, showing determined form as she swung her club from side to side, finished out her first hole, in twenty-two strokes.

"I like it," Bria said.

As miniature golf enthusiasts are quick to point out, there is often more going on at a miniature course than meets the eye.

For starters, the game is less disputatious than the full-size version, as *Castle & Windmill*, a magazine for the small-course set, recently noted in its "Top 10 Reasons Why Miniature Golf Is Better Than Golf." Among them: "No long boring discussions about 'which club will get the ball home.'"

Also, miniature golf is much more of a family game, noted Ben Jones, the head of Recreation and Entertainment Consultants, Inc., of Oakbrook Terrace, which designed the YMCA's hilly course, built with YMCA funds at a cost of $250,000.

Following current trends overseas, where miniature golf has become a serious competitive sport promoted by the World Minigolfsport Federation, which has forty thousand members, the "Y" course was designed in "garden style, to simulate a more realistic putting surface," Jones said.

Leaving out such traditional adornments as sphinxes, totem poles, smiling animals, mini-dinosaurs, castles, drawbridges, windmills, Buddhas with holes in their knees and spinning flowers that glow in the dark, this new type of course is built around "choice, chance and challenge," Jones added.

On several holes, putters are offered a choice of approach. Some are easy. Some, hard. Other holes, with twisty-turny tunnels, drop a ball who-knows-where. "Some holes," Jones said, "are challenging and reward a skilled player. On others, a five-year-old with luck can beat a parent." That, in turn, ties in with the sport's long-term appeal.

As historians note, miniature golf became a national fad in 1930, a year after the Great Crash, at a time when problems of everyday life had swollen beyond manageable proportions. Here, mini-golf suggested, everything was brought down to less-than-normal size, making it a place where a person could relax and feel more in control of the surrounding environment.

Though the game has sunk far below its Depression peak of twenty-three thousand courses, it keeps on. "After all," suggests Constance Bond, who often writes about this small pursuit, "what better activity can there be for teenagers on a first date, or for a family doing the 'Father Knows Best' routine?"

To make its own course, and by extension its neighborhood, more user-friendly, YMCA officials deliberately put greens out front, instead of behind the building on a more protected site, as some had suggested.

Fencing was kept low, to make the course "an inviting, natural gateway" to East 63d Street, Johnson noted. A pass-through window, where mini-golfers can easily sign up, was drilled through the YMCA building's outside brick wall "so you don't feel you have to know somebody inside," Jones said.

Already, YMCA staff members are talking of picnics, parties, even tournaments next spring, in the European style where players see the game as more like billiards, playing angles, banking shots, often against a time clock. Last August, one mini-golfer notes, championships in Denmark drew twenty-five countries.

"Walk five miles a day. Quit eating so much. Let your blood flow right. Come and take your exercise," urged Barrow, stating her good-health regimen as she started off around the course.

"All those who want to get in a quick eighteen holes, follow me," added "Jock" Johnson.

And many did.

September 24, 1997

Her mother remembered the ice. Huge chunks fell on the third-class deck. People were playing in it until an officer warned them away. In the lifeboat, they were told not to look, but everybody did. They saw the liner go down.

Just before, they saw Captain Smith, holding a megaphone, yelling across the roiling waters, "Get away from the ship! Get away from the ship!"

In a neat little house on a tree-lined street in Elgin, an elderly woman, now slowed by arthritis, told what she remembered—and has been told—about that ocean voyage. That includes her mother's story of how their dining-room steward had banged on their cabin door and said: "Put on your coats and follow me. There isn't any time to lose. The ship is sinking."

It was eighty-three years before we talked that Eleanor Shuman set out from Southampton, England, on the most famous ship in history, a doomed ocean liner built for a thousand crossings of the Atlantic but unable to complete even one.

"I have a memory," she began, as a reporter probed her for details of a night that she does not care to remember. "I was being held in my mother's arms," she said. "I was at a great height. I was crying. People were screaming. They were yelling. There was so much confusion."

These days, far from any ocean, a portrait of a majestic, four-funnelled ship — the R.M.S. *Titanic* — hangs on the wall of Shuman's living room, over "my *Titanic* corner," as she calls her collection of books on the disaster.

One of two surviving *Titanic* passengers known to be living in the United States, Shuman, now eighty-four, was eighteen months old on that clear, starlit evening of April 14, 1912, when the *Titanic* entered a thick field of ice, steaming at twenty-three knots, declining to slow down, determined to set a speed record to New York.

There have been worse maritime disasters, but none has ever had the haunting symbolism of what followed, almost four hundred miles off the coast of Newfoundland, a brutal collision between Man and Nature described by Canadian poet E. J. Pratt in his epic ode, *The Titanic*.

The iceberg, Pratt wrote, was born alone, in the stark isolation of the Arctic. Barely chipped, it sailed south after the crash, to melt. The ship, 882 feet long, eleven decks high, built by seventeen thousand workers, pronounced unsinkable, suffered a long tear in its hull. Its wreckage took hours to sink two-and-a-half miles to the floor of Canada's Grand Banks, a region of abysmal darkness, intense pressures and nearly blind ratfish.

That night, 1,522 people died. Only twenty lifeboats, the number required by regulations, plus some collapsible canvas dinghies, were on board for 2,227 passengers and crew.

At dawn, after a night out at sea, 705 people — including Shuman, her mother and her brother, Harold, then four — were picked up by the nearby vessel *Carpathia*.

"My mother didn't like to talk about it," Shuman said. "Whenever company came, it was the first thing they'd want to know." Many of Shuman's memories, she said, are based on her mother's reluctant reminiscences.

Nor, she said, was the aftermath easy for her. Growing up in St. Charles, classmates often "came up just to look at me." At one school, "the first day I got there, everybody was running down the sidewalk to greet me. I always felt different." But, she added, "I think about it an awful lot, especially around this time of year."

Shuman agreed to share her experiences as a favor to the producers of "Titanica," a ninety-four-minute film shot in the huge Imax medium which, starting Friday, will offer viewers at the Museum of Science and Industry stunning images of the world's most famous shipwreck, on a five-story Omnimax screen.

"The *Titanic* is such a great poetic disaster," said the film's director, Stephen Low, in a telephone interview from IMAX's offices in Toronto. Low worked with a crew of 150 people aboard the Soviet ship *Akademik Keldysh* for twenty-three days of filming in June 1991 using high-tech Russian submersibles, Imax cameras and halogen lights to pierce the ocean darkness.

"It was a lot wilder than comes across in the movie," he said. "Diving on a wreck in a submersible is the scariest thing a person could do."

Death, should equipment fail, was only milliseconds away. A leak, at pressures a thousand times heavier than at sea level,

Officer Lowe, towed collapsible D to the Carpathia.

(Above) Collapsible D approaches, overloaded and awash with icy ̶w̶a̶t̶e̶r̶. Her passengers include

would create a jet of water that could saw a person in two, he noted. But the sights were amazing.

The Titanic, he found, seems to be melting on the ocean floor, with rivers of red and orange rust flowing from its steel remains. Suitcases, seemingly preserved, lie outside. The nearby sand is littered with jewelry and coal.

"There was a mood of sadness," Low said, recalling the en-crusted first-class lounges, with their chandeliers intact, and the questing seastars on the long-abandoned bridge. "We saw the decay of a lost civilization."

As for Shuman's story, it began when her family received word that her mother's father was dying in Finland and had asked to see her mother. Her father, building a house at the time in St. Charles, couldn't make the trip. Shuman's mother and the two children set off.

On the return trip, accompanied by two teenage girls they met in Sweden, they hit a snag in London. Their passage back was canceled due to a coal miners' strike. The Titanic in South-ampton had space. They hopped a boat train — and got last-minute tickets.

"It was third class. We were locked down there. We couldn't go up to the upper decks," Shuman said. "When the Titanic struck the iceberg, why, tons of ice went on the deck, right out-side our cabin door.

"Mom and these girls went out to see what was going on. They were kicking the ice around, having fun with it. An officer came down and said, 'Everybody go back to your cabins. We'll be getting under way shortly.' After that, there was a rap on the door. Our table steward, from the dining room, got us up to the boat deck.

"There was a ring of officers around a dinghy. One officer beckoned to my mother to come through. I was in her arms. She stood on the edge of the deck. She was afraid. A man in the dinghy said, 'Don't look down. Close your eyes. Lean forward. I'll catch you.' He did and helped her to her seat.

"It was about to be lowered. Mom looked up. Ellen (one of the Swedish girls) was up on the next deck, holding Harold. Mom called her to drop him down. She was so afraid that she couldn't. A man beside her took Harold and dropped him down."

The dinghy, Shuman said, was the last lifeboat to be lowered from the *Titanic*. "One of the Swedish girls survived," she said, "but the one holding Harold went down."

Then, "Mom took her life jacket off and put it on Harold. She said, 'I'll look after Eleanor, but if we don't get through, Harold can tell what happened.' I had a wonderful mother."

At 7 o'clock in the morning, bitterly cold, "we were picked up by the *Carpathia*. Harold and I were hoisted up in mail bags. We couldn't climb up the ladder."

Besides that, the reporter asked delicately, how was the rest of the trip?

"Mother didn't go into much detail about the cabin — or the first three or four days," Shuman said. "Most of what she said was about getting off.

"But I did get a letter from a young man in Troy, New York, not long ago asking me, 'Did you enjoy the cruise on the *Titanic*?'"

What has she done of a *Titanic* nature over the years? "Mostly refused invitations," said Shuman, who worked at a local watch factory, served as a telephone operator and retired in 1962. Her husband, an engineer at International Harvester to whom she was married for forty-seven years, died in 1981.

"The Kiwanis Club wanted me to come and tell my story, and I get a lot of invitations to talk at schools," she said, "but I can't bring myself to do it." She knows of one other survivor in the U.S., a woman in northern Michigan, in her nineties, who refuses to talk about it at all.

For Shuman, the *Titanic* was her first and last ocean voyage.

Several years ago, in Florida visiting her son, who then was living in Fort Lauderdale, she went down to see the Atlantic Ocean, her first view of it since 1912. "I kept looking towards the east and thinking of the *Titanic*," she said. Was she tempted to board one of the cruise ships in the harbor?

"Oh, no," she said, quite firmly.

April 10, 1995

LIGHT POLE PAINTER
HAS A TRUE BRUSH
WITH FAME

"Why is all this happening at once?" wondered Ray Gregor, relaxing in the recreation room of his home on South Campbell Avenue in the Morgan Park neighborhood of Chicago's Far South Side.

Last week, there was a story in a community newspaper. Now, TV stations were calling.

"What are you going to do next?" asked a visitor, noting that Gregor was running out of what he has become famous for — light poles. His claim to fame, widely noted these days, is that he has painted five thousand of them — almost every one in Morgan Park, Mt. Greenwood and Beverly.

"Well, you could always go back and paint a stripe," suggested his wife, Laurie, as they sat discussing his hobby, a one-man civic improvement mission built along the lines of the biblical maxim that it is better to light a single candle than to curse the darkness.

Now seventy-eight, Gregor started out five years ago, irked by a rust-flecked pole outside his family-run print shop, Fernwood Printers Ltd., 3504 West 111th Street.

"Could use a touch of paint," he thought. After he turned his business over to the care of two sons, he showed up at the 19th Ward office at 10231 South Western Avenue, wondering if the city might spare some paint and a brush.

The answer was along the lines of, "But, of course."

From there, one pole led to another.

"I did 111th Street," he recalled, "then I had to pick some other street. So I did Central Park (Avenue) to 115th (Street), then I did other areas, little by little."

Slowly, he became known in the area.

"You've got to understand," explained his wife. "Ray likes to talk to people. He paints one pole and he talks to a hundred people."

"Yeah, I keep moving — so I never run out of an audience," Gregor added, noting that he likes his hobby because he keeps his own hours, nobody tells him what to do, he gets a

Tribune photo by Charles Osgood.

modest amount of exercise in the fresh air and he sets his own dress code.

Most of the time that means only shorts and shoes, a bare-bones costume that leads to, well, a certain amount of "wearing of the green," as some locals say.

That's the color of the paint supplied by the city. Under the Clean & Green program, the city provides supplies, including rakes, shovels and other equipment, to citizens and groups wishing to spruce up neighborhoods by removing clutter, planting gardens — and painting light poles.

It is a trend that is catching on in many areas of the country.

Last spring, for example, in the San Fernando Valley north of Los Angeles, some six hundred residents who took part in a neighborhood cleanup got free fruit trees to improve their backyard gardens. In Texas, volunteers in seven suburbs of Arlington got together on successive Saturdays to pick up trash from vacant lots. Each June, as one of the many activities of New

(LIGHT POLE PAINTER)   179

York's Neighborhood Week, neighbors of Mayor Rudolph Giuliani sweep the block around Gracie Mansion, his residence.

Yet, in terms of one man doing one community chore, probably few in the country can match Gregor's record for pitching in.

"We have many civic groups that do cleanup," noted Matt O'Shea, an administrative assistant to Alderman Virginia Rugai (19th), "but Ray came up with this on his own. He volunteered his time. And we've had some ninety-five-degree days this year when Ray was in picking up more paint."

Over five years, O'Shea said, Gregor has used four hundred gallons.

"It's wonderful. We should all be that civic-minded," said Lorraine Larson, pulling into her driveway on South Hoyne Avenue near West 110th Street on Monday afternoon as Gregor worked across the street, using a ladder to start twelve feet up and paint his way to the ground.

"Nice guy. It shows you there's still a sense of community around here," added passerby John Meyer, who lives several blocks away.

"He takes pride in those poles," noted wife Laurie. "We'll be riding down the street and he'll say, 'Look how nice they are,' and I'll say, 'They sure are.'"

Now, like the ancient Greek warrior Alexander the Great, who ran out of worlds to conquer, Gregor has run out of poles to paint. He doesn't want to go outside his ward. Yet, except for a few poles that, for technical reasons, he can't do, they've all been done.

On the other hand, he noted, the paint he uses has a warranty of five years.

Sooner or later, they'll all need doing again.

September 2, 1998

THE ULTIMATE
OUT-OF-TOWNERS

It's a big jump from the rain forests of eastern Indonesia to a dinner party in Winnetka, but thirty-five tribal members, in the Chicago area for a show at the Field Museum of Natural History, handled it just fine. The Winnetka police dropped by only once, to remind the visitors that local customs in this tree-lined village, on the North Shore, do not allow tribal chanting on the back patio, at least not after the sun goes down.

Otherwise, it was a great evening.

Good talk, in the French chateau-style home of their host, Indonesian Consul General P. Surahman. A hearty meal, of meat gumbo with bean sprouts, blackened beef and boiled eggs. Group dancing, as a full moon peeked through the swaying elms. And, for visitors from one of the least-known regions on Earth, a chance to discover one more startling thing about America:

Lawn sprinklers.

As dancers and artisans representing the Asmat, Dani and Sentani peoples of Irian Jaya, the western half of the island of New Guinea, now part of Indonesia, the troupe had motored north by bus, discovering, among other urban wonders, snarled expressway traffic. Much later, well after dark, they returned to explore their Chicago base, the Blackstone Hotel. It was all part of as grand an adventure as a person could have, plucked from a low-tech village and dropped, in succession, into Jakarta, Washington, New York, New Orleans and — now — Chicago.

For the past three months, it's been one thing after another, according to Arianto Reksoprodjo, a senior at the University of Indonesia and translator for the U.S. tour, which was put together by the Asmat Progress and Development Foundation, a Jakarta-based support group.

"Most of these people had never been in a high-rise building," noted Penny Fairchild, the foundation's international coordinator. That meant quick lessons in such urban skills as how to stop an elevator door from closing, and how to cross a busy street. Nor was the idea of traffic easy to grasp.

"Where are all these people going?" one tribesman asked her. "And why?"

"They are really bright — and gentle, considering their war-like past," added Robert Welsch, a Field Museum associate curator who has visited Asmat villages. "They put on costumes, but they are not primitive. Like Americans, once they find a place is safe, they like to go out and explore. They don't need to be coddled. Give them a few ground rules, and they're OK."

Indeed, by the time they reached Chicago, the tour's last stop, they had acquired substantial street smarts, along with shoes, T-shirts and other clothing that made them look like thousands of other neatly dressed tourists who visit the city each year. The difference was something in the eyes: an intensity that fastened on what was, to them, unusual.

Like vending machines. "Who wants a Coke?" shouted one tribesman, eager to press the buttons and hear a thunk every time he saw one.

Or hats with logos, like "Truckers of America" or "Born to Be Wild."

Or hotel rooms, with ceiling heat lamps, wall-to-wall carpeting, pull strings for drapes, taps for hot and cold water and a tub in each bathroom which was not, as some initially surmised, for the washing of clothing.

Or flush toilets.

"I told them, 'All of you, sit down,'" recalled group leader Tito Adonis, describing the start of a demonstration he gave for five nervous volunteers in a five-stall restroom before the group left their first big city, Jakarta. Then he moved on to the more difficult concept of locks and keys, unknown in the remote villages of Irian Jaya, a land alive with spirits and myths and watchful ancestors where theft is rare.

So what adventures have they had?

Well, for one thing, shortly after taking off from Jakarta, one tribesman, suffering motion sickness, threw up on group leader Adonis. Another, trying to open the air nozzle above his seat, pushed every button, which lit four lights and summoned a stewardess. People kept locking themselves in the washroom until they figured out how the bolt worked.

In Washington's National Airport, one tribesman walked into a plate glass window. "Heavy air," he muttered, holding his nose. In New Orleans, encamped in a Loyola University dormitory, so many tribal members gathered in one room to smoke

cigarettes, a habit spread centuries ago by European traders seeking spices, that they set off a ceiling smoke detector.

Badly startled, they tried to flee, overloading an elevator. That set off another alarm. Later, several slept outside, refusing to reenter a building they felt was infested with spirits ringing bells. Most also disliked American cigarettes.

In hotels, many of them worried about a strange humming. It took careful explanation to reassure them that the noise was from an air-conditioning system, not ghosts.

At one party, at the home of an anthropologist, an Asmat tribesman spotted a drum that had been taken from his village years ago. It was, he said, one of two used in a ritual dance. After the drum's loss, the dance had been abandoned. "He didn't want it back," explained tour publicist Foofie Axelrod, "but he wanted to show his host how to display it properly. He was happy when it was put in a place where it was respected."

They found the idea of ice unusual, but uninteresting. They liked wandering through a Wendy's Hamburgers, notably when a tour leader ordered "sixty-five—to go." Television was OK, especially religious programs and westerns, but the big electronic hit was cassette recorders. Many taped their own music at night and, during dull day stretches, played it back through headphones.

Other local customs also proved confusing. In Chicago, on their first morning at the Blackstone Hotel, many in the troupe came down to the lobby, found coffee and sweet rolls laid out and, assuming the crowd at the complimentary breakfast table had gathered to greet them, shook hands with everyone and said, "Hello, hello," bewildering the hotel's business travelers. Later, they got to see something of the city.

One concept that the out-of-towners found hard to grasp was landfill. That, they were told, was used to form Grant Park at a time when the waters of Lake Michigan lapped as far in as Michigan Avenue. "This was after a great flood?" one tour member asked.

"No, after a great fire," their guide replied, puzzling them.

Nor were the Asmat reluctant to recount, if properly approached, some daunting ideas of their own, among them that part of their rich heritage which involves head-hunting. The practice ceased about thirty years ago, as Yuven Biakai, thirty-six, a church deacon in his village, explained in English during a long interview, relaxing on a sofa in the lobby of the Blackstone.

"Not I, but my older brother did this," he said, describing in careful terms a ceremony of ritual decapitation, known as "daokus pokmbu," which he said was tied to a respect for the strength of an enemy and a wish to bring peace by imbuing two warring spirits in one self, that of the decapitator.

Had Biakai, the reporter wondered, known Michael Rockefeller, who had disappeared in 1961 after his catamaran raft had overturned during a fierce storm off the jungle coast near Asmat settlements? "No," Biakai said. Nor did he believe speculation that Rockefeller had been killed by Asmat tribesmen. "Probably, a big fish ate him," he suggested, noting that the area where Rockefeller was last seen swimming was known for its "alligators, sharks and man-eating whales."

So did the tribal members like America?

"Yes," said Anakletus Ciwicak, an Asmat wearing a green T-shirt from the Hard Rock Cafe in New York. "I knew it was far away, but I didn't know what to expect. I couldn't imagine it. It was too big for my thoughts."

Added Elly Hengda, a Sentani tribesman and bark painter: "Lots of high buildings. Beds — good. Bathrooms — good."

Yet, as more than one tribal member murmured, it will be good to get back to the forest.

July 29, 1991

RIVER'S FRIENDS GO
WHERE ONLY MOST
HARDY DARE

Edgily, the canoers pushed off from shore, aimed downriver toward Bubbly Creek, the kind of watery abyss that is the stuff of cheap horror movies.

Death, some felt, was but a boat-tip away.

Organized by the Friends of the Chicago River, this was one backwater expedition that needed all the friends it could get.

One woman, from the Lincoln Park area, carried along a private supply of anti-bacterial soap, rubbing it on her hands.

"Stinky, awful," she complained, nosing her bow away from the launch point by the Chicago River's southeast turning basin, near 2600 South Ashland Avenue. "Somebody," she said, "forgot to turn on the air-freshener."

"The water is kind of thick, like motor oil," agreed her boatmate, looking down. "And you can't help but notice the stuff floating around."

Others, who had paid fifteen dollars for what was billed as a guided two-hour trip of "our working river's wildlife, industrial architecture and new opportunities," took a somewhat sunnier view of the outing.

Paddling around barges moving sand and gravel, past sheets of corroded metal half-sunk in dank waters, then under the soaring white girders of the Ashland "L" station, they came upon an area of natural serenity.

It was a stretch where the green walls of trees hung down to the river's edge. Fairy-like black-winged damsel flies danced above the water. In the distance a pair of herons spread wings and flapped into the sky.

Only the dip of paddles broke the summer silence.

And the water, the optimists agreed, was better than it used to be.

Starting in the 1860s, as historians in the flotilla recalled, this fork of the Chicago, reaching down from where the river's South Branch joins the Chicago Sanitary & Ship Canal, serviced the nearby stockyards.

For almost a century, it received carcasses of dead animals

whose decaying remains, to this day, still bubble up tiny gas emissions.

Hence, Bubbly Creek, a stream at one time so ill-fetid that, as one friend of the river said, birds could walk across on congealed grease.

It was, another quipped, "truly offal."

Turning such a river around is no easy feat. But it is part of a mission that has engaged increasing support from environmental activists across the country. The much-reported phenomenon received a recent airing in *The Amicus Journal*, in an article titled "Trashed Urban Rivers and the People Who Love Them."

An environmental quarterly, the *Amicus* noted cleanup efforts on the Chicago as well as better days for New Jersey's Passaic River, which once flowed purple, yellow and green with textile mill dyes, for New York's Bronx River, until recently a cover for an underwater junk yard, and for waterfronts in Philadelphia, Hartford, Connecticut, and San Antonio, Texas.

"Yes, urban rivers are big right now," noted Christine Cercone, membership and volunteer program coordinator at the thousand-member Friends of the Chicago River, which was founded in 1979 and sponsors river outings, bank walks, nature classes and "river rescue" days for trash removal.

Many cities, Cercone added, are seeking a new direction for such liquid assets. Many of the slaughterhouses, factories or steel mills that used local rivers as industrial sewers have closed.

Now, local residents want to reclaim them for recreation and enjoyment.

"Today's pioneers no longer follow the rivers west with Lewis and Clark," notes Washington-based environmentalist Will Nixon. "They follow their block to the end, duck through a gap in the fence under the 'No Trespassing' sign and imagine a better future for their own river."

On banks near Bubbly Creek, for example, trails and canoe launching sites have been cleaned up and prepared over the last three years by volunteers from Chicago Youth Centers Fellowship House, 844 West 32nd Street.

The group calls itself "The River Rats."

Or, as happened this trip, a hundred people sign up to explore the Chicago's most-troubled branch and try to figure ways to make it more like the stream early French explorers found on paddles down from Montreal.

"You appreciate how clear the rest of the river is getting," said Don Pitzen. "It all used to run black."

Nearby, Patricia Groh, a librarian at the Skokie Public Library, said that friends had warned her, before she set out, that tipping into the river, at least in Bubbly Creek, would produce "instant death."

Still, she said, referring to a long-held dream of the late Mayor Richard J. Daley, "I always remember Richard J. 'Hizzoner' saying that one day people will swim and fish in this river.

"People laughed at him."

August 1, 1997

LOCAL TACTICS
IN THE RESTLESS
SEARCH FOR LOVE

SHRINKS IN LOVE

Like Sam Spade, she works out of an office with a frosted-glass door, upstairs in an old building in Hyde Park, sharing a floor with a tailor, a financial adviser, a barber and a gynecologist. Her clients pay her $175 every six months. She helps them look for people.

But April Abbott is no private eye. She's a matchmaker, the head of April Abbott's Social Adventures Ltd. Much of the time she handles certain people with certain needs: psychotherapists looking for love.

She has been at the dating game for eight years, enough time to see a lot of people come and go. What she has found, from a thousand clients, about 35 percent of them in the therapy professions, is enough to fill a book, which she's writing.

Guy walks in. Fills out the form. Wants a wife. Has three criteria. Must be willing to bear children, have a trim body and reach orgasms quickly.

He's a psychiatrist. He has been looking for twelve years.

Woman walks in. Leaves a photo of herself scowling and wearing a black-leather jacket. Later, she complains that few men chose her.

She's a psychologist. Tells Abbott she could use some therapy herself.

That's how it goes. No two therapists are exactly alike, Abbott said, but as she plunged into desk drawers, pulling out envelopes crammed with pictures and opening files filled with what has become a substantial body of anthropological research, certain themes emerged.

"Male therapists," she said, "usually are looking for thin, physically attractive women whom they can manipulate." Female therapists say they are looking for "commitment-oriented men who seem to be emotionally stable," but they spend much dating time checking for signs of pathology.

Female therapists frequently call her at home late at night after a date. "They want to tell me everything and hear what I have to say. When I pause, they say, 'Why did you pause?' They process everything," Abbott said.

Male therapists "rarely give feedback," she said. They look for "instant chemistry." If it isn't there, she said, they seldom go on, preferring to start fresh with someone new. One therapist told Abbott he had dated more than a thousand women in a dozen years.

Often, dates between therapists go badly, Abbott said. In restaurants, one male therapist suggested that meal checks be shared on a sliding scale, according to each party's earnings. His dates reported that he almost always overestimated their salaries, thus assigning them too large a share.

One female therapist liked to draw out men by listening to them, but later complained that "they talked too much." Another female therapist often turned men down on the basis of initial telephone conversations or, if she was interested, became obsessed with the possibility of rejection. She went out with one man, but he was mean to her, eventually refusing to take her calls, a situation she compared, in tears, to neglect by her father.

A third female therapist went back into therapy to find out why she kept falling in love with men who failed to respond. Eventually, she found someone, got married and called Abbott because "she wanted me to know her story had a happy ending."

In their profile descriptions, most male therapists think of themselves as strong on conversational skills. Yet on dates, Abbott said, they seem "to have a surprising disregard for women's feelings." Though successful at therapy, many seem to have difficulty shifting from a position of dominance, which they assume with patients, to an egalitarian stance, for dating.

One male therapist even requested a woman willing, as he put it, "to star in a supporting role as wife." Earlier, he told Abbott, he had written a singles ad that began: "Ahoy there and welcome aboard the journey through life. This is your captain speaking. I'm looking for a loyal and dedicated first mate."

Female therapists often undertake extensive psychological diagnoses of their dates, "at times carrying the 'rational' evaluation common to other women to an extreme," Abbott said. Some become judgmental, often in picky ways, complaining about dirty bathrooms or failures in the kitchen. Others, however, do use their professional skills to "listen carefully, make a man feel he is cared for and learn to develop a personal relationship."

Besides therapists, Abbott deals with lawyers, business executives, investors, professors, doctors, nurses, teachers and editors.

"I never thought I'd become a matchmaker," said Abbott, forty-three, who was raised in southern California and went to the University of Chicago to pursue a doctorate in religion and literature, after majoring in German at New York's Barnard College and the University of California at Irvine.

In Chicago, she took off-campus courses in therapy, which she liked but found vague. About ten years ago, she started conducting private classes for graduate students who needed help with reading German, a subject she still teaches.

Abbott got started in the dating game by running socials, picking up the idea from a California friend who was making "a nice living at it," she said. It didn't work out. Though she'd hoped to meet some nice people, she found herself spending more time stuffing envelopes, chopping carrots and moving chairs than mixing and mingling at her parties.

That led to matchmaking, which "turned out to be a happy medium between teaching German, which is very specific, and doing psychotherapy, which is not," she said. "Now, I interview people, discover interesting things about them and find a concrete solution to their problems. I get them dates."

Clients get a questionnaire, to pin down their interests and the type of person they seek. "I do not have a formal means of screening for mentally deranged people," she said. "However, I use my intuition and will not accept someone, usually a man, who seems strange."

Much of the selection work relies on photographs brought in by clients. Men usually supply pictures of themselves at work. Women prefer snapshots in more relaxed settings, taken with friends. Backgrounds are important.

"One woman was rarely chosen," Abbott said. "All we had was a Polaroid taken in my office. When she replaced that with a better picture of herself, with trees and Lake Michigan behind her, she was picked on a regular basis."

On dates, men often are tripped up by their bluntness, making such remarks as, "Let's get naked and party all weekend," "I have made love only three times since my divorce ten years ago," "Where does your dog sleep?" and, "I haven't dated much because I'm emotionally needy." But during the selection process, Abbott said, women more often comment on sexual compatibility. "Can I really see myself kissing him?" one woman, examining a picture, asked Abbott.

"A first date can be a virtual mine field for a man," Abbott said. "He is constantly being subjected to a variety of tests of which he is completely unaware." Some talk too much, others too little. One woman complained that a man kept drumming with his fingers the entire date. Another said a man brought along an attractive female houseguest who, he explained, was staying with him for the weekend. A third complained that her date wouldn't share his popcorn.

Nor do women always behave well. One woman went silent after she thought she spotted her ex-husband in a crowd. Another, her date complained, "kept saying, 'So much to do, so little time,' even though she didn't seem to actually do anything."

For therapists, as well as for others, Abbott argues that a dating service makes increasing sense. New people are hard to find. Singles ads draw blizzards of unscreened responses. There are ethical problems if therapists date clients.

Both sexes can be picky, Abbott said.

One client refused to date a woman who had a telephone answering machine on which she had recorded the words "No one is home" to a tune from Beethoven's Ninth Symphony. Men have been refused, or dumped, because of "silly sideburns," leaving inadequate tips in restaurants or drinking a date's orange juice and failing to replace it.

Another of her clients, Abbott said, refused to go out with a man when she learned that, like herself, he was a psychotherapist. Perhaps, a visitor suggested, a matchmaker could suggest that the two could date. But . . .

They should limit each date to exactly fifty minutes, and place strict rules on who gets to use the couch — and for what.

July 24, 1992

(THE RESTLESS SEARCH FOR LOVE)

ONE LANGUAGE NEEDS
NO TRANSLATION

"It's a fairy tale," whispered Margaret McMillan, sitting in Cafe Amore Mio in Skokie, listening to the singer and relating a story that began in Khabarovsk in the far eastern reaches of Russia, an industrial city near Vladivostok known for its waterfront esplanades.

That was seventeen months ago.

It was raining.

"I'm a dentist, from Tinley Park," McMillan began. "I had a young woman working for me as a dental assistant. She was from Russia. I was like her surrogate mom. She was heading home for the summer and she invited me to come, but I couldn't get a tourist visa."

McMillan turned to a non-profit, Washington-based group called the Citizens Democracy Corps, similar to the Peace Corps, but for businesses. Yes, they said, they could use an American dentist in Khabarovsk. A dental office wanted help in adapting its communist-style practice to the latest thinking in dental marketing and patient management techniques.

The trip was, well, nice — until her last Sunday there. Then, kaboom!

Her translator, Ilya, had planned a barbecue for her. It was rained out. On a Sunday, everything else in town was closed. Desperate for some going-away entertainment, Ilya turned to a friend, a local folk singer, Vyacheslav Kuznetsov, better known as Slava. "Sure, come over to my place," Slava said.

It was there that McMillan was hit, as the French say of romantic beginnings, by a coup de foudre, a thunderbolt. Or, as she describes the meeting, "It was a Kodak moment."

Not a woman who is normally swept away, McMillan, who had never been married, spent most of her remaining four days with Slava, accompanied by Ilya, the interpreter, for times when words were needed.

She left. After many hassles, Slava got a short-term visa to the U.S. After more wrangles, he got to stay. They were married in October at Church of St. Mary in Park Forest. "There were tears in many eyes," recalled a guest, as Slava sang a love song to his bride.

"That's amazing," said a visitor to the cafe, at 7931 North Lincoln Avenue, in Skokie, picking into a napoleon, a favorite pastry of Russian emigres who hang out there — despite being named for a French emperor who caused havoc in their homeland almost two centuries ago.

"Hey, Slava, do 'Moscow Nights,'" shouted Jasha Rubinovich, a fan at a table near the back of room. At the microphone, on a stage by the window, Slava did, in a baritone trained for opera, doing songs he has performed, as his agent notes, "throughout all the far east Russian area and into Siberia and Japan."

Much of his material is original.

"This one is called, 'Sweet Lies,'" McMillan said, as her husband swung into a sort of Russian blues that was not, as a visitor suggested, "about Washington." Rather, it was a plea for a husband to return from afar and personally whisper endearments in his wife's ear.

Other songs told of life and death and of a promised land of peace and plenty "somewhere beyond the sunrise" where "there's no war, no cursing, no stealing" and "a white boat will sail up to greet you" and "the grapes as big as apples grow."

Later, after completing a ninety-minute set, Slava confessed that he never expected to end up living in Tinley Park. Or singing at a cafe in Skokie almost every weekend. (He also has been doing private parties, mostly for Russian-speaking groups.)

And, both he and Margaret added, it has not been an entirely easy road.

"Neither of us spoke the other's language. We had only feelings," Slava said, recalling the rainy Sunday in Khabarovsk, "but there were many, many communications to the heart."

So, what were the challenges?

The problems involved adjusting to credit cards, the paperwork of buying a car and learning to trust a bank with one's money.

"I hit the language tapes. We did charades. We used dictionaries," added McMillan, "but we didn't have any way to communicate what was inside." Yes, she admitted, there were moments, shortly after Slava arrived, when she wondered what she had gotten herself into.

So, asked the visitor, what did she know and when did she know it?

"The moment I fell absolutely in love with him was one day when I was sick," she said. "I came home feeling awful and sent him to the pharmacy to get some medicine. He came home and thought I was sleeping. He put the medicine and a glass of water down on the night stand. Then he brushed my hair out of my face and covered me up.

"You never know," McMillan added, "how someone feels about you until you see them when they don't think you're watching."

December 23, 1998

SMALL DELIGHTS ON
THE ZEPHYR

I wish to speak a word in support of Amtrak, that curious, out-dated, quirky form of long-distance transportation that usually is in the news only after a crash or a funding crisis.

Two, three, sometimes four times a year, I take a train some-where, always staying in the coaches, overnight, with my regu-lar rituals that include taping a portable radio to the window.

With tiny earphones, I slide through the inky darkness, lis-tening to stations in the night.

For me, there is a sense of personal peace that settles in when I find myself, say, barreling across the sea of grass that is western Nebraska. Or snaking in a Vista-Dome beside the mountain rivers and landings where the Civil War once raged, west of Washington, D.C.

I bring books, newspapers, a bag of oranges and a journal to write in. I spread out on a seat that is bigger than any first-class seat on an airplane — and let things happen.

What I have found in my travels, just as Paul Theroux did when he set out from London for Asia to research his notable book, The Great Railway Bazaar, is that a train traveler may start out with a love of trains, but often ends up fascinated with the passengers.

I offer this small story.

It started eight days ago in Denver with the departure of the California Zephyr for Chicago. My prospects for a cozy trip looked less than promising at the start. I stood in the cavernous railroad station, preparing to share a train with hundreds of high school kids, all laden with backpacks, returning to the Midwest from their spring break.

One of my rituals, or train-smarts, is to use any excuse I can think of to preboard. "Dad, you're not," my daughter, who was twenty at the time, once whispered urgently in a station in Phil-adelphia when they announced that parents with children could get on first.

"Yes, we are," said I, a firm believer that you play the cards you get.

I have also been known to slip five dollars to a porter, or to claim old age, in order to get first crack at what, for me, is wonderful. That's a seat by a window in the middle of a car by the stairs where there is less sway, fewer jolts from the wheels and the freedom to recline your seat as far back as possible since there are no other seats behind you.

So, on the *Zephyr*, I did manage to wangle my way on early, arrange my space, then split for one of my two favorite places on the train, the dining car. I like it because one of the rules of Amtrak is that it arranges seating. Every space is filled. You can't sit alone.

For me, speaking to strangers is like diving into a swimming pool. Getting over the fear of coldness is the hard part: Once I'm in, even if pushed, I'm fine.

At dinner, I met a couple from San Antonio, en route to see their grandchildren in Ohio, and a strange young man from Boulder, Colo., with earrings, going to see his newborn son in Buffalo.

Hearing their stories, which I doubt I would have heard anywhere other than on Amtrak, I was reminded again of what Paul Theroux had written, that "anything is possible on a train: a great meal, a binge, a visit from card players, an intrigue, a good night's sleep, and strangers' monologues framed like Russian short stories."

That's the curious thing about Amtrak.

Even though it has its bad days, and unfortunate disasters, there is something about its protracted runs, overnight to distant cities, that is increasingly rare. People who don't know each other are stuck together long enough to start talking. That doesn't happen as much, I notice, on airplanes.

Also, back in the coaches, people are able to sack out in a kind of intercity sleepover, rolling through the night together in a way that always reminds me of a story I once did on a Chicago group called The Friends of the Parks. It had to do with what, to the watchful eyes of its executive director, Erma Tranter, constituted "a safe park."

"Having lots of people around," she told me, "and feeling comfortable enough to take a nap there." And that's how I feel about all my trips on Amtrak.

In my many nights in the coaches, I have never seen or heard any "trouble," as they call the kind of incidents that regularly happen in other places where strangers find themselves together late at night. Mostly, there is, as they say, a sense of trust.

For example, as I moved back from the diner through swaying cars, I saw that the seat next to mine, over which I had spread my stuff to protect my elbow-room, had been taken up by a rather attractive woman. She was reading a book much like the ones I had brought with me.

She had been placed there by a conductor, she said. The other seats were all taken up by "da yout," as we call them in Chicago. They were settling in as the car softened into its dark-hours decor of reading lamps, winking off, and the palest of aisle illuminations.

She was, she said, a first-grade teacher in Iowa.

We talked, for an hour, about kids, books, travel, challenges.

Then she unfolded a blanket and asked, in the softest of voices, if I'd like to share it. Underneath, working toward a comfortable position on our seats, we arranged ourselves, after several shifts, into the two-spoons position. We both fell asleep, somewhere east of Fort Morgan, Colo., she first, with a delicate feminine purr, as I drifted off on a cloud of calm, with a moon in the sky, a girl in my arms and, on my shortwave radio, a dance band from Paris.

She got off the train the next morning in Osceola. Nothing like that ever happened to me on United Airlines.

March 28, 1999

IN TOUCH WITH SEX

To many people, the words "sex therapist" bring to mind a prune-faced teacher who sits beside a bed, brandishes a pointer, raps toes for clumsy moves and, for moments of success, flashes a sign that says "9.5!" Others think of an inspector in a chocolate factory.

Such images are false. So says a soft-spoken woman in a business suit who spends her days counseling couples on the nuances of physical and emotional pleasuring. She is Barbara Vaughan. She plies her trade around a coffee table in tasteful quarters on an upper floor of Lake Point Tower, at 505 North Lake Shore Drive. She has yet to see a client undress.

Unlike many in sex fields, such as best-selling authors who portray men and women interacting like clanking boxcars, Vaughan does not go for gymnastics, screaming, moaning or the kind of kinky behaviors seen in many neighborhoods on videotape. Of the hundreds of sex experts and marital counselors practicing in the area, she is the only Chicago therapist trained by William Masters and Virginia Johnson, the St. Louis researchers who mapped physiological sexual experiences in their pioneering 1967 work, *Human Sexual Response*.

Contrary to popular myths, Vaughan's work does not include providing partners for single clients, commonly known as sexual surrogates. Nor does she speed from motel room to motel room, checking how her couples are coupling. She deals with adult couples. She offers rapid treatment of "here and now" problems. Her therapy is based on simple maxims: Represent your feelings. Take risks. Open up to your partner.

"Concentration is necessary," she added. She does not treat deeply depressed people or psychotics unable to follow her instructions and exercises.

What does Vaughan know? When does she know it? And then what? "One word to describe my therapy," she said at the start of a long interview, "is communication — on all levels."

Most couples are referred to her by other professionals, such as psychiatrists, neurologists, endocrinologists, internists or psychoanalysts. She urges couples to pick a time period when they are not working, not seeing friends or family and can be really together and focusing. Often they arrive at severe odds. "Many tell me, 'If this doesn't work, we're going to get a divorce,'" she said.

Vaughan starts with a thirty-minute evaluation, which is free, using that time to explain costs and procedures. Her charge is twenty-eight hundred dollars and, if the couple agree to proceed, she meets one, the other or both partners for two hours each day for two weeks. She is on call between meetings. One first task is to calm them down. "Actual sexual dysfunction is often easy to reverse, assuming there is no physical disimpairment," she said. "It's the verbal issues that allow — or block — the whole process."

There are ground rules. "I tell them, 'Don't intentionally hurt each other, physically, emotionally or verbally,'" Vaughan said. No drugs are allowed, except those prescribed during the therapy period. Alcohol use is limited, because it lowers libido, impairs function and brings out hostility. Both partners are ordered to "stay in the present." Nor are they allowed to utter sentences beginning, "You never . . . ," "If you only could."

Four sessions are used to take personal histories. "I want to sense where they are coming from," Vaughan said. How do they see their partner? Their families? What about affection? Education? Sex education? First sexual experiences? How much do they know about bodily functions? What complaints do they have? How do they see the problem? What are their goals? During the fifth session, she mirrors back information she has gathered, reviews how the two "got to where they are" and offers diagnosis and prognosis.

"You can't 'work' at sex," she said. "You can't be in a corner, worrying and watching." Instead she sends partners into private encounters with exercises designed to improve verbal skills, focus senses and get comfortable. Occasionally Vaughan will lend a vibrator but only for overnight. Mechanical aids, she finds, produce strong physical response but also can overfuse a sensitive area, producing a numbing experience.

A better way to heighten erotic experiences, Vaughan advises, is to become more aware of one's own sensations. "The largest sexual organ is skin," she said. "Don't focus on breasts and genitals." Another goal is to play down judgments. Still another is to teach each partner to "stay in touch with feelings." One technique: Have people hear themselves, by repeating back their own words, as they tell their partner what that partner should feel, think and do. That's wrong. "Often,"

Vaughan said, "despite good intentions, such a caretaking role causes trouble. The emphasis should be on individual feelings, taking responsibility for oneself."

At the beginning of therapy, each couple is asked to refrain from direct sexual interaction. "This approach," Vaughan said, "helps remove performance pressures." Instead, partners are introduced to "sensate focus" and encouraged to touch each other. They are urged to develop an awareness of textures, contours, temperatures and contrasts, doing what interests them, not guessing what a partner does or doesn't like. "The purpose," Vaughan said, "is not to be sexual but to establish an awareness of touch sensations."

Therapy usually ends between the twelfth and fourteenth sessions, a time by when, Vaughan finds, most partners have met their own personal goals. "They learn a private, intimate, revealing way of talking, not to be shared with others," Vaughan said. "We then talk about how to integrate this into their lives."

Often, she finds, she can be helpful in debunking sexual myths. For example, many women, influenced by male imagery of orgasms as fireworks and erupting volcanoes, are not sure if they can properly identify their own orgasms. Vaughan reassures them. For females, she says, orgasmic images should run to water and wave movements, which may range from gentle to crashing. Nor should female orgasm be frightening. "If I really let go, I worry I may go crazy," one client told her. Replied Vaughan: "I told her that won't happen. She then began to 'own' her experience, in her unique way."

In turn, males worry about penis size. "The female vagina accommodates to the size of the male," she tells them. In size, are some races better endowed than others? "There is one difference," she said. "For tropical and genetic reasons, the African male has a penis which does not retract into the body as much as that of Nordic man. There is a good natural reason. If sperm, kept in the testes, becomes too hot or too cold, it is destroyed. Thus, the penis of the tropical African male hangs low so it will be air-conditioned and maintain sperm. Aroused, at intercourse, all men are about the same."

For disabled people, a significant percentage of Vaughan's practice, there are other concerns. For example, people with spinal injuries that paralyze parts of their bodies must cope with an abrupt array of emotional and physical sexual readjustments. One first task is presenting facts. Male paraplegics,

Vaughan said, can ejaculate and reproduce but do not have "erective security." Male quadraplegics, who have lost use of both arms and legs, have erections and even intercourse but feel nothing in the genital area and cannot reproduce. Female quadraplegics conceive and bear children but, unable to feel pain, may miss noticing the start of labor.

"They are all concerned about partners," Vaughan said. "They wonder, 'Will I be able to have sex? Will my partner stay? Will I still be loved?'"

Vaughan teaches disabled clients to identify their own pleasurable areas, spots where they have intense sensation, often their "border areas," places near their paralyzed limbs where sensation begins and ends. Such erotic areas constantly shift as feelings change, blood flow varies and temperatures fluctuate, but clients are urged to explore their bodies with their partners helping. Breasts and genitals, areas of the body that often bear mixed messages from childhood days, are off limits.

Can one reach an orgasm during such mapping adventures? "Yes," Vaughan said. Through use of focusing techniques, she reported, her clients — abled and disabled — have triggered what they describe as "brain orgasms" by concentrating on, among other areas, the mouth, ears, inner arm, neck, lips, tongue, eyes and shoulders. No one as yet, she added, has told her of a back orgasm, but, she added, there is no reason why it should not be possible.

A member of the American Association of Sex Educators, Counselors and Therapists, Vaughan offers a five-page resume of professional achievements, including training at Chicago's Adler Institute and the Institute for Psychoanalysis, the University of Michigan Hospital and New York's Eileen Ford Model Agency, where she worked from 1954 to 1956. One of sixty-four people to study "in-house" at the Masters and Johnson Institute, she is the only graduate practicing in Chicago.

"They collapsed an eighteen-month training program into six months," she said, recalling her intense training period. "It was seven days a week, starting at 8 A.M." The first hour each morning was spent in the institute library with Masters, putting questions about therapy and research to a medical professor whom Vaughan described as having "a wonderful way of focusing ideas and putting them into carefully defined language." Institute students then studied specific cases, four to six hours a day, consulting with other staffers, including psychologist Virginia Johnson, whom Vaughan called "warm, sensitive, intuitive and creative."

Some critics, such as psychoanalyst Leslie Farber, have complained about the Masters and Johnson technique of using "colored motion-picture photography to record in absolute detail all phases of the human sexual response cycle, a movie which was, wisely I think, a silent one." In Farber's view, sex under the requirements of an orderly laboratory — on a table, disrobed, before staffers, during weekday working hours — bore little resemblance to natural field conditions in which sex often occurs late at night after dances.

In reply, Vaughan, reflecting Masters and Johnson's findings, notes that her files bulge with case histories where sex lives of clients, helped by a combination of physical information and emotional counseling, have improved dramatically. Samples:

— One man found that he was aroused by feeling women's underwear stolen from public laundries. He started therapy after his wife, whom he loved, discovered boxes of strange panties in their bedroom drawer. Encouraged to take the risk of sharing feelings, the husband was able to transfer the eroticism of an abstraction, in this case underpants, to intimacy with his wife.

— A business executive began a practice of disrobing in his office, exposing himself to women in nearby buildings and masturbating. Worried that he would be caught, he entered therapy. Growing up in an emotionally distant family under a stern father, he developed poor social skills but was aroused as a youth by watching a neighbor woman undress. Now, pressured by increasing professional success, he turned to liquor, undercut his sexual ability at home and reverted to earlier pleasures. When he learned to limit alcohol intake, improve communications, work on focusing techniques and feel "safe" with his wife, his exhibitionistic urges disappeared.

— One woman complained that she was not able to experience vaginal orgasm though she could peak manually. During history-taking, her husband said he was a premature ejaculator. The couple's complaints were treated simultaneously. The husband was taught how to delay; his wife learned to experience her own body and trigger orgasm.

Abuse of drugs and liquor causes many sexual problems. Each week Vaughan lectures at the Martha Washington Hospital treatment center, telling alcoholics and addicts about such matters as impotence, a disorder that affects 50 percent of all alcoholics. Cocaine, she added, helps maintain male erection and delay orgasm. Both heroin and cocaine, especially during the "big rush" of early use, provide sensations similar to orgasm. "People try to get back to that," she said, suggesting one cause of addiction. "It's seductive."

Vaughan described a typical drug scenario. "A man and a woman use cocaine together. Sex is terrific. They need more and more. Ultimately the man says, 'The lady has to go. I can't afford this for both of us.' Cocaine takes over the woman's role."

When the hour was up, a group of thirty men and women kept Vaughan for fifteen extra minutes, asking detailed questions. Does lubrication indicate the level of a woman's arousal? "No," she said. "Only the front one-third of a woman's vaginal wall lubricates anyway." Do moisture creams help when vaginal dryness impedes sexual intercourse? "Yes, but those with vaseline or other oil bases are dangerous. They coat the vagina wall, allowing for bacterial growth." Is oral sex harmful? "No, not if both parties have a clean bill of health."

Such straight talk reduces anxiety, a major cause of sexual dysfunction, Vaughan believes. It helps people to relabel their expectations, she added, and not judge everything they do as success or failure. "Orgasm is a brain experience," she said, a sentence upon which she plans to expand considerably in coming years.

With researcher Michael Maliszewski, Vaughan has undertaken an eight-year project to study sexual experience and phenomena, such as shifts in emotions and perceptions, feelings of self, imagery and transcendent states. "People engage in sex," Maliszewski said in an interview. "But we don't know exactly what they experience." Literature is filled with paeans of poets, but most impressions are emotion-laden and lack specificity. Details are needed.

"What," Maliszewski asked, "are pleasurable experiences? We know what happens physically, but what happens spiritually?" As always, the answers, soon to become a major book, are sought with discretion and taste. Over a three-week period, participants fill out a forty-page questionnaire. They mail them back anonymously.

Neither Maliszewski nor Vaughan sees them undressed.

April 14, 1987

ALGREN AFFAIR TO
REMEMBER LIVES AGAIN

Art Shay, a longtime friend of gritty novelist Nelson Algren, was a Chicago-based staffer for *Life* magazine many years ago when Algren was courting, of all people, Simone de Beauvoir.

The romance started when the famed French feminist philosopher, on a cross-country tour, found herself at loose ends in what is now the Chicago Hilton & Towers hotel. Looking for divertissement, De Beauvoir rang up Algren. He, not knowing anyone with a French accent, hung up. De Beauvoir called back, mentioning two mutual friends, writer Mary McCarthy and philanthropist Peggy Guggenheim. Algren, impressed, did not hang up again.

And the rest, one might say, is history — and now a play.

At least, that's what the odd coupling became this week when Shay, now a freelance photographer and writer, unveiled his own take on what was to be a seventeen-year romance. His 110-page script, *Breaking Rule 3*, drew a full house to Highland Park's Apple Tree Theater.

The evening was a reading staged by director Mike Nussbaum, featuring actress Carmen Roman and actor Jim Leaming and set during Algren's longest stretch with De Beauvoir, the summer of 1950 at Algren's bare-bones cabin at Miller Beach, Ind.

It was there that Algren asked De Beauvoir to marry him and forget her other boyfriend, existentialist guru Jean Paul Sartre. She, for complicated reasons later spelled out in several books, declined.

"He kept inviting me out for weekends swimming, but I was busy with *Life*," recalled Shay, now seventy-six, musing on his long-ago role as a witness to a relationship that continues — almost half a century later — to inspire a considerable amount of literary fallout.

This year, for example, has seen the publication of *A Transatlantic Love Affair: Letters to Nelson Algren by Simone de Beauvoir*. Also recently out are new biographies of both writers, with attention to a Paris-Chicago liaison that, if not dangerous, was certainly wordy.

Last year, a British television channel taped a documentary on the affair, titled *A Walk on the Wild Side*, after one of Algren's best-known titles. French television ran a docudrama on De Beauvoir's life, using two dozen pictures by Shay of the couple, early in their romance, exploring elements of Chicago not usually included in night-life tours for visitors.

As part of his own show, Shay projected scenes he captured at seedy pool rooms, skid-row bars, garbage-strewn street corners and police-station lineups — places where Algren took De Beauvoir to expose her to far-from-the-lake local ways of life. His pictures greeted audience members as they filed into the 180-seat suburban theater, on the second floor of a shiny new strip mall.

"And what was Rule Three?" a visitor asked, as the house lights dimmed.

"Never go to bed with a woman whose problems are worse than your own," whispered Shay. It was, he said, a maxim Algren often repeated after passing on two other exhortations: "Never eat at a place called Mom's" and "Never play cards with a man named Doc."

Later, the consensus of the crowd, an older group who got free tickets with subscriptions to Apple Tree's regular offerings, was that Algren should have followed his own rules.

"Why did she have to mention Sartre so often?" wondered one woman, during the post-reading comment time, referring to De Beauvoir's obsessive quoting of Sartre, the existentialist with whom she maintained a fifty-year, frequently-abusive relationship.

"What happened to the cottage?" wondered another audience member, asking about the Indiana site of what some today see as a laboratory where De Beauvoir expanded her thinking in *The Second Sex*, her breakthrough book, developing the ideas that established her as a feminist icon.

"Nelson paid fifteen thousand dollars for it. He sold it years later for fourteen thousand dollars. It was one of his better business deals," Shay said, recalling that Algren regularly plunged into debt playing poker.

Though Shay's play was clearly a work in progress, many saw possibilities.

"You did a great job with Simone's being a lover — and playing at being a lover. I think you're about 80 percent there. The dialogue is great," noted Maud Lavin, a non-fiction writer.

"There's a real love of the history of this (relationship)," added Bill Lederer, a playwright, though he, and others, urged a closer examination of why the chemistry sizzled, then fizzled.

Scholars have raised many theories over the years about Algren, who had been married and divorced twice before De Beauvoir came along, and De Beauvoir, who never married.

One dowager theatergoer, unswayed by the appeal of Miller Beach, offered a simpler explanation of the split. "At least he could have offered to put her up in the city," she huffed.

March 3, 1999

PORN STAR MISSY
IS GRAPHIC ABOUT
SAFE SEX

Nobody ever went broke underestimating popular taste, P. T. Barnum once proclaimed, which might explain the arrival here last week at the Limelight club of Missy, the nation's first "safe sex" porn star and an emerging figure on the late-night lecture circuit. She is a former aide to Sen. Orrin Hatch (R-Utah) and describes herself as an "actress/activist."

The purpose of her trip was to speak to several hundred assembled patrons in the grand ballroom of the nightclub, at 632 North Dearborn Street, where, in a twenty-minute monologue, she talked about the technical problems of filming the nation's first "safe sex" movie, her debut picture, *Behind the Green Door: The Sequel* and the reasons why precautions have become necessary in what, until recently, was considered an era of license.

A second reason was to promote her new video, a thirty-minute lecture tape, with an all-clothed cast, called *Missy's Guide to Safe Sex*. Available at a lobby desk at the Limelight, it is one of a growing number of videocassettes suggesting practical measures to reduce the risk of contracting acquired immune deficiency syndrome, or AIDS. It was selling for $9.95.

Pushing "safe sex" through the medium of adult movies, with adult movie stars as spokesmen, might strike some as trying to go backward and forward at the same time. But Missy, whose real name is Eliza Florez, described her work as "a statement." In recent months, she has brought her message to readers of *Playboy*, US magazine and the *Atlantic Monthly*, where she received lengthy mention in an eighteen-page report on "Heterosexuals and AIDS: The Second Stage of the Epidemic."

As *Atlantic* noted, the *Green Door* sequel last summer was the country's best-selling adult home video. Its selling proposition was a costume budget heavily devoted to condoms, gloves and other latex devices. "The government just isn't about to do anything," Missy told the *Atlantic*. "I remember sitting in on Senate hearings a few years ago when funding was cut for Planned Parenthood. Some senators objected to the explicitness of the sex-education films for teenagers. Well, we're out to reach people who are promiscuous, have multiple partners and still want to live their fantasies."

Such print exposure led to an appearance on WLS-Channel 7's syndicated *The Oprah Winfrey Show* show. Missy was spotted by Cindy DeMarco, a booker for Limelight who "called up Oprah and said, 'I want to have a safe-sex party. Is there any way you can help me out?' They gave me her number." DeMarco lined her up for the three-hour stint here — the lecture plus mingling and talking with patrons — to be followed by a similar outing at the Limelight's New York outlet. Next month Missy, who is twenty-five, is going to the Cannes Film Festival.

For a young woman who looks like a slightly raffish prom queen, her original brown hair now swept up into blonde spikes, these are heady times. Dressed in a flowing floor-length gown by Deborah Winn of San Francisco, a protege of Hollywood designer Bob Mackie, she talked of her life and cause during a long interview conducted on a couch in a Limelight office.

"I usually wear pink, the color of love, or salmon, the color of love and strength," she explained. "Tonight, we thought black would be better."

She began by defining her cause — "the need for safe sex practices in this Age of AIDS, a scourge of potentially major proportions, not just to the homosexual community, but to the public at large." Her own role, she added, is "to translate the phrase 'safe sex' into terms and actions that can be routinely incorporated into day-to-day living."

She was asked whether there had been a decisive moment in her life, a point when she decided to stop being, as *Playboy* put it, "a sweet girl with impeccable GOP credentials" and turn into, again in *Playboy*'s words, "Missy, Republican Porn Star!!!"

"I still think about doing the right thing," she said. "I know that sounds Republican, but I really think I am. I'm helping save lives. The government will sit around with thumbs up their noses for years. It takes people from the private sector, like myself, to get out and do something. I've seen people die of AIDS. It's horrifying."

Born in Salt Lake City, the daughter of a prominent Republican, she was raised a Catholic. She went to Washington at fifteen to be a Senate page. She became an intern and a staffer for Hatch, who has said he remembers her as "an excellent worker" who "worked long hours trying to elect Republican candidates." She remains, she said, a Reagan Republican.

"I was a very conservative girl when I went to Washington," she said. "I was a page. I wore a blue-and-white uniform every day. I went to Georgetown University. I got a bachelor of political science degree. I wanted to get a master's in anthropology so I went out to Berkeley. An old boyfriend of mine introduced me to my new boyfriend, Artie Mitchell."

He is one of two Mitchell brothers, the country's best-known adult film producers, who began their San Francisco-based empire in 1970 with Marilyn Chambers, who went from posing for the picture on Ivory Snow packages to the Mitchells' first hit, *Behind the Green Door*. Last year, with the adult film industry confronting a situation potentially dangerous to its own health — AIDS — the Mitchells decided on a sequel, to show that "safe sex" is "both smart and sexy."

Not everyone is happy with the result, which is heavily into latex and, one critic suggested, is about as titillating as open-heart surgery. Upset, for other reasons, were Missy's father and stepmother, who didn't speak to her "for a whole year." Also displeased: Judith Martin, also known as syndicated columnist Miss Manners. Martin filed suit to stop Missy from being known as Missy Manners. "I'm just Missy now," Missy said. "We agreed to a cease-and-desist order. It cost me sixty thousand dollars."

Currently, she said, her primary marketing aim is to promote "Missy's Guide to Safe Sex," a tape that "tackles this important problem with sensitivity to the human experience, a sense of humor, and direct specific information that the public needs to begin the gradual task of making safe sex an integral part of their daily lives." During the evening, she also showed samples of the Missy Safe-Sex Kit, a white box whose contents include latex gloves, a tube of nonoxynol-9 antiseptic foam and condoms. It sells for six dollars. Two Limelight bartenders demonstrated proper methods of pulling on gloves.

Boyfriend Artie accompanied her to Chicago. The two have lived together for two years. "We're quite the couple around San Francisco," Missy said. Then, it was off to New York. "I was supposed to be on *Larry King Live* on Friday, but I was bumped," she complained. "They got Oral Roberts' son instead."

Well, as they say, it's always something.

April 12, 1987

MARRIAGE AN OPEN BOOK
FOR LOGGINS, WIFE

"For the most part, we're doing pretty good," reported singer Kenny Loggins, starting off a reading Monday night at Transitions, a New Age bookstore at 1000 West North Avenue in Chicago. And that, in a nutshell, was what the standing-room-only crowd wanted to know. Does it really work?

"He's not going to sing, is he?" wondered Tom Andrade, in a row at the back. "No, I guess he's going to talk about gettin' along with his wife. Like, maybe he's got the magic word."

"Are you as excited as I am? My knees are shaking," Gayle Seminara-Mandel, a co-owner of the store, had confessed when she introduced the evening, reflecting the inner feelings of 350 people in the room before cautioning them, "Please, no lighting of matches."

It was, indeed, very much an evening for the flickering-flame crowd.

It was a time to hear, against a background of water gently lapping over a display of tabletop fountains, Loggins and his second wife, Julia, discussing their manual on relationships, *The Unimaginable Life.*

Many women came with thumbed copies of the book, shouting out page numbers when Kenny Loggins was looking for passages to read. Men seemed less certain.

Written in the form of journals kept by both Logginses, the book, as one critic has observed, does not follow a "don't ask, don't tell" policy. Quite the opposite.

"The book," Kenny Loggins noted, "is about our lives together, our falling-in-love time, how we became conscious to things that allow us to speak to the truths inside ourselves, all the time."

The result, he said, has been a relationship where both partners say absolutely everything they think, when they think it, repressing nothing. Both also take care to probe where their feelings, when perceived as negative, might have originated in their separate histories.

Like, other critics have noted, sure.

"Morning disc jockeys get very confused with the idea, especially men," Kenny Loggins noted, speaking of encounters on the road promoting the book. "They say, 'Wait a minute, you can't tell the truth all the time, to a woman.' And, yes, I know where they're coming from."

But, he retorted, "you can tell the truth all the time. You can be yourself. Not be what others want you to be. Or what you think they want you to be. You should risk everything. Be honest. Get in touch with what it is that rattles you. Give up trying to control."

Married for eight years, the Logginses, their book confides, have brought up everything from his premarital doubts about his capacity for monogamy to her pain during "their first time together," a burning sensation later attributed to "the wrong spermicide foam."

Last year, Julia Loggins worked through worries about body fat she retained after the birth of their daughter. Meanwhile, Kenny Loggins' mind, though apparently not his body, has known sexual temptation.

"The road to love is lit by the lamps of fear," he told the crowd, before taking questions. "Let trust lead to love and fear slowly fades away."

Apparently, in their case it does. They nuzzled repeatedly during their seventy-five-minute talk, with Julia Loggins taking time out, at one point, to nurse their daughter, who was carried onstage by a nanny.

One of the major acts at Taste of Chicago, Kenny Loggins, fifty, is known for soundtrack hits from three movies, *Footloose*, *Top Gun* and *Caddyshack*. He has sold forty million albums during a twenty-five-year career, winning two Grammys.

Yet, it in an age marked by skepticism, one person's path to wisdom can be another's psychobabble, as Loggins and his wife, forty-three, a nutritional counselor and colon hydrotherapist, found out long before they showed up at Transitions.

Indeed, when it comes to their venture into self-help, the mainstream press has been, some at the gathering observed, vicious.

The *Washington Post* dismissed their book as "drivel." The *Toronto Sun* made fun of the couple's introduction, in 1984, before a session on colon hydrotherapy, a form of alternative therapy akin to an enema.

"One day," the paper speculated, "they will get to shock and sicken their kids with the story of how they met."

"Yes, he was my client," Julia Loggins told the crowd, adding in a whisper, "It's a good way to meet someone."

On a larger issue, total honesty, the crowd split along gender lines.

"It got to me. It was so personal," said Mikki Dobric.

Later, in the darkness of the parking lot, Anton Antoszek murmured, "Well, I'm not going to be that truthful all the time, because I know what the repercussions are."

July 8, 1998

OH, TO BE A
FISH (OR CAT)
IN CHICAGO

FINNED FRIENDS CHEER
LONELY GUESTS

Hungry? Angry? Lonely? Tired? Stuck in a hotel room far from home? How about a little chicken soup from room service and (for company) a pet goldfish?

That's the ticket for guests at the Hotel Monaco, a trendy updating of the old Oxford House Hotel, at 225 North Wabash Avenue, which has opened with a flourish — and a novel idea.

"Would you like a fish?" the desk clerks at the Monaco ask persons checking in, a question that the hotel management suggests, in a staff memo, should be posed "as if it were absolutely normal, even a bit blase." The objective, often reached, "is to make jaws drop."

Indeed, a common reaction, before new arrivals are handed a flier explaining the Monaco's policy of what it refers to as "Guppy Love," is along the lines of "Say, what?"

The idea of offering a companionate low-maintenance pet, as a way of easing loneliness and providing diversion for a dispirited guest, actually originated in 1997 at the Monaco's sister hotel, the Hotel Monaco in Seattle. There, one night, 170 of its 189 rooms ordered fish.

In Chicago, the idea has been slightly slower to catch fire, but something like one-fifth of all guests, offered a fish, have been saying "yes" to the gold-coated wigglies.

"It seems to be something people find dear," said Michael DeFrino, general manager of the Chicago operation, which for a week has been filled with conventioneers attending Pack Expo at McCormick Place, a gathering of the Packaging Machinery Manufacturers Institute.

That was by way of a test run for the 192-room hotel and its start-up pool of 120 fish. With considerable hoopla, the hotel's "o-fish-al" opening day, as DeFrino called it, was Tuesday.

Helped by the John G. Shedd Aquarium, which is providing expertise on how to maintain such an operation, the guts of the Hotel Monaco's fish venture is a hundred-gallon tank set up, along with towels, sheets and soaps, in the basement quarters of the hotel's housekeeping department.

There, swimming about, warming up for work, are "small

Tribune photo by Charles Osgood.

fish, usually of a reddish or golden color, of the same family as carp," as ichthyological manuals usually describe them.

"Basically, we're acting as consultants," noted Daniel Christopher, collection supervisor at the Shedd, which also houses eight thousand other aquatic specimens, including eels, sharks, sea otters and whales.

Hotel staffers, Christopher said, have been trained in the nuances of tank maintenance, water-changing, diet and trauma-free transfers to bowls which are carefully carried, with hands on the bottom of the bowl, along the hotel's corridors to the rooms of guests who want them.

Each bowl comes with rocks and a small sign saying, "No Fishing."

"Goldfish are pretty hardy," Christopher said. "They tolerate a wide range of temperatures and can go for a day or two without eating." That gives the goldfish a fair chance at survival, if guests follow directions not to feed them or set their bowls on hot radiators.

"It's really been a team effort to get this up and running," noted DeFrino, lauding the work of housekeeping coordinator Teresa Guillen, who sets up bowls and delivers, and assistant executive housekeeper David Stoner, who organized the holding tank, stocked it from a local goldfish emporium and keeps the fish going between their upstairs gigs.

Guests and staff have named many of them.

"My favorite is Madonna, of course. She's the showy one," said Stoner, as a tail-wiggling fish swam up to the tank glass, apparently eager to have her picture taken. Another is "Dorothy," after ice-skater Dorothy Hamill, "because she swims backwards."

"Has anybody taken to swallowing them?" a visitor asked, referring to another hazard for goldfish, encounters with out-of-control college students. "Not so far," reported DeFrino, noting that guests get only one fish per room, hardly enough for pranks.

"I love the fish idea. It's awfully clever, really," said guest Mary Oldfield, in from Seattle. Others agreed with the hotel's flier, that "our goldfish will be happy to provide you with the perfect kind of companionship, relaxed and quiet."

Cost to the hotel of the fish service is minimal, DeFrino said. In Seattle, startup expenses were thirty-one hundred dollars, with operating outlays of about thirty-five cents per fish-enhanced room per day.

But there is, as with all living things, a down side.

A manager at the Hotel Monaco in Seattle had to personally blot the tears of a little girl whose fish "checked out before she did," as he delicately put it. Thus far, no fish have died on duty in guest rooms at the Monaco, though, as DeFrino concedes, "it's inevitable."

With floaters, hotel staffers are informed to quickly assure guests, "Oh, I see you have an extra sleepy fish. We'll bring up a more perky one."

A bar adjoining the hotel is available for grief counseling.

November 11, 1998

ANIMAL LOVERS
FERRET OUT A UNIQUE
HALFWAY HOUSE

When a Gold Coast mother recently asked her veterinarian what she should do with two ferrets no longer needed by her older son, she was told to call a certain number, drive west along a certain expressway, turn south into a certain suburb, ring a certain bell and ask for Mary.

Despite the secrecy surrounding it, there is nothing illegal about the Chicago area's first halfway house for ferrets. It's just that Mary Van Dahm prefers that her neighbors not know that her ranch house on a quiet tree-lined street is alive with inquisitive furry creatures. Van Dahm keeps fourteen ferrets of her own in a spare main-floor bedroom. In her basement are sleep and play spaces for sixty more ferrets that are looking for, or are between, owners.

All this started eighteen months ago when a group of concerned Chicago-area ferret-lovers got together to form the Greater Chicago Ferret Association. Van Dahm, the only founding officer with a basement, was asked to run the association's shelter. She thought it over for about a minute and said yes, which is why, these days, she lives, breathes, talks and plays with more ferrets than most people would dream of meeting in a lifetime.

Van Dahm's own ferrets all have names and regular access to a kind of ferret health club with ramps, velour tubes, hollow balls and other ferret-oriented athletic equipment such as a dollhouse with windows suitable for climbing in and out of. Van Dahm lets them tear through her house for two hours a day, though one hour is devoted to cleaning. "They try to help," she said. "They follow me around and check out what I'm doing."

Visiting ferrets, 220 in all so far, live and play in twenty cages neatly stacked in the basement. Their spaces are equipped with crawl tubes, toy balls and lounging blankets. "We've gotten ferrets from all over the country," Van Dahm said in an interview. Some were transported from New Jersey. A group came from Kentucky after animal-welfare officials there seized nineteen ferrets from a suburban Louisville woman who kept them cramped in a backyard shed. Other people voluntarily give up ferrets when they move into smaller quarters or into buildings that do not allow pets.

Some become disenchanted. "It was not what I expected," one woman said, returning her ferret and complaining that it did not like to sit in her lap to be stroked like a cat or small dog.

Yes, Van Dahm admits, ferrets are different — but fun. "They are more exotic than dogs or cats," she said. "They are good for apartment dwellers because they are small and can be kept in cages most of the time. They also have a bit of a wild look, and they don't provoke allergies." They sleep fifteen to twenty hours a day but spend their up hours "banging off the walls."

They also like to frolic, dig in planters, hide behind furniture and burrow. So far, she added, they have caused no problems in her household, which also has three cats, a snapping turtle, an iguana, two fish tanks, a husband and a stepson who keeps a tarantula in his bedroom. Her husband's views? "He likes ferrets," Van Dahm said, "as long as I take care of them."

Of the nation's five million pet ferrets, about ten thousand live in the Chicago area, according to Janice Miller, an account representative for AT&T, who, in private life, is president of the Greater Chicago Ferret Association and maintains sixteen ferrets in her apartment in a western suburb. "So much was unknown," Miller said, explaining why the association was founded. "We wanted to say, 'Hey, these little guys aren't so bad.'"

That was seconded by another association founder, Dr. Susan Brown, a Westchester veterinarian who specializes in ferrets and other exotic animals and birds and has eight ferrets of her own. "They have a strong will to survive," she said. "They are easy to work with. I'm seldom bitten. In fact, I'm bitten far more often by iguanas and birds."

Unlike squirrels, which are rodents, ferrets are related to skunks, weasels and minks. Like cats, they can be trained to use litter boxes and can eat cat food. According to historians, ferreting, the use of ferrets to destroy rats and other vermin or to drive rabbits from holes, was known in Roman times. Modern pet ferrets, however, are dependent on their owners. They cannot survive on their own and die within several days if let out into the wild. Their coats, too short from indoor living, are not sufficiently thick to handle outside temperatures. Nor can they recognize natural sources of food.

Ferrets do like to party, as the Greater Chicago Ferret Association, which now has 275 members, found out at their annual Christmas gathering at the Warren Park Community Center at 5631 West 16th Street in Cicero. The top costume prize, accompanied by much applause, went to four ferrets dressed up as a bridal party, playing a bride, groom, maid of honor and, well, best ferret.

It was an afternoon of much hilarity. Two ferrets, Ralph and Icky, owned by Joanne Miglore of Arlington Heights, wore small Amish outfits. Rosemary Wolski's ferret, Amadeus, posed with a human Santa Claus while wearing a top hat, cape and scarf. Another ferret, lured by the promise of a raisin, did a trick that involved rolling over on a towel and pretending to sunbathe.

The prize for "Breeder of the Year" went to Jill Shumak of Sharon, Wis., who raises about three hundred ferrets a year that are bred, she said, for short heads, husky bodies and small ears. Along with T-shirts and ferret toys, association operatives also sold copies of *Off the Paw*, a quarterly newsletter (available from P.O. Box 7093, Westchester, Ill. 60153) with news of upcoming ferret shows, ads for ferret-boarding agencies, and obituary notices. Sample: "Butch, 1982–1988. What you brought was the wonder with which you greeted each new day and a joy that filled our lives with sunshine."

"The average ferret owner is single or divorced and has no children. A lot of our attitudes are a bit 'different.' People say we are a little strange," observed Mary Van Dahm, who also does ferret phone counseling (at 968-3189), helping people whose ferrets have such problems as missing the litter box.

Van Dahm grew up in LaGrange Park. Her father was allergic to dogs and cats. So her mother raised exotic turtles — as many as fifty-five at a time — and sold them to, among others, the Shedd Aquarium. Van Dahm worked as a meat wrapper for Jewel Food Stores in Darien and Lombard for fifteen years, but she quit last year to devote her full time to ferrets. "It used to be a family joke," she said, referring to her early months running the ferret shelter. "By day, I'd take dead animals and sell 'em to people. By night, I'd take live animals and sell 'em to people."

Now it's ferrets full time, and husband Kurt is pitching in, too. Among his good-sport plans for 1989: take enough photos for a possible ferret-of- the-month calendar.

December 29, 1988

268 PAWS TUG AT HER
HEARTSTRINGS

No lap goes unused in the big house in Ravenswood where Sister Marijon Binder lives with sixty-seven cats. "If you want to sit down," she said, welcoming a visitor, "you'll have to move a cat."

Does one need, say, a cat traffic controller for such a menage?

Not at all, noted Suzie Buzzo, one of a cadre of devoted helpers who keep the place purring. "It doesn't even seem like all that many. They each have their own special place."

But the story of Sister Marijon Binder, the founder of a not-for-profit foundation called Cats-Are-Purrsons-Too, Inc., goes far beyond mere cat-o-philia. Her mission in life, as she sees it, is to help older people who, for a variety of reasons, none pleasant, have to give up "companion animals" and don't want to see them, well, put to death.

So it is these days that every flat space in a clapboard house on a tree-lined side street is occupied by a contented hairball. That wasn't even counting the under-the-bed crowd.

Cats were on top of the refrigerator. Above the TV. On the radiator covers. Others, languidly crossing the kitchen, moved out a cat door, edged down a covered walkway and entered a back-yard screen-house which also had good places to sit, lie, stretch, yawn, nap and bird-watch.

One, noted Sister Marijon, likes to stretch out on a fresh newspaper each morning.

Living with sixty-seven cats might seem, as the French say, *un peu excessif*.

Yes, she loves cats. But as she was quick to point out, her mission has more to do with humans, especially older ones. "What you see here is only the end part of our ministry," she explained, describing work that starts with the idea that "companion animals" are important outlets for love in a modern-day society where people feel increasingly cut off.

"Sometimes a cat is their whole family," she said, talking of the difficult situations that occur as human abilities fail, when cat boxes become too hard to clean or, in the worst-case scenarios, when people move into retirement facilities that limit or prohibit animals.

These days, in a world that loves kittens, the odds seem stacked against the older cat that, through no fault of its own, after many years of faithful companionship, often faces a be-adopted-or-die policy when sent as a last resort to an animal shelter.

"I've had three cats for ten years. The home will let me keep one. How can I decide which two should be killed," cried one woman who recently called Cats-Are-Purrsons-Too.

"So we took in two more," reported Sister Marijon, who has spent a dozen years running what is licensed by the city as "a cattery," or a home with many cats. Thus far, no neighbors have complained. Even inside, there isn't much odor. Smells from twenty litterboxes, scooped daily, are kept under control by the use of pine shavings, a scent-absorbing form of cat litter now being field-tested there by a Southern manufacturer.

Now fifty-nine, Sister Marijon started convent preparatory school in California at the age of thirteen and later went into the novitiate of the Order of the Sisters of St. Joseph. For eighteen years, she taught sixth grade in San Francisco, eventually specializing in social studies. In 1975, she was moved to Chicago, to write children's textbooks for a large publishing company.

"All my elderly neighbors had pets," she went on. Over back alley fences, she listened to stories of woe. "One big problem was that they couldn't ever downsize, move into a nursing home, or retirement community, because they couldn't stand to give up their animals."

Sister Marijon started making house calls, assisting the elderly in caring for their four-footed friends. "What's really important," she said, "is that we gave them peace of mind by assuring them we would take in their animals permanently — if need be."

These days, volunteers include Eleanor Fuchs who, after a stroke, moved in with her own twelve cats. Now much recovered, Fuchs folds clothes, washes dishes, bottle-feeds kittens and uses a brush to fetch toys from under furniture, an operation of interest to cats who line up to watch.

A neighbor, Kolbjorn Haugen, comes in at 4:30 A.M. to fill food bowls, change water and start off each day for a community that, over the years, has been home to about a thousand cats.

Another neighbor, Joann Gurley, who has had veterinary training, helps with medical problems, though the tougher cases are treated by the Arlington Cat Clinic in Arlington Heights, whose husband-and-wife veterinarians, Bob and Gloria Esbensen, have been longtime supporters.

"We need volunteers, adopters and donations," Sister Marijon said, as a visitor brushed himself off, preparing to leave. Current residents of Cats-Are-Purrsons-Too go through about two thousand dollars a month in food, litter and the odd catnip party.

"We do a lot of begging," she added, gamely. "I haven't been a nun all these years for nothing."

May 8, 1998

PAWS PUTS FURRY FACES
IN THE ADOPTION MARKET

Put dogs and cats in fancy store windows along North Michigan Avenue and Oak Street.

Dress up volunteers in yellow T-shirts with the logo "See Me to Adopt This Dog" and send them out, walking dogs, to parks and beaches of the Lincoln Park area on weekends.

Set up a storefront on a busy stretch of North Clark Street. Fill it with dogs, plus a selection of serene, mature cats, many of them purring, all of them eager for a lap.

"It's all Marketing 101," said Paula Fasseas, chief planning and development officer of the Metropolitan Bank Group, talking of her after-hours obsession, snatching the city's unwanted pets from the jaws of death and directing them toward warm, loving homes.

PAWS, an acronym for Pets Are Worth Saving, her booming dog-and-cat operation, scarcely four months old, reflects a maxim of retailing, "location, location, location."

But it is more than that.

"People need to see these animals. Look at their faces. See their eyes. These are wonderful, quality pets, not damaged goods. But they are tucked away in shelters. Shelters can't afford good locations. And they don't have money to market what they have," Fasseas began, when a visitor asked to hear the story of PAWS.

What Fasseas and her crew do, early each Saturday morning, is to make a station-wagon run to the city pound, at 2741 South Western Avenue. There, they fetch a dozen dogs and a dozen cats.

Most are chosen on the basis of their seniority at the pound, a status that, to put it delicately, is not a good thing for an animal to have.

"She and her group are literally lifesavers," said Gene Mueller, a veterinarian and executive director of the Chicago Commission on Animal Care and Control, the city agency that runs the ever-crowded pound, where forty thousand dogs and cats are put to death each year.

About half are suitable for adoption, Mueller said. Many are pets turned over to the pound by owners who move or no longer want them. The problem is matching such animals with new owners, few of whom know about the pound or want to go there.

"We're known in neighborhoods down here," Mueller said, "but what we really want to do is to market our pets throughout the city of Chicago." That kind of outreach, he hopes, in a goal shared by Fasseas, might someday make Chicago a "no-kill city."

Toward that end, the PAWS dream is to open more centers, pull in animals from more shelters, push for low-cost spaying and neutering, keep down the number of unwanted animals and help find homes for all "angels with tails" who need them.

It's a cause that, for Fasseas, started with a small shaggy dog she saved from death last winter while she and her husband, Peter, the bank group's founder, were vacationing with their children on the Greek island of Crete, where police routinely poison strays.

The dog, a Scotty-looking animal now named Pippen, came home with them even though, as Fasseas noted, "we'd never had a dog. We've always lived in high-rise apartments."

Pulling together friends, plus an ad agency (Ogilvy & Mather) to do pro bono work designing fliers and a program, Fasseas called up stores on Michigan Avenue and Oak Street, asking them to participate in "PAWS Chicago: Angels With Tails Walking Tour."

The event, in late May, put pets from three shelters and the pound in windows of such retailers as Pavillon Christofle, Escada, Ralph Lauren, FAO Schwarz and Barneys New York.

"We opened our shelter in late July, just before our second event, on West Armitage," Fasseas said, giving a tour of what is now the PAWS adoption center, at 2337 North Clark Street.

Open on weekends, plus weeknights for cats only, its two rooms are filled with volunteers answering phones (at 773-244-3248) and grooming animals. "I've taken all of them out for a walk today," said Arya Barirani, a volunteer. "People stop me, ask what kind of a dog it is and how old, I give them fliers and encourage them to come here."

Adoption charges run from $42 to $56.50, the same fees the pound charges.

"We had a sheep dog, but we had to put him down several months ago," noted browser Valerie Gangas, taking away a Polaroid snapshot of a possible replacement.

Thus far, PAWS has placed four hundred animals, including two dogs to a couple who said, "We're going to our beach house in Maine for a month. Do you think the dogs would mind going?"

"I think they could handle it," Fasseas told them.

September 30, 1998

GOLD COAST PAYS TRIBUTE
TO ITS STORIED VET

Few benefits attract a following as diverse and passionate as the one that shows up each year to support the Lake Shore Foundation for Animals, but the crowd at this brunch at the Drake Hotel had a purpose beyond raising funds to protect creatures of the land, sea and sky.

They came to give a standing ovation to Dr. Lloyd Prasuhn, adviser and healer to Chicago's most elegant dogs and flossiest cats — as well as birds, gerbils, hamsters, mice, snakes, fish, turtles, rabbits and the occasional domesticated rat. Prasuhn is, as they say, much loved in the community and, as master of ceremonies Ken Nordine noted, "he's had a tough year."

His problem is ill health, but that did not prevent Prasuhn from personally greeting most of the 425 guests (who paid thirty dollars a ticket), remembering their names, asking after their pets, also by name, keeping an eagle eye on the proceedings or laughing at — what else — animal stories.

It was an afternoon of yaks and yowls. Federal district judge Ilana Rovner told of her cat Justice who, for some reason, hated male lawyers and bit any who came near her, usually on the forehead.

Skyline columnist Ann Gerber spoke of Zsa Zsa, a Skokie-based squirrel who came to her back door seeking peanut butter and macadamia nuts, became a fast friend and later, just before she died, brought around one of her offspring for Gerber to inspect.

WLS-Channel 7 anchor Joan Esposito remembered the chaotic day her cat, Lester, inadvertently got its tail sucked into an IBM Selectric typewriter. A two-vet squad arrived from the Lake Shore Animal Hospital with tools, freed the cat and took it in for repairs. Cat, tail and machine survived.

WBBM-Channel 2's Phil Walters also talked about cats, notably Retardo, his fourteen-year-old tabby who rarely hits its litter basket. *North Shore Magazine* columnist Bobbi Goldblatt told of her love for all black animals ("they exude mystery") and WMAQ-Channel 5's "Big Al" Lerner told about his cat, Harry, mauling his upper lip. Lerner had to explain to a confused emergency room doctor, preparing to put in stitches, why his mustache could not be shaved off. ("I need it for my work.")

But it was actress Robyn Douglass, after telling how she once saved a wounded duck from death on her way home from kindergarten, who struck a common chord when she noted: "Like a lot of you, I have always had the curse of seeking out the underdog, or cat, or horse."

Such concerns have been the life mission of Lloyd Prasuhn, a drawling, gregarious Ohio State graduate whose turf, the Lake Shore Animal Hospital, a buckskin-brick building at 225 West Division Street, is a healing facility that rivals many human institutions. With his wife, Mary, handling administration, Prasuhn oversees an operation that boasts its own diagnostic and therapeutic radiology facilities, obstetric and other specialty wards, operating suite, recovery rooms and individual housing for two hundred patients.

Besides their for-profit veterinary practice, the Prasuhns also have invested considerable energy since 1966 on the Lake Shore Foundation for Animals, a nonprofit humane society that has rescued thousands of tired, poor huddled masses of fur or feather with nowhere else to turn.

Prasuhn was raised in Greenville, an Ohio farm town thirty-nine miles northwest of Dayton. Today he works in an office cluttered with memorabilia: a framed bloc of animal stamps from Brooks McCormick Jr., a dog portrait fashioned from shredded wine corks from Wanda Szathmary, a photo of the doctor examining one of his seventy thousand patients — advertising star Morris the Cat. ("He'll bite you," says Prasuhn. "He's real nasty.")

Of more serious veterinary concern, Prasuhn also has amassed the largest private library in the country, with aisles of slides, video tapes, books, publications and case records. Eight years ago, he was the first Chicago veterinarian to use acupuncture to relieve arthritis (in a rabbit). He has fixed broken legs for birds, using Scotch tape. ("It's just thick enough and they heal real fast, generally in a week.") He has helped a snake who wouldn't eat. (The snake, it turned out, was merely cold.) And over the years, he also has been of help to physician colleagues with pet problems.

When one medical doctor rushed in with his dog, convinced that a thick lump under the animal's leg was a tumor, Prasuhn came up with his own finding: a wad of bubblegum. When a neurologist moaned "my cat is dying," Prasuhn asked about symptoms. "She's scooting across the floor? Crying? Screeching? Acting in pain? Sounds like it's in heat."

Anyway, this was the man who stood shyly by a pillar in the Gold Coast Room of the Drake Hotel, smiling as a room full of clients, supporters and friends came to their feet in applause. Each had a story, or more.

"He's wonderful," said one admirer. "I had to call him over a Fourth of July weekend when Noonie, my Siamese cat, ate my macrame yarn." Added another: "I phoned him once at 3 A.M. He told me, 'Come on over.' If it was me in trouble, not my dog, I couldn't reach my internist at that hour."

"He loves pets. He loves people. And he understands them both," noted a third. "That's why he has that sign in his waiting room. 'Please be patient. The doctor will be with you shortly. Sit! Stay!'"

November 13, 1988

THE MEANING
OF LIFE?
DON'T ASK

SUDS, SANCTUARY
ARE MATCH MADE
IN HEAVEN

Nothing stays the same for long at the Truth & Deliverance Christian Center, now one of the larger spiritual spots along West Madison Street in the South Austin neighborhood.

Take, for example, its carwash.

"Yes, it was a great idea," said Rev. John T. Abercrombie Jr., pastor of the eight-year-old church Tuesday, showing a visitor through a building that has morphed, over the years, from an automobile showroom to a five hundred-seat religious sanctuary, with TV lights.

"No, I'd never seen anything like it. It was just something I was inspired to do," he added, telling the story of how his fast-growing ministry became probably the first, possibly the only, institution in the Chicago area to combine religion and motor laundering.

It was, some might say, an idea that updated an old religious maxim, taking the value of "a clean mind in a clean body," adding in the joy of "a clean car." It also reflected an old piece of Chicago street wisdom: "Play the cards you get, not the ones you want."

In this case, Truth & Deliverance, which began in 1991 in a tiny storefront on South Lavergne Avenue with only eight members, found itself, after four years of growth, in possession of a crumbling two-story building at 5151 West Madison Street, once a Pontiac car dealership.

Its membership, by then in the hundreds, started by repairing the roof.

They then appraised the building's assets and found that the rear area, once the dealership's service department, had drains in the floors, working air hoses and pipes for water spray.

Outside, Abercrombie made another discovery. Residents often were afraid to go to carwashes, fearing they might be hassled if they left the safety of their cars.

Thus it was, early last year, that the Christian Car Wash opened for business.

"We wanted to bring something to the community. A place where people wouldn't have to feel afraid, where they could leave their cars, be comfortable, not feel threatened," Abercrombie explained. Drawn by an awning over the sidewalk on South Laramie Avenue that proclaimed "Clean Inside. Christian Car Wash," patrons spent the wash time in a waiting room stocked with comfortable chairs and, in the air, "soft Christian music," Abercrombie said.

The operation provided a dozen jobs for washers, all of whom had to promise to join a church, though not necessarily that one. "We tried to bring the spirit of excellence. That's what our ministry is about," Abercrombie said. The place was an immediate success.

Were there any problems? Like soapy water running into the pastor's offices?

"No, everything—the drains, the air hoses, the water sprays—worked perfectly," Abercrombie said. "And, yes, it was a moneymaker. In fact, it was very profitable."

So why, in late fall, did the city's first Christian carwash close down?

"Our emphasis here is not on profit, but on souls," the pastor said, describing other works of the center, which now has its own magazine, a food pantry, outreach programs and an annual tent crusade in the parking lot which, he says, is the biggest of its kind on the West Side.

"We took over the (carwash) space because now we have a congregation well over eleven hundred," he said. "And we needed the space for television production."

Last month, after a frantic eight-week renovation carried out entirely by members, the church held its first worship service in what was once the carwash. Now it is a five hundred-seat sanctuary, suitable for weekly services and a weekly TV program, aired on WJYS-Channel 62 on Saturdays at 7 P.M.

"I was flabbergasted. Talk about a transformation," said Tracey Brim, the congregation's administrator. Churchgoing carpenters put down a plywood floor and covered it with carpet. Others hung burgundy-colored drapes to serve as walls. Still others built an altar and TV stage. What was once the carwash waiting room became the church foyer.

Even that won't be there for long.

Already on the drawing boards are plans for a permanent fifteen hundred-seat auditorium, to occupy part of the back parking lot and a building next door.

(THE MEANING OF LIFE?)

When construction starts, workers will tear down the awning, the last artifact of the "Clean Inside. Christian Car Wash."

A good idea will be history.

January 8, 1999

A GENERATION TRIES
TO REMEMBER . . . SOMETHING
OR OTHER

Some true tales for that whadda-ya-call-it, you know, the journal of short-term memory loss:

Woman, fifty-something, double-parks outside her house on West Wolfram Street in New Town. Runs in to check the mail. Gets distracted. Decides to take a bath. Sinking into the water, she hears loud honking from the street.

Man, in his late forties, home from hard day at the office, makes a cup of tea. Walks into the den to slump in front of TV. Finds two other cups there, neatly set out, filled with tea that he's already made.

Woman, sixty-four, working out on a jogger-cycle in a Gold Coast health club, hears a guy shouting, "You took my key." She is stunned. "Well, just look," he retorts, pointing at the cloth loops dangling from her wrist. To her chagrin, she is wearing not one, but two locker keys.

It's "oops" or "my-my" — for sure. But with increasing public knowledge about severe, degenerative memory loss, most notably Alzheimer's disease, more than a few people approaching middle age or beyond may wonder whether their own lapses are cause for concern — or just garden-variety forgetfulness.

In short, is it normal, at a certain age, to start forgetting assignments, names of colleagues or phone numbers of bridge partners?

Or can such slips be worrisome evidence that storage areas of the mind — our crucial link to the real world — are starting to erode? Is it a cranial meltdown, brought about by the modern need to remember an ever-increasing blizzard of passwords, entry codes, area codes, Social Security numbers and whereabouts of dry cleaning?

To put it practically, when is it time — as recall fades into "where'd-I-put-the-car-keys" — to call in the psychological Marines?

"I'm a clinician. I see hundreds of people because they worry about memory problems," noted Dr. Sandra Weintraub, a psychiatrist at Northwestern Memorial Hospital and director of the clinical core of its Alzheimer Disease Center. What's needed, Weintraub said, is a sense of what is normal aging — and what is something worse.

To her, warning flags fly when memory loss is "persistent, gets worse and begins to interfere with daily living activities."

At the losing-the-keys level, short-term memory loss is probably not a way station on the road to Alzheimer's disease, said Edward Truschke, president of the Alzheimer's Association, which offers advice on memory-related concerns through a Chicagoland branch, at 847-933-1000.

"With age-related memory loss, you will eventually be able to complete a task," Trûschke said, "but with Alzheimer's you will not. You will forget how to do simple things like open a door, pay bills or get dressed." It is normal, he adds, for "busy people to get distracted from time to time and leave carrots on the stove.

"People with Alzheimer's disease could prepare a meal, forget to serve it, even forget they made it," he said. Similarly, "anyone can misplace a wallet, but eventually find it by reconstructing where they could have left it. A person with Alzheimer's disease may put things in inappropriate places, such as an iron in the freezer, or a wristwatch in a sugar bowl, and be unable to retrieve them."

For those who suffer from persistent memory loss, decline in mental abilities, disorientation or bizarre behavior — not normal parts of the aging process — professional help should be sought, Truschke advised.

As psychologists note, intelligent behavior could hardly exist without remembering, because experience influences subsequent behavior. Even such a simple matter as crossing a street, they point out, is based on remembering many earlier experiences. In prehistoric times, they add, those who remembered what an ominous noise meant — and fled — tended to survive and pass genes to similarly good-memoried progeny.

On the other hand, suggests Northwestern's Weintraub, no one would want to remember everything. For example, she says, "you can listen to an operator give a seven-digit phone number, put it in your memory for a short time, then trash it." Otherwise, she notes, "your brain would fill up" with minutiae — another route toward dangerous mental overload.

As other researchers suggest, an ability to forget has such useful consequences that it may well have been programmed into humans as part of the process of natural selection. Forgetting brings relief from painful experiences. It helps humans place events in time, because old memories fade and new ones tend to be more vivid. It keeps them up-to-date, as fresh thinking replaces dated approaches and solutions.

To offset ordinary forgetfulness, many doctors remind patients to watch out for undue stress, anxiety or lack of sleep. Others, such as Dr. Joseph Mendel of the Memory Institute in Philadelphia, recommend card games, crossword puzzles or even learning a foreign language — all ways to keep the aging mind and memory as active as possible.

Some theorists on aging, among them Robin West, associate professor of psychology at the University of Florida, suggest "external aids," such as lists, calendars, diaries and notebooks to focus the aging mind. West recommends a "memory basket," to hold important reminders, and "designated spots" for such oft-misplaced items as keys and glasses.

"Much of the time we're on automatic pilot and not aware of what we are doing," adds Danielle Lapp, memory researcher at Stanford University. She advises the memory-impaired to "stop and focus on what you're doing. Say aloud, 'I'm putting my glasses on the night table now.'" When reading, Lapp adds, stop to review key points and relate them to past experiences, building on an established knowledge base.

One study, on the University of California campus at Berkeley, found that older professors, sixty-one to seventy, were less adept than younger colleagues, thirty to forty-four, in pushing computer buttons after instructions were flashed or in matching faces to names after a single viewing.

Yet the senior staffers held their own in memory tests requiring mental planning, organization and problem solving. According to the researchers, the older professors were able to devise their own memory strategies to work around biological glitches of their aging brains.

Someday, chemical means may be available to bolster memory and counter short-term memory loss, but thus far no "memory pill" for short-term memory loss has emerged, Weintraub reported.

Meanwhile, some even joke about the syndrome, telling of a mean-spirited doctor who greeted each of his first-time patients by noting, "Well, as we discussed last time, you will probably experience some short-term memory loss." The story is probably an urban myth.

In any case, nobody can remember his name.

March 9, 1997

SONG HELPS REKINDLE
SPARK IN ALZHEIMER'S
PATIENTS

"This is important. I want you all to frown during the performance. It's not fun to be up here," joked music therapist Kathy Schellin, in a pep talk to the "Swingin' Singers" before they swung into action.

It was a bit of reverse psychology, not lost on sixteen members of what might be the nation's only chorus composed exclusively of Alzheimer's patients.

Yes, their voices were a bit frail and attentions wavered as they moved through "Sentimental Journey" and "Good Old Summertime." But even if they had to frequently resort to lyric sheets, no one failed to beam, even before applause rang out for their show stopper, "Climb Every Mountain."

Seated in a courtyard, wearing hats to ward off the August sun, with eyes fixed on conductor Shari Floss, the Swingin' Singers were the hit of a party to toast the Wealshire, a facility in Lincolnshire that bills itself as "the only free-standing community in Illinois dedicated solely to residents with Alzheimer's disease and other forms of dementia."

The place, on twenty wooded acres, has some novel ideas, not the least of which involve the use of live music to jog fading memories and pull together a group whose members, too often, wander apart.

"We work hard. I'm right on top of them," said conductor Floss, in an interview after the group finished its nine-number turn. "They know I expect them to perform as a chorus, to sound as one. I care and they know I care. They are my chorus, not a bunch of people with Alzheimer's."

"It was a great show," said Gail Seidel, whose mother is a patient. And, added Florence Davis, a patient herself, "a beautiful day."

Shortly, the chorus, not content with entertaining family and friends, will do their first traveling gig, performing at a nursing home in Buffalo Grove.

"Here we say, 'Let's focus on what they can do' and not make what they can't do a big problem," said Carly Hellen, the home's

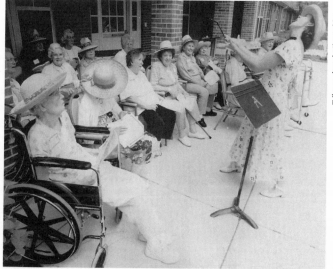

director of Alzheimer's care, talking to a visitor on an afternoon of balloons, punch, pastries, poetry readings and awards for staff and patients.

"Consider what it's like," she began, reaching for a simile. "It's like being abandoned in the middle of China, knowing neither the language nor the customs. That's why they're so frightened a lot of the time."

About four million people now have some form of Alzheimer's disease, an incurable degenerative disorder that affects memory, language and motor skills and now makes up about 60 percent of all cases of dementia.

Most receive care from a relative, usually from a spouse (one notable example these days is Nancy Reagan), a daughter or a daughter-in-law.

But according to thinking at the Wealshire, one-to-one situations, often overwhelming for caregivers, are not necessarily the best way for patients to maintain increasingly fragile links to the present and past.

The idea of group living is to encourage the afflicted, by being together, to maintain social skills, assisted by staffers trained to help them get over often-startling gaps in ability to handle daily life.

Routine tasks, such as brushing teeth, are broken down into a series of movements. Attendants help with forgotten steps, carrying in a bath towel and soap, for example, to cue a patient when bath time is at hand.

(SONG HELPS REKINDLE SPARK)

At the dinner table, utensils will be placed in a patient's hand, to help recall a sequence in eating. Or staffers will demonstrate actions, encouraging a patient to "mirror." Self-reliance is encouraged.

"It's 'doing with' a person, rather than 'to' or 'for' them," Hellen said, a philosophy that covers a whole range of keep-in-touch activities, from cooking and folding wash to sharing memories and going on outings.

"You realize the importance of the simple here," Hellen said, recalling benefits of a trip to an upscale supermarket where patients were able to share a concern about the soaring price of chicken.

Or an hour on a Lake Forest beach, where an elderly volleyball player, once a pro, now a patient, swapped tips with kids about fifty years younger.

Or eating at a restaurant where one patient, a retired industrialist, insisted on grabbing the tab. Staffers arranged with waiters to let him sign the checks, bolstering his self-esteem, then bill the home later.

"It's a different philosophy. You need to create a special ambience for people with this disease," said Wealshire's president, Arnold Goldberg.

What works with dementia, he finds, is tying in with the familiar, a way of dealing with a major patient concern, feeling safe at a time when they feel abandoned as they lose the ability to speak or be understood.

According to a recent article in *Contemporary Long Term Care* magazine titled "Designing for Dementia," Alzheimer's patients do best in facilities which are homelike, with a foyer for coats, living rooms near the entryway, small dining rooms instead of cafeterias and no central nurse stations.

Besides that, at the Wealshire, where annual fees run from fifty to sixty-five thousand dollars, bedroom hallways are short, so residents have less guessing about which room is theirs. Outside each room is a mailbox with a name and photo.

Often, at the home, patients confuse taking the property of others with going shopping. Instead of remonstrating, explained one staffer, "we simply run around and put things back." Rather than ban pets, as most such institutions do, the Wealshire employs a staff golden retriever, Kelly.

Trained to ignore hits from canes, walkers or wheelchairs, the dog, who carries $150,000 in bite insurance, is calm enough to allow endless fussing, fetching and combing from patients remembering their own pets.

And there is music, from sing-alongs to drumming circles.

As therapist Schellin said, "it brings back memories. 'Sentimental Journey' will lead some to talk of ice-cream parlors, of old romances." Yes, she added, "they do have problems, such as remembering lyrics. But singing's like riding a bike. It comes back — if you do it."

"You're an angel," said one Swingin' Singer, during a recent rehearsal. Conductor Floss demurred. "Well," countered the patient, "you do a good job of being a human being because you treat us like human beings."

Alzheimer's "is a hideous disease. I hate it," added Floss, after leading her charges through their show. "But you have to look beyond it. There is always something left. We have to find that spark."

August 20, 1997

NEAR-DEATH EXPERIENCES
SHARE COMMON THREAD

They sat in a large circle in a church basement, sharing stories — strangely similar — of a dark tunnel, a door, a blinding white light, then feelings of calmness, love and support.

One woman told how she had been horseback riding on a North Shore trail when "my horse walked onto a stretch of concrete, freaked and bolted." Thrown, she looked down on the scene during her ambulance trip to Evanston Hospital, as if she were in a helicopter.

A teenager recalled slipping into a coma in an emergency room, then "getting up and leaving, in total darkness, seeing an opening and, through it, orchids and trees bathed in pink light. I usually hate pink," she added, "but it was so beautiful."

During a severe asthma attack, one young man found himself "looking down on a group of people around a table." He had "no body, just a viewpoint." Around him, floating in a place of peace and calm, were faces of deceased relatives. The vision receded, he said, "after a voice told me, 'You have more to do,' and I woke up surrounded by doctors."

Recently, as they do on the second Saturday afternoon of every month, two dozen members of the Chicago-area branch of the International Association of Near-Death Studies met for two hours at Unity Church on the North Shore, at 3434 Central Street in Evanston.

On the agenda was coffee, cake — and other-worldly talk.

The aim of the group is to offer support, advice and study opportunities for people who find themselves in an unusual situation. They have gone through a life-altering experience, one that has affected, according to a Gallup survey, some fifteen million Americans.

When they talk about it, and many don't, the reaction from friends, relatives, even religious advisers, is often "this is the nuttiest thing I've ever heard."

That, despite a growing body of professional interest, dating to 1898 when geologist Albert Heim started collecting accounts of near-death from climbers in the Swiss Alps.

It is a field, now known as thanatology, the study of death

and dying, that has expanded considerably in recent years. Some of the interest was sparked in the 1970s by GIs, caught in murderous back areas of Vietnam, who later offered their near-death accounts.

In Chicago, psychiatrist Dr. Elisabeth Kubler-Ross, working out a pattern of stages of death and dying, culled similar stories from patients on the wards of Cook County Hospital.

Tens of thousands of case histories have been collected at the University of Connecticut, home base of the International Association of Near-Death Studies, which now publishes two journals, the scholarly *Journal of Near-Death Studies* and the popular *Vital Signs*.

"These people are telling the truth. The truth has a ring to it. You can feel it," said Diane Willis, a professional flutist who heads the Chicago-area chapter of the association, as the circle of local members offered testimony, sometimes for the first time.

"I think the work is really important," said Willis, adding that the group, now almost two years old, has had people call for information (at 847-251-7270) and "come to meetings right out of the hospital."

Almost always, near-death stories include moving through a dark space or tunnel, experiencing intensely powerful emotions, from terror to bliss, encountering a light, usually described as golden or white, and having a sense of the meaning of life.

"I've only shared this with a few friends," added a mother, who was given morphine after delivering a baby, then had trouble breathing. "First, it was dark. Then I came into a bright light. It was wonderful! Then the nurse said, 'Wake up, Barbara.'"

Besides sharing, what members found useful, they said, were Internet addresses, allowing them to connect with headquarters, at www.iands.org, and read the latest thinking on what the association itself says is a phenomenon "that cannot yet be explained."

"There seems to be agreement that these are not hallucinations or psychotic episodes or even conclusive proof of life after death," the association reports in its frequently-asked-questions section. Nor, it seems, are near-death visions related to dreams.

"Dream content is wide ranging, with scenes changing randomly. Near-death content seems to follow a story line dictated by some other agency," it notes. Dreams focus on living or composite figures, rarely on dead people. Near-death images seldom include the living.

Also notably absent, researchers report, are accounts by near-death survivors of scenes of judgment or hellfire, of the kind predicted by Christian dogma. Instead, the common elements of the experience have included "a figure of light guiding the dying person" and a "life review, being shown one's life and asked to evaluate it."

Often, trivial details are noticed. One victim of a heart attack floated up to the ceiling of an emergency room and saw dust on top of the light fixtures. "I thought, 'Boy, somebody's going to catch it for this,'" she later remembered, as she watched doctors working frantically to revive her.

September 29, 1999

THE MEANING OF LIFE?
DON'T ASK

It's not easy being a human these days. There's so much to do. Pick up the laundry. Sort your books. Get the car serviced. And high up on any thinking person's list of "Don't Forgets" is a nagging reminder: Find out, before it's too late, the meaning of life.

Now there's a newsletter to help you.

It's called *The Meaning of Life*, runs sixteen pages an issue, comes out quarterly and costs ten dollars a year. The publisher, Robert H. Lichtenbert, who holds a doctorate in philosophy, sat down the other day in his tiny basement office at Loyola University's Lewis Towers, across the street from Water Tower Place, to talk about it.

"It is a rather grand topic, but the most important one we have," Lichtenbert began, noting that many of the planet Earth's current roster of five billion people will spend their lives worrying about such day-to-day scufflings as football and home decoration, never tackling such larger issues as why are we here, where did we come from, where are we going?

Unlike the questions of, say, mathematics, many of whose answers can be looked up in a book, the solutions to philosophical inquiries can prove elusive. "When I taught a course on 'The Meaning of Life' at Harold Washington College," Lichtenbert recalled, "one student wanted to know the answer right away. She was kind of disappointed."

Instead, what Lichtenbert has in mind is a continuing dialogue, his newsletter acting as a springboard for discussion of such ideas as "Values and Meaning," "Finding Meaning in Love" and "Making Life More Meaningful." In recent issues of *The Meaning of Life*, he has written on all these topics, as well as on "Meaning from Social Problems," "The Meaningful" and "Subconscious Freedom as the Meaning of Life in the Paintings of Jackson Pollock."

Does he like doing a newsletter?

"Yes. It stimulates me and helps me get my ideas down and apply them to life. That's the point of studying or teaching philosophy, to make life better," Lichtenbert said.

"We need an alternative to materialism. I think we miss out on a lot in our society. I want to make the abstract, the spiritual, as real and as obvious as the materialistic. That's my life's goal."

How's it going so far? As with much of publishing these days, the road is bumpy.

Lichtenbert markets his newsletter by sending flyers to professors, libraries and other people who might be interested. Production costs are minimal; his wife, Mary, a secretary with a Loop law firm, sets copy on a computer. But revenues have been sluggish. Until he can figure out how to generate some money for subscription promotion, he said, circulation of the newsletter will likely remain the same, in the middle two-figures or, to put it bluntly, "about fifty copies an issue."

Though philosophers often make more money than poets, financial reward has never been a big draw, said Lichtenbert, who also lectures at Barat College in Lake Forest and Elmhurst College.

Nor is philosophy a hot draw on campus, he said. These are times of sagging enrollments, staff cuts and waning student interest in the tangled thickets of philosophy as an academic pursuit.

"A lot of people are dishonest with their lives," Lichtenbert said. "They don't admit their lives lack meaning. Others have trouble with ideas in general."

To pull in students, he said, "I tie the philosophy courses I teach to life, to thinking about how to lead a good life."

To Lichtenbert, the meaning of life is really a search for the meaningful, a guide for personal action that "includes every major consideration in a person's life." That thought, and the philosophical fallout from it, occupy the first four pages of the current issue of *The Meaning of Life*, now in its fourth year.

Born in the Humboldt Park neighborhood, Lichtenbert, forty-five, studied at De Paul University and later at the graduate school of Tulane University in New Orleans. "One big endless party down there," he said. A shy man who makes eye contact like a curve ball brushing the corner of home plate, Lichtenbert started teaching in the early 1970s, "just as the youth revolution was petering out." Its buzz words were "dialogue" and "community," he said. In his view, neither of those desirable goals has yet been reached.

"Dialoguing is the best way to learn about life," Lichtenbert said. "Talk! Don't read so much. Words are abstract. It's in the

(THE MEANING OF LIFE?)

give-and-take between humans that you learn what ideas you value.

"The level of serious dialogue in our society is appalling. Listen to people talk at cocktail parties. People are burned out by their work. They have a lot of dissatisfactions. Not many feel they are accomplishing much."

Because one purpose of Lichtenbert's newsletter is to encourage and direct the philosophically impaired, each issue ends with a section called "Nuggets of Meaning," for those who wish to go deeper. Among recent thoughts:

> "Living a meaningful life is difficult in a world where over-population and technology (especially television) dominate the individual and threaten him with insignificance, even among his closest associates."

> "What will you do tonight? We need to plan the most meaningful thing we can, instead of haphazardly drifting through life."

> "The highest meaning in social relationships is to meet a Thou, another person whom you respect highly and can engage in dialogue."

> "On the personal level, a meaningful life can be constructed in a few minutes of thought. To implement these often takes much longer."

So has Lichtenbert come to any conclusions after three decades of study, two decades of teaching and three years of newslettering? Is there meaning to life, a subject the Monty Python comedy troupe once explored in a notable movie? If so, is there news we can use?

One clear message is that it is hard to mount a successful newsletter about the meaning of life. "Maybe," the publisher noted ruefully, "I'll have to make some door-to-door calls."

Another is that, without meaning, life is unbearable. "We all have to have some meaning," Lichtenbert said, "or we'd end it all."

A third is that the currents of philosophy affect everyone, even Elvis Presley, who was, as a recent issue of *The Meaning of Life* pointed out, "in a strong sense, an existentialist in that he was very alienated from society and did feel a sense of the absurd and anxiety in his dark side."

Robert H. Lichtenbert's newsletter offers these ten tips for a meaningful life:

1. Talk to people.
2. Know your neighbors.
3. Develop a sense of place.
4. Know the history of your neighborhood.
5. Help out where and when you can.
6. Form a meaningful community.
7. Don't waste time.
8. Don't try to escape a sense of meaninglessness by turning to alcohol, drugs, TV or "just relaxing."
9. Create a vision of your own life.
10. Discuss.

December 3, 1991